The Seventh Trumpet

THE GOOD NEWS PROCLAIMED

by Mark Link, S.J.

Argus Communications A Division of **DLM,** Inc.
Niles, Illinois 60648 U.S.A.

ACKNOWLEDGMENTS

Scripture texts used in this work are taken from *The New American Bible*, copyright © 1970 by the Confraternity of Christian Doctrine, Washington, D.C. and are used by license of said copyright owner. No part of *The New American Bible* may be reproduced in any form without permission in writing from the copyright owner. All rights reserved.

Excerpts from *The Outline of History* by H. G. Wells. © 1970 Doubleday & Company, Inc, and G. P. Wells. © 1949, 1956, 1961 by Doubleday & Company, Inc. © 1920, 1931, 1940 by H. G. Wells. Reprinted by permission of Doubleday & Company, Inc., A. P. Watt & Son, and Professor G. P. Wells.

Excerpt from *A Study of History* by A. J. Toynbee, abridged by D. C. Somervell. © Oxford University Press, 1954. Reprinted by permission of the Oxford University Press.

Excerpt from *The Life of Jesus* by Ernest Renan. © 1972 Belmont-Tower Books, Inc. Used with permission.

Excerpts from *The Founder of Christianity* by Charles H. Dodd. Reprinted by permission of Macmillan Publishing Co., Inc. and William Collins Sons & Co. Ltd., London and Glasgow. © 1970 by Charles Harold Dodd.

Excerpts from *Jesus: A Gospel Portrait* by Donald Senior. Pflaum/Standard Publishing. © 1975 by Donald Senior. Reprinted with permission.

Excerpts from *Roots* by Alex Haley. Copyright © 1976 by Alex Haley. Reprinted by permission of Doubleday & Company, Inc. and Hutchinson Publishing Group Ltd.

Excerpt from *New Horizons* by Barnabas M. Ahern. Reprinted with permission of the publisher Fides/Claretian, Notre Dame, Indiana.

Excerpts from *Invitation to the New Testament* by W. D. Davies. Copyright © 1966 by William D. Davies. Reprinted by permission of Doubleday & Company, Inc. and Darton Longman & Todd Ltd.

Excerpts from *Saint Matthew* by J. C. Fenton. (The Pelican New Testament Commentaries, 1963.) Copyright © J. C. Fenton, 1963. Reprinted by permission.

Excerpt from *Saint Luke* by G. B. Caird. (The Pelican New Testament Commentaries, 1963.) Copyright © G. B. Caird, 1963. Reprinted by permission.

Excerpt from *A New Look At An Old Book* by Luke H. Grollenberg. Translated by Richard Rutherford. Paulist Press. Used by permission.

Reprinted with permission from *Light On the Gospels* by John L. McKenzie, © 1976. Published by the Thomas More Association. Chicago, Illinois 60601.

Excerpt from *A Modern Scriptural Approach to the Spiritual Exercises* by David Stanley. Reprinted by permission from The Institute of Jesuit Sources.

Excerpt from "Where Jesus Walked" by Howard LaFay. *National Geographic* Magazine, September 1967. Used by permission.

Excerpts from *Jesus and His Story* by Ethelbert Stauffer, translated by Richard and Clara Winston. © 1960 by Alfred A. Knopf, Inc. Used by permission.

Excerpt from "The Birthday of the Unconquerable Sun" by John M. Scott. Published in *Today's Catholic Teacher* Nov.-Dec. 1971. Used with permission from the publisher.

Excerpts from Howard LaFay in *Everyday Life in Bible Times*, © National Geographic Society, 1967, 1976, 1977. Reprinted by permission.

Excerpts from *Lord of History* by Vincent Novak. © 1966 Holt, Rinehart and Winston, Publishers. Used by permission of publisher.

Excerpts from "Hidden in Jesus Before the Father" by George A. Aschenbrenner. *Review for Religious,* January 1975. Reprinted with permission.

Excerpt from *Daily Life in the Time of Jesus* by Henri Daniel-Rops. © 1962 by Hawthorn Books, Inc. By permission of Hawthorn Books, Inc.

Excerpts from *In the Steps of the Master* by H. V. Morton. Dodd, Mead & Company. Reprinted by permission from H. V. Morton.

Excerpts from *The Gospel of Luke* (Daily Study Bible Series) by William Barclay. Published U.S.A., 1957 by The Westminster Press. Used by permission of The Westminster Press and The Saint Andrew Press, Scotland.

Excerpt from "Language of Christ Still Buys Loaves, Fishes in Maalula" by Ray Vicker. Published in *The Wall Street Journal,* May 3, 1976. Reprinted with permission.

Excerpt from *New Testament History* by F. F. Bruce. Copyright © 1972. Reprinted by permission of Doubleday & Company, Inc.

Reprinted by permission of G. P. Putnam's Sons from *Alone* by Richard E. Byrd. Copyright 1938 by Richard E. Byrd; renewed 1966.

Excerpt with deletions from page 51 of *Jesus: The Man Who Lives* by Malcolm Muggeridge. Copyright © 1975 by Malcolm Muggeridge. Reprinted by permission of Harper & Row Publishers, Inc. and Rainbird Publishing Group Ltd.

Excerpts from *Jesus of Nazareth* by William Barclay. © 1977 William Collins & World Publishing Company. © RAI & ITC Inc. Television Co. LTD and William Barclay. Reprinted with permission.

Excerpt from "Why Drive When You Can Walk?" by Doug Alderson. Reprinted by permission from *Campus Life* Magazine, Copyright © 1976, Youth for Christ International, Wheaton, Illinois.

Excerpt from *Man's Search for Meaning* by Viktor Frankl. Rev. ed. © 1963 Beacon Press. Reprinted by permission from Beacon Press and Hodder & Stoughton Ltd.

Excerpt from *A Shorter Life of Christ* by Donald Guthrie. Copyright © 1970 by Zondervan Publishing House. Used by permission.

Excerpt from Kee, Young, and Froelich, *Understanding the New Testament*, 3rd ed. © 1973, pp. 49–50. Reprinted by permission of Prentice-Hall, Inc., Englewood Cliffs, N. J.

Excerpt from *Dictionary of the Bible* by John L. McKenzie. Copyright © 1965 Bruce Publishing Company. Used by permission.

Excerpt from *Am I Free?* by Catherine Fletcher. © 1975 Argus Communications. Published in the U.S.A. under license from the National Christian Education Council, Robert Denholm House, England.

FIRST EDITION

Cover Design: Gene Tarpey
Book Design: Gene Tarpey, David Povilaitis
Illustrations and Maps: David Povilaitis

© Copyright 1978 Argus Communications, A Division of DLM, Inc.

Argus Communications
A Division of DLM, Inc.
7440 Natchez Avenue
Niles, Illinois 60648

International Standard Book Number: 0-89505-014-5
Library of Congress Catalog Card Number: 78-53943

0 9 8 7 6 5 4 3

PHOTO CREDITS

ACKNOWLEDGMENTS *(continued)*

Excerpt from *Stride Toward Freedom* by Martin Luther King, Jr. Copyright © 1958 by Martin Luther King, Jr. Reprinted by permission of Harper & Row Publishers, Inc. and Joan Daves.

Excerpt from *In God's Underground* by Richard Wurmbrand. © 1968 Diane Publishing Company. Used by permission of Richard Wurmbrand.

Excerpt from *Report to Greco* by Nikos Kazantzakis. Copyright © 1965 by Simon & Schuster, Inc. Reprinted by permission of Simon & Schuster, a Division of Gulf & Western Corporation, and Helen Kazantzaki.

Excerpt from "When You Pray, Say: Abba!" by Dorothy Dawes, *The Bible Today Reader.* Published by The Liturgical Press. Copyrighted by The Order of St. Benedict, Inc. Collegeville, Minnesota.

Excerpt from "It Happened One Night on the River Kwai" by Ernest Gordon and Clarence Hall. Condensed from the *Christian Herald,* June 1960. © 1960 Christian Herald Association.

Excerpt from *Hungry for God* by Ralph Martin. Copyright © 1974 by Ralph Martin. Reprinted by permission of Doubleday & Company, Inc.

Excerpt from "The Magic of Good Posture" by Warren R. Young. *The Reader's Digest,* November 1971. Copyright 1971 by The Reader's Digest Assn., Inc.

Excerpt from "The Gospel of St. Matthew" by David Stanley in the *New Testament Reading Guide.* Published by The Liturgical Press. Copyrighted by The Order of St. Benedict, Inc. Collegeville, Minnesota.

Excerpt from "The Gospel According to Matthew" by John L. McKenzie. Brown, Fitzmyer, and Murphy, eds., *The Jerome Biblical Commentary,* © 1968, p. 105. Reprinted by permission of Prentice-Hall, Inc., Englewood Cliffs, N.J.

Excerpts from *The Living Reminder: Service and Prayer in Memory of Jesus Christ* by Henri J. Nouwen. © 1977 by The Seabury Press, Inc. Used by permission of the Publishers.

Excerpt from "The Friday Incident" by Drew Duke. Copyright 1974 Guideposts Associates, Inc., Carmel, N.Y. 10512. Used by permission from *GUIDEPOSTS MAGAZINE.*

Excerpt from *The Life of Christ* by Guiseppe Ricciotti. © Christian Classics 1952.

Excerpt from "A Death in Jerusalem." Reprinted by permission from *TIME,* The Weekly Newsmagazine; Copyright Time Inc. 1971.

Excerpt from *God In An Age of Atheism* by Paul Shilling. © 1969 Abingdon Press. Used by permission.

Excerpt from *Who Is Christ?* by Anthony Padovano. © 1967 Ave Maria Press. Used by permission.

Excerpt from "Those Who Lie in Jail." Reprinted by permission from *TIME,* The Weekly Newsmagazine; Copyright Time Inc. 1951.

Excerpt from *The Amazing Results of Positive Thinking* by Norman Vincent Peale. © 1959 by Prentice-Hall, Inc. Published by Prentice-Hall, Inc. Englewood Cliffs, N.J. Used with permission.

Excerpt from *But That I Can't Believe* by John A. T. Robinson. © 1967 The New American Library. Reprinted by permission from The Rt. Reverend Dr. J. A. T. Robinson.

Excerpt from *Who Do You Say I Am?* by Edward J. Ciuba. © 1974 Alba House. Used with permission.

Excerpt from *The Winter of Our Discontent* by John Steinbeck. Copyright © 1961 by John Steinbeck. Reprinted by permission of The Viking Press.

Excerpt from *Salvation History: An Introduction to Biblical Theology* by Neal M. Flanagan, Copyright 1964, Sheed and Ward, 1964.

Excerpt from *An Analytical Approach to the New Testament* by F. B. Rhein. © 1974 Barron's Educational Series, Inc. Used by permission.

Excerpts from ". . . A Quest for the True Jesus." *NEWSWEEK,* April 11, 1966. Copyright 1966 by Newsweek, Inc. All rights reserved. Used by permission.

Excerpt from *Mere Christianity* by C. S. Lewis. © 1954 Macmillan Publishing Co., Inc. Used by permission from Macmillan Publishing Co., Inc. and William Collins Sons & Co. Ltd.

Excerpt from *God of the Oppressed* by James H. Cone. © 1975 The Seabury Press. Reprinted by permission from The Seabury Press and the Society for Promoting Christian Knowledge, London 1977.

Also available
THESE STONES WILL SHOUT
A New Voice for the Old Testament
by Mark Link

CONTENTS

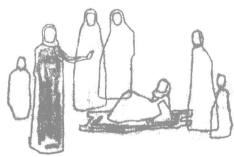

THE GOOD NEWS PROCLAIMED

Then the seventh angel blew his trumpet.
Loud voices in heaven cried out,
"The kingdom of the world
now belongs to our Lord and his Anointed One,
and he shall reign forever and ever."

REVELATION 11:15

This vision, recorded by John, is the one
that guided the early Christian community.
Jesus' victory was their victory.

Strife from within and persecution from without
never dimmed the vision.
Above the threatening sound of thunder
was always heard the seventh trumpet.
The darker the stormy skies,
the brighter shone the rainbow of hope.
John Knox put it well:

The primitive Christian community
was not a memorial society
with its eyes fastened on a departed master;
it was a dynamic community
created around a living and present Lord.

It is this dynamic vision
that the modern Christian community
must recapture and share with the world.
For the kingdom begun by Jesus
was left to his followers to complete:

Go, therefore,
and make disciples of all nations . . . .
And know that I am with you always
until the end of the world.

MATTHEW 28:19-20

Easter, 1978   Mark Link, S.J.

Second-century Roman aqueduct near Caesarea-on-the-Sea.
Caesarea was built by Herod the Great (39–4 B.C) to honor Augustus Caesar (27–14 B.C.)
Later it became the residence of Pontius Pilate (A.D. 26–36).

PART ONE

INTRODUCTION PRE-MINISTRY

1

Phenomenon
of Jesus

Like all people
who spend their lives planting seeds
that grow to greatness only after they die,
Jesus was largely overlooked by historians.

Modern chroniclers have gone far, however,
to correct this oversight.
H. G. Wells, for example, ranks Jesus first
among history's greatest people.

_____"The Three Greatest Men in History"
H. G. WELLS

I am speaking of him as a man . . . .
The historian must treat him as a man
just as a painter must paint him as a man. . . .

Of course the reader and I live in countries
where to millions of persons,
Jesus is more than a man.
But the historian must disregard that fact.
He must adhere to the evidence
that would pass unchallenged
if his book were to be read
in every nation under the sun.

Now it is interesting and significant
that a historian . . . like myself
who does not even call himself a Christian
finds the picture centering irresistably
around the life and character
of this most significant man.

Why is the picture centering around Jesus?
Why is he deserving of "first place"
as history's greatest individual?

That place is his by virtue of the . . .
profound ideas which he released—
the profound importance
of the individual under the Fatherhood of God
and the conception of the kingdom of heaven.

It is one of the most revolutionary
changes of outlook
that has ever stirred and changed human thought.
No age has even yet understood fully
the tremendous challenge it carries. . . .
But the world began to be a different world
from the day that doctrine was preached
and every step toward wider understanding
and tolerance and good will
is a step in the direction
of that universal brotherhood Christ proclaimed.

The historian's test of an individual's greatness
is "What did he leave to grow?"
Did he start men to thinking along fresh lines
with a vigor that persisted after him?
By this test Jesus stands first.

JEWISH CHRONICLERS

An ancient chronicler who did not overlook Jesus
was the Jewish historian, Josephus.
Josephus began public life as an army officer.
His military career ended in A.D. 67, however,
when he was captured in a revolt against Rome.
Later, Josephus turned to writing history.
He said of Jesus:

_____Jewish Antiquities
FLAVIUS JOSEPHUS

There lived a wise man—
if, indeed, we can call him a man—named Jesus.
A wonder-worker

2

and a teacher of those who search after truth,
he attracted crowds of both Jews and Gentiles.
He was the Christ.
Nevertheless, Pilate, at the urging of our leaders,
sentenced him to death on the cross.
His disciples remained faithful, however,
and after 3 days he appeared to them alive.
This and many other marvelous things
had been foretold about him by the prophets.
The Christian sect, named after him,
still flourishes to this day.

For centuries, this passage from Josephus
was widely quoted and accepted.
But critics later began to challenge it.
They felt it odd a Jewish, nondisciple of Jesus
would identify him flatly as "the Christ" (messiah).
They suggested that some pro-Christian editor
may have tampered with the manuscript.

Others countered, however, saying that Josephus
was reporting on widespread popular belief,
not his own personal belief.
The present attitude toward the text is, generally,
one of acceptance until definitely proven otherwise.

ROMAN CHRONICLERS

Two ancient Romans who mention Jesus
are Tacitus and Pliny the Younger.
They treat him only incidentally and indirectly.
Nevertheless, a glance at what they do say
proves interesting.
Consider Tacitus (A.D. 55–117).

TACITUS

Writing sometime after A.D. 110,
Tacitus refers to Jesus
in reporting the worst fire in Rome's history.

Occurring in Nero's reign in A.D. 64, the fire
swept out of control through the narrow alleys
and winding streets of old Rome.

Single Figure

Putting his signature to a massive study
of history, a modern scholar wrote of Jesus:

A Study of History
A. J. TOYNBEE
abridged by D. C. SOMERVELL

When we set out on this quest,
we found ourselves moving in the midst
of a mighty host,
but, as we pressed forward, the marchers,
company by company,
have all fallen out of the race. . . .
And now, as we stand
and gaze with our eyes on the farther shore,
a single figure raises from the flood
and straightway fills the whole horizon.

Another scholar wrote:

The Life of Jesus
ERNEST RENAN

There are pillars that rise towards the sky,
and bear witness to a nobler destiny.
Jesus is the highest of these pillars
which show to man
whence he comes and whither he ought to tend.
In him was condensed
all that is good and elevated
in our human nature.

3

All exits leading from the burning sector
were clogged with hysterical people,
fleeing for their lives.
When a number of survivors reported
seeing men with burning torches,
rumors spread about that Nero had the fire set.

After almost a week of burning,
the fire was finally brought under control.
But then, another massive fire broke out
in another area of the city.
Now rumors spread faster than the flames
that Nero was, indeed, behind the burnings,
"seeking to build a new capital
and to name it for himself."

In the weeks that followed,
Nero did his utmost to squelch the rumors.
But they refused to die.
Finally, he decided upon a desperate move.
He would find a scapegoat to blame,
thus shifting attention away from himself.
For his scapegoat,
Nero chose a religious sect called Christians.

Describing the sect's origin,
Tacitus says they took their name from Christ,
"who was executed during Tiberius' reign
by sentence of Pontius Pilate."
He then details Nero's purge of the Christians:

Annals
_____
TACITUS

First, known members of the sect were seized.
Then, on their information, crowds were seized,
not so much on arson charges as out of hate. . . .
Unusual brutality attended their execution:
they were dressed in animal skins
and torn to pieces by enraged dogs;
they were put on crosses, and at nighttime,
burned as torches to light up the darkness.
Nero sponsored the exhibitions in his Gardens.

He also held performances in his Circus,
mixing with the crowds
and dressed in the garb of a charioteer. . . .

Although the sect deserved some punishment,
a feeling of pity developed for them.
For it seemed clear to many
that they were executed not for the state's sake,
but because of the madness of one man.

PLINY

Pliny's reference to Jesus
comes in a letter written around A.D. 110.
Addressed to the Roman emperor, Trajan,
it deals with problems Pliny was experiencing
as a Roman administrator in Bithynia (now part
of modern Turkey).

The Founder of Christianity
_____
C. H. DODD

He had on his hands strikes,
municipal scandals, and political disaffection.
There was also some religious unrest.
Many temples, he reported,

were practically deserted, and in some,
services had been discontinued.
There was a slump in agricultural markets,
because people were no longer buying beasts
for sacrifice as they should.

It was all the fault, so his informants said,
of some people called "Christians,"
who formed a secret society . . .
and who were certainly disloyal to the empire,
since they refused to offer sacrifice
to the god-emperor.
So a number of Christians were arrested
and brought to trial.

Pliny himself described the procedure followed
against Christians.

Letters To Trajan
PLINY

I questioned them, personally,
asking them if they were Christian.
If they said they were, I repeated the question,
informing them of the penalty involved.
If they persisted, I ordered them punished.

Those who denied being Christian, I released—
but only after they acknowledged the gods,
honored your image, and defamed Christ. . . .

Some affirmed they had once been Christians,
but no longer were. . . .
They also admitted meeting regularly at sunrise
on a stated day to pray to Christ as to a god.

First Christians

Condemned to be thrown to the beasts
to entertain spectators, a Christian wrote:

Letters
IGNATIUS OF ANTIOCH (c. A.D. 100)

I am God's wheat
and shall be ground by the teeth of wild beasts,
so that I may become God's pure bread.
Pray to Christ for me. . . .
The time for my birth is close at hand.

Roman Colosseum,
where many early Christians were put to death.
Huge awnings protected spectators from the sun.
It could be flooded for water spectacles and
held 45,000 people.

Finally, they admitted taking a solemn oath,
not with criminal intent, but to refrain from fraud,
theft, adultery, and betraying a trust
if called upon to do so.

After their sunrise meeting, they broke up.
But they reconvened later the same day
to share together in a harmless meal. . . .

I now want your personal advice on this matter,
because of the growing number of offenders. . . .
This contagious superstition has infected
not only the cities,
but also the towns and countryside.
But, I am confident we can still contain it.

FIRST FOLLOWERS

Pliny's belief that Christianity could be contained
recalls earlier efforts to control it.
After the resurrection, Jerusalem authorities
forbade the apostles to teach in Jesus' name.

To this, Peter and the apostles replied:
"Better for us to obey God than men!"

When the Sanhedrin heard this,
they were stung to fury and wanted to kill them.
Then a member of the Sanhedrin stood up,
a Pharisee named Gamaliel, a teacher of the law
highly regarded by all. . . .

"Fellow Israelites, think twice
about what you are going to do with these men. . . .
Let them alone.
If their purpose or activity is human in its origins,
it will destroy itself.
If, on the other hand, it comes from God,
you will not be able to destroy them
without fighting God himself."

ACTS 5:29, 33–39

2

Book of Jesus

If you could choose only one of the following,
which would you take:

☐ a documentary film of all that Jesus
did and said during his lifetime or

☐ the 4 gospels?

Answering the question, a biblical expert said:
"Without hesitation, I would take the 4 gospels."

REPORTER *You imply there is no comparison*
between the 2 choices.

EXPERT *Not the slightest.*
The 4 gospels are more valuable
than any film could ever be.

REPORTER *Why is that?*

EXPERT *Often Jesus' own disciples did not*
understand something Jesus said or did.
For example, they did not understand
Jesus' passion prophecy. (Mark 9:32)
Nor did they understand the Palm
Sunday episode. (John 12:16)

REPORTER *What happened to Jesus' disciples later*
to help them understand these things?

EXPERT *Exactly what Jesus said would happen:*
"The Holy Spirit whom the Father
will send in my name
will instruct you in everything

and remind you of all that I told you."
(John 14:25, 16:13)

REPORTER *In other words,*
what makes the gospels invaluable is
that they were written in the light of
the Holy Spirit's coming on Pentecost.

EXPERT *Precisely!*
Pentecost gave Jesus' followers
their faith-insight into Jesus' life.
It is this insight
that is recorded in the gospels.
John's gospel, especially,
reflects this new perspective. (John 2:22)

REPORTER *Now I see.*
Lots of people saw what Jesus did
and heard what he said,
but missed the point of it all.
In the same way,
if we had a documentary film of Jesus'
life, but no gospels,
we might miss the point, too.

EXPERT *Right!*

GOSPEL ORIGINS

Jesus
DONALD SENIOR

On the wall of my office hangs a painting
that I treasure;
it was a gift from my parents
when I received my doctoral degree.
The painting is a copy of a medieval portrait
of the evangelist Matthew. The scene is familiar.

Matthew,
a venerable old man with a flowing beard . . .
bends over a writing desk
where a large parchment scroll
is spread before him. The evangelist is alone.

A classic angel
with wings and flowing white garment
stands beside Matthew,
one arm around the evangelist's shoulder
and the other firmly guiding his hand. . . .
Few of us would have trouble
interpreting the message of this painting.
Matthew is writing his gospel.
The angel symbolizes
the divine guidance or 'inspiration'
that certifies that the gospel Matthew is writing
is not an ordinary book
but our Sacred Scripture, the word of God. . . .
The problem with the painting's image
is not the value it seeks to communicate
but the process of composing the gospel
that it implies.

The evangelists were not simply secretaries.
The process of gospel composition
is much more complex—and much richer.
Divine guidance, for example, began long before
the evangelist picked up a pen to begin writing.

In fact, many parables and stories
that the evangelist wrote down
had a definite shape and form already,
as a result of being preached so often
by the apostles.

The 4 gospels, as we find them in today's bible,
passed through 3 stages before reaching this form.

FIRST STAGE

The first stage was the actual life and teaching
of Jesus himself.
About the unparalleled life of Jesus,
an unknown poet wrote these memorable words:

He never wrote a book. . . .
He never owned a home. . . .
He never went to college. . . .
He never traveled two hundred miles
from the place where he was born. . . .

People Move People

No matter how beautifully expressed,
abstract ideas rarely move people.

"Pastoral Letter"
CARDINAL DUVAL

But let a person come forward,
a living person, capable of speaking to the heart;
let truth flow from the person's life,
and let the person's power
be matched by an equal gift of love;
then people will listen to the good news . . .
and the dawn of better days . . .
will brighten our skies.

While still a young man,
the tide of popular opinion turned against him.
His friends ran away. . . .

He was nailed to a cross. . . .
When he was dead, he was taken down
and laid in a borrowed grave. . . .

Nineteen wide centuries have come and gone
and he is still the centerpiece of the human race.

The first stage in the formation of the gospels
was the actual life and preaching of Jesus himself.

SECOND STAGE

The next stage
was the preaching of Jesus' life and message
by the apostles.
This stage began on Pentecost. (Acts 2:14)

Wherever they could find a soapbox and a crowd,
Jesus' followers shared the "good news"
of Jesus' life, death, and resurrection.
And what they preached was what they themselves
had seen and heard as eyewitnesses.
John underlined this point:

We proclaim . . .
what we have heard,
what we have seen with our eyes,
what we have looked upon
and our hands have touched—
we speak of the word of life. . . .
What we have seen and heard
we proclaim in turn to you
so that you may share life with us.

1 JOHN 1:1, 3

With burning urgency,
Jesus' followers carried the "good news"
beyond Jerusalem's walls and Galilee's hills
to Greece—and even Rome itself.

Part of the urgency stemmed from the conviction that Jesus' "second coming" would take place when his message was preached to every nation. Some of Jesus' followers thought this to be possible during their own life.

"Why record Jesus' words, if the end is near?" they would have reasoned.

The gospel's "oral" stage lasted about 30 years. During this period, parts of the gospel began to take the shape they now have. One reason for this was the Lord's Supper, celebrated in Jesus' memory. (Luke 20:17)

Part of each meal was given over to recalling Jesus' life and teaching. Events closely linked to the Supper's meaning were reviewed in a special way:

the wine miracle at Cana,   John 2:1
the bread miracle by the sea,   John 6:1
the Last Supper,   Luke 22:17
the "breaking of bread" at Emmaus. Luke 22:13

Christians also recalled Jesus' words and works on other special occasions. One was when they gathered to anoint and pray for the community's sick members. A first-century plate, unearthed in Palestine, recalls the instruction of James:

Is there anyone sick among you?
He should ask for the presbyters of the church.
They in turn are to pray over him,
anointing him with oil in the Name (of the Lord).
                              JAMES 5:14

Archaeologists believe the plate was designed specifically for use in this ceremony. The ceremony was also enriched, no doubt, by recalling Jesus' miracles related to healing.

Christians recalled Jesus' teaching, also, when they met to discuss problems related to daily life in the world in which they lived.

For example, Jesus' followers were criticized for showing concern for sinners and outcasts, for ignoring certain sabbath observances, and for paying taxes to Rome. The community answered these criticisms by recalling what Jesus did or taught concerning sinners (Mark 2:16), the sabbath (Mark 2:27), and taxes (Mark 12:17).

Finally, when missionary work expanded, and communities welcomed new members, instruction became necessary. This gave rise to further "oral" formulations of Jesus' life and teaching.

Before concluding our discussion of the oral stage, an observation is in order. It is hard for us in this age of the "printed word" to appreciate the role that the "oral word" played in certain civilizations. Alex Haley can be a help here.

As a boy, Haley used to sit on the front porch of his grandmother's house in Tennessee and listen to her tell stories about his ancestors. The stories went all the way back to *"Kin-tay,"* who had been kidnapped into slavery while chopping wood near *"Kambay Bolongo."*

Fifty years later, Haley went to Africa to try to learn his ancestry. He talked with villagers in the backcountry.

Roots
ALEX HALEY

They told me something of which I never dreamed,
of very old men, called griots . . .
who told on special occasions the centuries-old
histories of villages, of clans, of families . . .
and there were certain legendary griots
who could narrate facets of African history
literally for as long as three days
without ever repeating themselves.

9

Haley eventually found his ancestral village
and consulted with the village *griot:*

The old man sat down, facing me. . . .
Then he began to recite for me
the ancestral history of the Kinte clan. . . .
I was struck not only by the profusion of details,
but also by the narrative's biblical style,
something like: . . . and so-and-so took his wife
so-and-so, and begat. . . .

Two hours later, the griot came to the 1700s.
All of a sudden, Haley heard the name
he was listening for: "Omorro Kinte begat Kunta."
More amazing was the detail that followed:
"Kunta went away from his village to chop
wood . . . and he was never seen again."

Haley says:

I sat as if I were carved of stone.
My blood seemed to have congealed.
This man whose lifetime
had been in this backcountry African village
had no way in the world to know
that he had just echoed what I had heard
all through my boyhood years
on my grandma's porch in Henning, Tennessee.

Through a similar "oral" process,
the life and teaching of Jesus was preserved
by the apostles.

THIRD STAGE

Finally came the "writing" stage.
It began when it was clear
that Jesus' "second coming" would not happen
during the lifetime of his original followers.
Guided by the Holy Spirit,
the evangelists decided to collect, edit,
and record the oral traditions about Jesus.
Luke alludes to the process:

New Testament Books

The New Testament could fit
into a *New York Times* Sunday Supplement.
Composed of 27 short writings, called books,
it divides into 4 sections.

Gospels The 4 gospels ("good news") are
so called because they announce the good news
of God's entry into history in Jesus
to free us from evil.
The first 3 gospels—Mark, Matthew, Luke—
are known as the "synoptic gospels."
Synoptic (*syn* "together" and *opsis* "seeing")
indicates they are so similar, in parts,
that they can be put side by side for study.

Acts of the Apostles This book was
written by Luke as a sequel to his gospel.
It describes the early Christian community
and traces its westward expansion to Rome.

Letters There are 21 letters. Thirteen bear
Paul's name; 9 are addressed to churches:
Romans, Corinthians 1, 2, Galatians, Ephesians,
Philippians, Colossians, Thessalonians 1, 2.
The remaining 4 are addressed to individuals:
Philemon, Timothy 1, 2, and Titus.

Seven other letters are by other writers:
James, Jude, Peter 1, 2, and John 1, 2, 3.
A final letter to the Hebrews is anonymous,
though early writers linked it to Paul.

Revelation The writing style of this book
confuses us, but was familiar to early Christians.
Called apocalyptic ("to unveil"), the style
overflows with symbolic visions and images.
This book, written by John,
exhorts Christians persecuted
by the Emperor Flavian (A.D. 69–96) to persevere,
and assures them of final victory in Christ.

Synoptic Gospels

MARK

Six days later,
Jesus took with him
Peter, James, and John
and led them up a high mountain,
where they were alone.

As they looked on,
a change came over Jesus,
and his clothes
became shining white—
whiter than anyone in the world
could wash them.

Then the three disciples
saw Elijah and Moses
talking with Jesus.
Peter spoke up. . . .

MARK 9:2–5 (TEV)

LUKE

About a week after
he said these things,
Jesus took Peter, John, and James
with him and went up a hill
to pray.

While he was praying,
his face changed its appearance,
and his clothes
became dazzling white.

Suddenly two men
were there talking to him.
They were Moses and Elijah,
who appeared in heavenly glory
and talked with Jesus. . . .

LUKE 9:28–31 (TEV)

MATTHEW

Six days later
Jesus took with him Peter
and the brothers James and John
and led them up a high mountain
where they were alone.

As they looked on,
a change came over Jesus:
his face was shining like the sun,
and his clothes
were dazzling white.

Then the three disciples
saw Moses and Elijah
talking with Jesus.
So Peter spoke up. . . .

MATTHEW 17:1–4 (TEV)

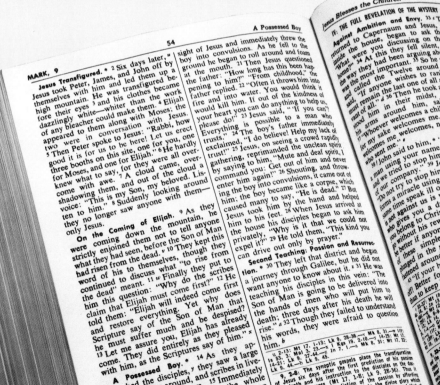

Many have undertaken to compile a narrative
of the events
which have been fulfilled in our midst,
precisely as those events were transmitted
to us by the original eyewitnesses
and ministers of the word.
I too have carefully traced
the whole sequence of events from the beginning,
and have decided to set it down in writing
for you, Theophilus,
so that Your Excellency may see how reliable
the instruction was that you received.

LUKE 1:1-4

Each evangelist assembled the oral traditions;
then, guided by the Holy Spirit, molded them
into the unique form each gospel now takes.

At times, we can see where this or that writer
stitched together a series of memorized events
about Jesus.

Expressions such as "one day" or "once"
are frequently telltale seams where the writer
sewed together 2 oral traditions about Jesus.
(Luke 5:12, 17, 6:1)

This helps to explain why we can easily divide
the gospel into handy "reading packages"
for use in liturgical worship.
The reason is that sections of the gospel
are made up of prepackaged readings,
originally used by early Christians
as part of their worship and catechesis.

In summary, the gospels went through 3 stages
in their formation:

> what Jesus did and said,
> what the apostles recalled and preached,
> what the evangelists recorded.

An analogy or comparison might be helpful.

The floor of the ocean is littered with sea shells.
Only some of these are swept onto the shore.
There wind and rain smooth away rough edges.
The sunlight brings out rich coloring.
A man finds them there,
gathers them up and forms them into a vase,
beautiful in shape and color.
To appreciate the exquisite beauty of the vase
we not only gaze at its whole contour
and color pattern, but we study also
the graceful turn and delicate tint of each shell.

It is the same with the gospels.
Our Lord's life was like an ocean bed
filled with words and deeds in such abundance
that books could not contain them. [John 21:25]
Only some of these reached the shore
of the primitive community.
There the wind and light of the Spirit
shaped the telling of each deed
and illumined its deeper meaning.
The evangelists gathered together these living
memories and molded them into a gospel
under the light of the Spirit.
No two gospels are the same;
each has its own contour and coloring.

3

Perspectives of Jesus

When each evangelist sat down to write,
he found himself in a situation
similar to that of a committee of students
considering the format for the school yearbook.
On the table are boxes of photographs,
ranging from photos taken on the first day
to others taken during the last week.

Some of the photos deal with sports events;
others, social events;
and still others concern the school plays.
Finally, there are random photos of people
doing all sorts of things.

Eventually
the time comes to decide on the book's format.

One group suggests
that the format follow an exact time sequence.
That is, each photo should appear in the order
in which it was taken.
Thus, the book would act as a picture "history"
of the year as it unfolded.

Another group suggests making the book
into a kind of "biography" of the typical student
going through the school year.
This would give the book a personal touch
that a picture "history" would not have.

A third group suggests dividing the book
according to a "theme" like "Self-Discovery."
The idea would be to treat each year differently.
For example, freshmen would be shown
getting acquainted; sophomores, getting involved;
juniors, taking over leadership roles;
and seniors, preparing college and work forms.
The idea would be to show how each year
involved something new for each student.

The evangelist faced a similar situation
when it came to the life and teaching of Jesus.
He had many "word pictures" of Jesus' life:
miracles, parables, and events from Jesus'
passion, death, and resurrection.

The question each writer faced was this:
How should I arrange these "word pictures"?
Should I choose an approach that is primarily:

☐　historical,

☐　biographical,

☐　theological.

Guided by the Holy Spirit,
each of the 4 evangelists chose the final option.
Each one opted for a faith-presentation of Jesus'
words and works.
Their reason:
they wanted not only to inform people of Jesus,
but also to invite them to *believe* in him.
Stressing the point,
John says of the events in Jesus' life:

These have been recorded to help you believe
that Jesus is the Messiah, the Son of God,
so that through this faith
you may have life in his name.

JOHN 20:31

To dramatize the purpose of the Scriptures,
this story is often told.

An old rabbi met a member of his congregation,
who began to boast:
"I have been through our Torah many times."
Rather than praise him, the rabbi said gently:
"The important thing is not how often
you have been through the Torah,
but how often the Torah has been through you."

In brief, the purpose of the 4 gospels
is not to recreate the words and works of Jesus,
but to let them recreate us.

FOUR GOSPEL VIEWS

Each gospel reflects a unique faith focus.
Each was penned at a different place,
at a different time, for a different audience.

Most agree that:
Mark wrote his gospel in Rome before 70,
mainly for Christians of gentile background;
Matthew, in Antioch (Syria) between 70 and 90,
mainly for Christians of Jewish background;
Luke, in Greece between 70 and 90,
for Christians of a Greek background;
and John, in Ephesus (Asia Minor) after 90
for Christians of a general background.

MARK'S GOSPEL

Mark's brisk account of Jesus' life and teaching
has been called the "Gospel of Jesus-on-the-Go."
Jesus is always going somewhere: to Jericho,
to Nazareth, to Capernaum, to Jerusalem.

A provocative technique Mark occasionally uses
is to ask a question and leave it unanswered.
When Jesus casts out an unclean spirit,
bystanders ask: "What does this mean?" (1:27)
When Jesus forgives the paralytic his sins,
Pharisees ask:
"Who can forgive sins except God alone?" (2:7)
When Jesus calms the sea, his disciples ask:
"Who can this be?" (4:41)

Little is known of Mark, personally.
Some think he was the young man who showed
the disciples to the upstairs room (his house?)
where they ate the Last Supper. (Mark 14:14)
Afterwards, he followed them to Gethsemani,
narrowly escaping arrest. (Mark 14:51)

Mark eventually went to Rome with Peter.
There he wrote his gospel for Christians
suffering under Nero's bloody persecution.
Perhaps this explains his stress on Jesus' role
as the suffering messiah.

Invitation to the New Testament
W. D. DAVIES

Mark's Jesus is the stark Son of Man,
destined to set his face to Jerusalem and die. . . .
The Jesus of Mark is the Jesus of the Passion.
He stands before us
in the glare of the fires lit by Nero. . . .
The strong, authoritative
and yet suffering Messiah of Mark bursts forth
upon his readers with the stark clarity and force
of a painting by Goya.

Mark opens his gospel with the words: "This is
the Good News about Jesus Christ, the Son of God."
These words point to Mark's 2 main concerns:
Jesus as "Christ" and Jesus as "Son of God."
Appropriately, Mark's gospel divides in 2 parts.

The geographic focus of the first part is Galilee.
The faith focus is Jesus as "Christ," that is,
"the promised messiah of Israel."
The first part ends with Peter saying to Jesus:
"You are the Messiah." (8:29)

The geographic focus of the last half is Jerusalem.
The faith focus is Jesus as "Son of God."
The last half ends with a Roman saying of Jesus:
"This man was really the Son of God!" (15:39)

MATTHEW'S GOSPEL

Some years after Mark recorded his gospel,
Matthew set to work on a similar project.
Writing a more detailed account than Mark,
he seems to have had Mark's gospel at hand
when he wrote.
He utilized parts of it almost word for word.
(Mark 9:2–13 and Matthew 17:1–13)

But Matthew also included new material
not found in Mark. (Matthew 1–2)

Matthew designed his gospel beautifully.
He cast the teaching of Jesus into 5 sections.
Each section has 2 parts: narrative followed by
instruction.
Each section, also, ends with a similar formula:
"When Jesus finished his teaching. . . ."
(7:28, 11:1, 13:53, 19:1, 26:1)

Matthew introduced the 5 teaching sections with
a prologue of Jesus' early years, and ended them
with an epilogue of his passion and resurrection.

Matthew's five sections of instruction
call to mind the 5 books of the Jewish Torah.
Matthew presents Jesus' instruction
as the new Christian Torah.
The heart of Jesus' instruction is God's kingdom:

its demands,	5:1–7:28
its proclamation,	10:5–11:1
its development,	13:1–13:51
its community,	18:1–19:1
its completion.	23:1–26:1

Matthew's fondness for order
appears, also, in his prologue and his epilogue.
His prologue quotation from Isaiah,
"God is with us,"
is matched with his epilogue quotation from Jesus,
"I am with you always." (1:23, 28:30)
Similarly, Jesus' birth is matched with
his resurrection (rebirth). (2:1, 28:1)

Jesus' baptism is matched with his passion,
which Jesus called a baptism. (Mark 10:38, Luke 12:50)
Lastly, Jesus' prologue temptation in the desert
is matched with
his epilogue temptation on the cross.
Satan and the mob make the same proposition,
"If you are the Son of God. . . ." (4:3, 27:40)

Poets call such a matching pattern a chiasmus:
1, 2, 3:3, 2, 1. An even clearer example of it
is Jesus' quote of Isaiah:

Sluggish indeed is this people's heart.
They have scarcely heard with their ears,
they have firmly closed their eyes,
otherwise they might see with their eyes,
and hear with their ears,
and understand with their hearts.

MATTHEW 13:15

The end-words form a chiasmic pattern:
heart, ears, eyes:eyes, ears, heart.

Saint Matthew
J. C. FENTON

It may be that Matthew has ordered
the whole of his Gospel
so that it forms one great chiasmus. . . .

The first teaching section (5–7) and the last (23–25)
are similar both in length and in subject matter
(entry into the kingdom);
similarly the second (10) and the fourth (18)
are of much the same length, and whereas
the former describes the sending-out of apostles,
the latter describes the receiving of people
who have been sent in Christ's name.
In the same way, the beginning
of the whole Gospel matches the end.

Writing mainly for Jewish Christians,
one of Matthew's main concerns was to show
how everything about Jesus

15

New Testament Canon

Who determined the New Testament *canon?*
Who decided that these 27 books, and only these,
were inspired?

Christians believe the same Spirit who guided the
writing of the books guided their determination.

History shows
that the determination process began early.
Sometime after John's gospel was written,
it was placed along with the other 3 gospels
into one volume called "The Gospel."
Around A.D. 115, Ignatius, bishop of Antioch,
referred to "The Gospel" as being authoritative.
No doubt he had in mind this volume.
Fifty years later, Tatian wove the 4 gospels
into one, continuous narrative called
"The Gospel Harmony."

Concerning the Acts of the Apostles,
evidence indicates it was first appended to Luke.
It received independent literary existence
when the 4 gospels were put in one volume.

Concerning Paul's letters,
they are already mentioned in 2 Peter 3:15.
They were also referred to in writings
by Ignatius and Polycarp around A.D. 115.

New Testament "lists" circulated early.
Around A.D. 160, the "Muratorian Fragment"
bears evidence to the 4 gospels,
13 Pauline letters, John 1, 2, and Revelation.
About A.D. 250, Origen indicates a concensus exists
concerning the 4 gospels, 13 Pauline letters,
John 1, Peter 1, and Revelation.
He indicates a concensus is lacking concerning
Hebrews, John 2, 3, Peter 2, James, Jude.

Finally, in A.D. 367, Athanasius compiled a list
of the 27 New Testament books.
In A.D. 393, a Church Council approved it officially.

matched with Jewish expectation and teaching.
Thus, he took great pains to link key events
in Jesus' life with Old Testament prophecies.

Describing Jesus' return from Egypt, he says:
"This was done to make come true
what the Lord had said through the prophet."
(Matthew 2:15)

Describing the slaying of the infants, he says:
"What was said through Jeremiah the prophet
was then fulfilled." (Matthew 2:18)

Matthew's point is this: Jesus is the messiah,
the fulfillment of the Old Testament prophecies.

LUKE'S GOSPEL

Whether Luke wrote before or after Matthew
is disputed by scholars.
Luke identifies himself and his purpose
in a brief preface. (Luke 1:1, Acts 1:1)

> Saint Luke
> G. B. CAIRD

Luke
had something of the poet in his makeup
and an artist's ability
to depict in vivid pen-portraits
the men and women who inhabit his pages.
He delighted in marvels and was a little inclined
to emphasize the miraculous element in his story.
He was more interested in people than in ideas.
He had a lively
social conscience and an inexhaustible sympathy
for other people's problems.

Tradition says Luke came from Antioch (Syria).
He traveled extensively with Paul.
His travel diary makes up much of Acts
and reflects clearly when he was with Paul
and when not. (Acts 16:10–17, 20:5–21:18, 27:1–28:16)
It is Paul who tells us much about Luke.

16

This "Rylands Fragment" of John 18:31–33
is the oldest bit of New Testament known to exist.
Found in Egypt in 1920, it dates from about A.D. 130.

This sketch shows how the Rylands Fragment
fitted into the original page of Greek text.

New Testament Manuscripts

Only copies of the original manuscripts exist.
One of the oldest copies dates from A.D. 200.
Called the Bodmer II papyrus,
it contains most of John's gospel.
Another ancient copy is the Beatty papyrus.
Dating from the 3rd century,
it contains most of the New Testament books.

When parchment became widely used,
copies of the New Testament became widespread.
This led to problems, since scribes sometimes
updated archaic words, rewrote awkward phrases,
and inserted clarifications.

Now scholars are studying all ancient copies
to try to produce a single master copy.
This study process is called textual criticism.

A New Look at an Old Book
LUKE H. GROLLENBERG

εἶπον αὐτῷ οἱ Ἰουδαῖοι Ἡμῖν οὐκ ἔξεστιν
They said to him the Jews for us not it is possible
ἀποκτεῖναι οὐδένα· ἵνα ὁ λόγος τοῦ Ἰησου
to kill no one that the word of Jesus
πληρωθῇ ὃν εἶπεν σημαίνων ποίῳ θανάτῳ
might be fulfilled which he said indicating the kind of death
ἤμελλεν ἀποθνήσκειν. Εἰσῆλθεν οὖν πάλιν
he was to die he entered therefore again
εἰς τὸ πραιτώριον ὁ Πειλᾶτος καὶ ἐφώνη
into the praetorium Pilate and he called
σεν τὸν Ἰησοῦν καὶ εἶπεν αὐτῷ Σὺ εἶ ὁ βα
for Jesus and he said to him you are the
σιλεὺς τῶν Ἰουδαίων;
King of the Jews?

"Textual criticism"
as an independent branch of science
first began to flourish in the 19th century.
Investigators traveled all over Europe,
Asia Minor, Palestine and Egypt to track down
old Greek manuscripts of the Bible. . . .
By the turn of the century they had located
about 4,000 containing the New Testament,
either in its entirety or in part.
All these texts were carefully compared
with each other.
If in a number of copies the same variant
was observed, this was an indication
that they had a common "ancestor."

The goal of producing a master copy continues.
Much has been accomplished already;
much more still remains to be done.

Paul says Luke was a gentile by birth
and a doctor by profession. (Colossians 4:10–11)
As a gentile,
Luke sought to tell gentiles about Jesus.
Luke's writing reflects that his readership
is ignorant of Palestinian geography.
He explains town names and locations. (4:31,
23:51, 24:13)
He also explains Jewish customs. (22:1, 23:56)

Besides his contact with Paul, where did Luke
learn about Jesus? Again, Paul helps us.
He tells us that Luke had contact with Mark.
(Colossians 4:10)
He suggests, also, that he may have met Peter
in Antioch, Luke's home town. (Galatians 2:11)

Luke's own writing
suggests another interesting source: Manaen,
"who was brought up with Herod." (Acts 13:1)
This would explain Luke's remarkable coverage
of certain events involving Herod. (Acts 12,
Luke 9:7–9, 23:6–12)

Writing mainly for gentiles,
Luke underscores the fact that Jesus fulfilled
not just Jewish dreams, but also gentile dreams.
Luke also underscores Jesus' special concern
for the "second-class citizens" of society.

Concerning women, for example, Luke records
4 incidents that are found in no other gospel:

the widow of Naim,	7:11–17
Joanna and Susanna,	8:1–3
the woman and the lost coin,	15:8–10
the widow and the unfair judge.	18:1–8

Similarly, Luke notes Jesus' concern
for sinners and religious outcasts.
This group included those who were "unclean"
because of occupation.

Artists' Symbols

I was caught up in ecstasy.
A throne was standing there in heaven. . . .
At the very center . . .
stood four living creatures. . . .
The first creature resembled a lion,
the second an ox;
the third the face of a man,
while the fourth looked like an eagle in flight.

REVELATION 4:2–7

Ancient artists linked the 4 living creatures
with the 4 evangelists:
the desert lion with Mark,
whose gospel opens with a "voice in the desert";
the sacrificial ox with Luke,
whose gospel opens with sacrifice in the temple;
the man with Matthew,
who opens with a record of Jesus' ancestry;
and the eagle with John,
who opens with a hymn to Jesus,
who alone looks on God's face,
just as the eagle alone looks on the sun's face.

Artists also linked the creatures with Jesus':

incarnation (man),   resurrection (lion),
redemption (ox),   ascension (eagle).

The lion and eagle symbols
need some explanation.
According to medieval folklore,
the lion slept with eyes open, thus symbolizing
the resurrection when
Jesus' divinity kept eyes open,
while his humanity slept.
The eagle, according to medieval folklore,
soared beyond the highest cloud,
thus symbolizing the ascension
when Jesus soared beyond the earth.

Sculptured panel above the main doorway
of the Cathedral of Chartres in France.

*Those whose occupations
brought them into contact with Gentiles
were proscribed as officially unclean
and incapable of keeping the Law:
toll collectors, traders. . . .
Others, like shepherds, bore the stigma
of popular suspicion for dishonesty. . . .*

*Such suspicion banned them
from the temple worship
and from being able
to give testimony in a court of law.
And, of course, public sinners. . . .
had absolutely no hope of achieving fidelity
under the law.*

Thirdly, Luke underlined Jesus' deep concern
for the poor:

*Blest are you poor;
the reign of God is yours.
Blest are you who hunger;
you shall be filled.
Blest are you who are weeping;
you shall laugh.*

LUKE 6:20-21

"The Jesus of Luke," says W. D. Davies,
"might well have uttered the words written
on the Statue of Liberty in New York Harbor:

*'Give me your tired, your poor,
your huddled masses yearning to breathe free. . . .
Send these,
the homeless, the tempest-tost to me.'"*

In conclusion, we might point out
that the general flow pattern of Luke's gospel
is similar to that of Mark and Matthew:

1 infancy prologue,	1:5–2:52
2 ministry prelude,	3:1–4:13
3 Galilean ministry,	4:41–9:50
4 Jerusalem journey,	9:51–19:27
5 Jerusalem ministry,	19:28–21:38
6 death-rising epilogue.	22:1–24:53

JOHN'S GOSPEL

John's opening prologue tips us off
that he approached Jesus' words and works
differently than did the other 3 evangelists.
John used the story format less than they did.
Moreover, when he did use it,
he was more interested in the symbolism
underlying it than he was the story itself.

A case in point is the miracle stories.
Mark devotes 200 of 425 verses of chapters 1–10
directly or indirectly to miracles.
John, on the other hand, describes only 7.
Moreover, John refers to miracles as signs.
This suggests that his concern
lies elsewhere than in the miracles themselves.

One of John's concerns is to show the link
between Jesus' ministry of signs (miracles)
and the church's ministry of signs (sacraments).

For example, Jesus' instruction to Nicodemus
concerning rebirth
inspires the church's ministry of baptism. (3:5)
Jesus' forgiveness of the paralyzed person
becomes a model of the church's forgiveness
of its own members. (5:2)
The hillside supper,
at which Jesus and his disciples minister,
becomes a sign of the Lord's Supper. (6:11, 32–35)
Jesus' anointing of the blind man's eyes
becomes a model of the church's rite
of anointing the sick of the community. (9:6)

John climaxes Jesus' ministry of signs
with the raising of Lazarus to new life. (11:11)

Thus it sums up, symbolically, Jesus' mission:
that all may have life and have it to the full. (10:10)

John's gospel
relates Jesus' ministry of signs (miracles)
to the church's ministry of signs (sacraments).
He sees both bringing the fullness of new life.

Jesus
DONALD SENIOR

*The picture of Jesus that the gospels present
is not a videotape but a portrait.
And we have not one portrait but four.*

*Thus the best way to learn about Jesus
is not to spend much time
attempting to retell from beginning to end
the life story of Jesus. . . .*

*A much richer way,
one that fits the nature of the gospels,
is to see the common features that cut across
all four New Testament portraits of Jesus.
What is there about the person and ministry
of Jesus that each of the evangelists, no matter
what the particular situation of his church,
felt compelled to include in his gospel message?*

4

Expectation of Jesus

Had *Time* magazine
been a part of the Roman scene in 64 B.C.,
it might have voted Pompey its "Man of the Year."

Pompey's star first began to glow in the heavens
when he swept the Mediterranean of pirates.
Earlier, these same pirates had kidnapped
a young Roman noble named Julius Caesar.

Next, Pompey marched his armies into Syria
and won a stunning victory.

Finally, Pompey marched on Jerusalem.
He took the city easily.
Some say that he entered it on the sabbath
and therefore encountered little resistance.
Only a handful of militants opposed his entry.
These militants eventually holed up inside
the temple area and held out for over 3 months.

Roman occupation of Jerusalem
ushered in a new era for the Jews of Judea.
For the next 135 years they suffered and bled
under the ever-poised claws of the Roman eagle.

JULIUS CAESAR

Upon his return to Rome,
Pompey struck up a political friendship
with the young military genius, Julius Caesar.
The elder Pliny described Caesar as being

Sign of Rome

Roman armies carried this standard
wherever they went.
When Pompey conquered Jerusalem,
his engineers set up similar emblems
in all public places.
The eagle stood for power,
the wreath for victory,
and the letters SPQR for *Senatus Populusque
Romanus* (The Roman Senate and People).

"most dynamic" in personality and character.
He was open, frank, and popular with troops.
Another chronicler says of him:

Caesar
SEUTONIUS

*He was skillful with sword and horse,
and had amazing powers of physical endurance.
He always was at the head of his army,
more often walking than riding,
and went bareheaded both in sun and rain.
When he encountered rivers too deep for wading,
he would either swim
or propel himself across on an inflated skin.*

But Pompey's alliance with Caesar was doomed.
By intrigue and plot, the corrupt Roman Senate
turned the 2 young leaders against each other.
Pompey fled Rome; Caesar followed in pursuit.
With the help of Antipater, an Idumean Jew,
Caesar routed Pompey and his forces.

Returning to Rome, Caesar had Antipater
appointed administrator of Judea.

Next, by astute political arm-twisting,
Caesar took control of the Roman Senate.
By 44 B.C., he was Rome's undisputed boss.
Shakespeare described Caesar's power
in this unforgettable dialogue:

CASSIUS: (whispering to Brutus)
*Why man,
he doth bestride the narrow world
like a Colossus,
and we petty men walk under
his huge legs and peep about
to find ourselves dishonorable graves.*

March 15, 44 B.C.
dawned like any other day in ancient Rome.
It was 3 days before Caesar's trip to the East,
and he had an appointment with the Senate
in Pompey's theater.
(The Senate's meeting hall was being repaired.)

When Caesar arrived, he was greeted politely.
Then something happened.
A crowd of senators rushed upon Caesar.
Seconds later, 23 daggers plunged into his body.
A stunned Caesar slumped in a pool of blood
at the foot of Pompey's statue.
In his hand, according to one report,
was a note warning him of the plot.
Someone had handed it to him on his way to the
theater, but he had neglected to read it.

AUGUSTUS CAESAR

Civil war broke out after Caesar's assassination.
Two of the assassins, Brutus and Cassius,
led one side.
Octavian, Caesar's adopted 18-year-old son,
and Mark Antony, one of Caesar's lieutenants,
opposed their bid for power.
In 2 quick battles, the assassins were crushed.

The victory catapulted young Octavian—
or Augustus, as he was later called—
into the political limelight.
Besides the power of his father's name,
Octavian seems to have been rather striking
in appearance. One of his chroniclers
describes him in this highly personal
and informal way.

Augustus
SEUTONIUS

He was quite handsome. . . .
Sometimes he would clip his beard;
sometimes he would shave it.
While his barbers were at work on him,
it was not unusual for him to read or write. . . .

His eyes were clear and radiant. . . .
His complexion was between dark and fair.
Though only five feet, six inches in height . . .
his shortness was not too noticeable
because of the good proportions of his figure.

While Octavian was growing in political stature,
so was Mark Antony.
Among the latter's political friends was Herod,
Antipater's son.
After Antipater's death by poisoning,
Antony helped Herod eventually get the title
"King of Judea."

But Antony's days of power were numbered.
He and Octavian began to disagree openly,
and a showdown took place at Actium in 31 B.C.
Octavian triumphed, but Antony managed a
spectacular escape to Egypt.
There, months later, he and his famous lover,
Cleopatra, ended their lives in suicide.

When Herod got wind of Antony's death,
he knew his own kingship now hung by a thread.
He decided upon a bold move.
Seeking an audience with Octavian, he took off
his crown and placed it at the leader's feet.

23

Mark Antony (83–30 B.C.) delivered an impassioned oration at Caesar's funeral. He divorced Octavian's sister to marry Cleopatra.

Herod's theatrics worked according to plan.
Octavian picked up the crown
and returned it to Herod, saying in effect:
"Serve me as faithfully as you did Antony."
Herod did just that, from that moment forward.

In 27 B.C. Octavian became Rome's first emperor,
taking the name Augustus Caesar.
Although he wore platform shoes to look taller,
Augustus turned out to be a giant, politically.
In later years he boasted—not incorrectly—
that he found Rome in bricks and left it in marble.

GREAT EXPECTATIONS

Something new and strange began to happen
during Augustus Caesar's reign in Rome
and Herod's reign in faraway Judea.
It seems to have been felt about the same time
in both places.
Historical records show a widespread feeling
of expectation among the masses.

The Founder of Christianity
C. H. DODD

There was something of a religious faith about it.
It invoked oracles and prophecies,
ancient and modern.
It was often associated with the figure of a 'savior'
or deliverer—a great man, perhaps a superman
with something of divinity about him. . . .

Millions of subjects of Rome saw
the emperor himself as the divine deliverer. . . .
He had given unity to a distracted world. . . .
Under Augustus it really did seem to many
as if a golden age might be round the corner.

But Augustus passed into history,
and by the time Tiberius came to power,
it was clear that the golden age
had either tarnished or vanished completely.

JUDEAN EXPECTANCY

A similar expectancy
was stirring in the winds of Herod's Judea.
Jewish masses sensed deep down in their bones
that a good time was on the way.
Unlike the Romans, the Jews could pinpoint
a concrete reason for the expectancy.

The Founder of Christianity
C. H. DODD

In the distant past, Jews believed,
the great God had revealed himself
to Moses and the prophets;
he had acted
in the deliverance of Israel from Egypt
and the restoration after the Babylonian conquest.
There was a deep longing that at this time of need,
when Israel was again oppressed,
he would again manifest himself
in appropriate action.

Jewish holy men and holy books
kept alive these memories of Israel's past.
And now there was a new wind blowing,
a new hope for freedom from Roman oppression.

This new hope found expression, especially,
in the second-century B.C. Book of Daniel.
It indicated that a glorious day was on the way.

The glorious day took the form of a coming king.
In the popular mind of the everyday Jew,
this king would catapult Israel
into first place among the nations of the world.

The Founder of Christianity
C. H. DODD

He would be the Caesar of a Jewish empire
no less universal than the Roman. . . .
To this ideal figure
was often given the title "Messiah." The term
was suggestive rather than precise in meaning.
In itself
it means no more than a person "anointed.". . .
In historical retrospect, David,
the idealized founder of the Israelite monarchy,
was 'the Lord's Anointed' (Messiah),
par excellence, *and the coming deliverer*
was some sort of second David.
Such seems to have been the most popular form
of the "messianic" idea.

It is against this background of expectancy
that both Matthew and Luke open their stories
of Jesus.

INFANCY NARRATIVES

The first 2 chapters in both Matthew and Luke
are often called the "infancy narratives."
This is because they treat Jesus' birth
and his early years.

These narratives cannot be considered
eyewitness accounts in the same sense
as the other chapters in Matthew and Luke.
The reason has to do with the way the gospels
came to be.
Recall the 3 stages of their development:

what Jesus did,
what the apostles preached,
what the evangelists recorded.

The second stage was especially important.
When the apostles gathered to pick
a replacement for Judas, after the resurrection,
they specified that it had to be someone:

. . . who was with our company
while the Lord Jesus moved among us
from the baptism of John
until the day Jesus was taken from us.
ACTS 1:21-22

In other words,
the second stage dealt with the period
between Jesus' baptism and his ascension.
Repeatedly, sermons in the Acts of the Apostles
confine themselves to this period. (Acts 2:22–36)

Thus it happened
that both Matthew and Luke ran into trouble
when they began their gospels.
Both wanted to introduce their works
with a short survey of Jesus' life
prior to his baptism.

Since the preaching of the apostles in stage two
was not too concerned with this period,
information about it was in short supply.

To remedy this situation, Matthew and Luke
went to 2 other sources for help:
old people and the Old Testament.
What did the families of Mary and Joseph recall
about this period?
What did the prophets say about the messiah
that might shed light upon Jesus' early life?
These two sources had a profound influence
on the content and style
of the first 2 chapters of Matthew and Luke.
Consider Luke's gospel.

It is the most picturesque of the 4 gospels.
No other evangelist has furnished more images

for artists and poets than Luke.
Luke's portrayal of Jesus' birth is especially picturesque.
In light of what has been said,
we know why it turned out to be so picturesque.

WORD PORTRAIT

Lacking a "word photograph" of Jesus' birth,
Luke painted a "word portrait" of it.
Moreover, to stress its historical significance,
he painted into his portrait a number of symbols.
An analogy might help.

Light on the Gospels
JOHN L. McKENZIE

*There is not much reason for thinking
that the childhood of Jesus
was any better remembered than the childhood
of any member of the poorer classes.
In our own history we can mention
Abraham Lincoln and even George Washington
who did not belong to the poorer classes;
and both of these men were born
in a time and place
where written records were better kept
than they were in Palestine in the first century.
Details of the lives of famous men become
interesting only after they become famous;
and when they have achieved fame, most of those
who knew them as children are dead. . . .*

*The birth of George Washington was not,
strictly speaking,
the birth of the Founder of his Country;
it was the birth of a male infant
to Washingtons of Virginia.
The event was fraught with historic significance,
if you wish, but no one knew it.
The artist or writer who wishes to portray
the event with its historic significance
will have to use artistic symbolism.*

This stained-glass window at Chartres
shows Matthew riding piggyback on Isaiah.
It was not the whim of a playful artist.
Rather, it dramatized for medieval Christians
an important biblical truth: the New Testament
rests upon the foundation of the Old Testament.

26

This, says McKenzie, is how we must view
Luke's "word portrait" of the birth of Jesus.
To view it in any other way would be a mistake.
It would be doing something
Luke never intended.

McKenzie ends his comparison between
the verbal symbolism of the evangelists
and the visual symbolism of the artists this way:

I have referred elsewhere to Christian artists
as the best analogy of the infancy narratives.
The symbolism
which the Gospels created by words
the artists portrayed in line and color.
Both were attempting to portray the event
in its full significance.

Another scholar says of the infancy narratives
of Matthew and Luke:

A Modern Scriptural Approach to
the Spiritual Exercises
DAVID STANLEY

In the absence
of any authoritative testimony by the Twelve
regarding the facts of Jesus' infancy
or their authentic interpretation,
the evangelists have gathered
family reminiscences, vaguely remembered
and have filled out the sketchy data . . .
by a rather generous introduction
of Old Testament themes and quotations.

Because they wrote
as Christian authors for Christian readers,
our evangelists,
besides recording certain facts about Jesus' life,
have attempted to provide us with insights
of a Christological nature.

5

Birth of Jesus

A popular technique in TV drama
is to present several stories at the same time,
switching back and forth between them.
In other words, the stories are interlaced
and flow along together.

Luke uses a similar technique
in portraying the early life of Jesus.
He interlaces it with stories from the early life
of John the Baptizer.
The 2 early lives flow along together:

John's birth announcement,	1:5–25
Jesus' birth announcement,	1:26–38
canticle about John's birth,	1:67–79
canticle about Jesus' birth,	1:46–56
birth of John,	1:57–66
birth of Jesus,	2:1–20
youth of John,	1:80
youth of Jesus.	2:40

Moreover, within a given episode,
Luke sometimes continued this parallelism.
The most striking example
is his birth announcements of Jesus and John:

both involve an angel,	11, 26
both cause fear,	13, 30
both cause questions,	18, 34
both identify the child,	13–17, 31–33
both give confirmation signs.	20, 36

Luke apparently paralleled these narratives
for theological reasons:
to stress the relationship between John and Jesus,
and to preview the role
that each would play in the drama ahead.

John was Jesus' herald,
sent to prepare people for Jesus' coming. (1:16)
Jesus was David's heir,
sent to rule God's people forever. (1:32)
John, the final star of the Old Testament night,
announces the sunrise of the New Testament day.

ANNOUNCEMENT OF JESUS' BIRTH

A look at the way Luke announces Jesus' birth,
in particular, reveals further theological intent:

NARRATOR *The angel Gabriel was sent from God*
to a town in Galilee named Nazareth,
to a virgin betrothed to a man
named Joseph, of the house of David.
The virgin's name was Mary. . . .

ANGEL *Rejoice, O highly favored daughter!*
The Lord is with you.
Blessed are you among women.

NARRATOR *Mary was deeply troubled . . .*
and wondered what his greeting meant.

ANGEL *Do not fear, Mary.*
You have found favor with God.
You shall conceive and bear a son
and give him the name Jesus.
Great will be his dignity
and he will be called
Son of the Most High.
The Lord will give him the throne
of David his father. He will rule over
the house of Jacob forever. . . .

MARY *How can this be*
since I do not know man?

ANGEL *The Holy Spirit will come upon you*
and the power of the Most High

will overshadow you;
hence, the holy offspring to be born
will be called Son of God. (Luke 1:26–36)

The unusual term "overshadow" occurs also
in the Book of Exodus.
There it describes the mysterious cloud
that "overshadowed" the ark of the covenant
and filled it with the "glory of God." (40:34)

Luke's choice of this special term underlines
a theological insight:
Mary is the new "ark of the covenant"
filled with the new "glory of God."
The glory of God
now resides in Israel in the *person* of Jesus,
instead of in the *symbol* of the ark.

BIRTH RECORDS

The infancy narratives of Matthew's gospel
show a similar concern for theology.
An example is the genealogy of Jesus,
which introduces Matthew's infancy section.
Matthew writes:
"A family record of Jesus Christ,
son of David, son of Abraham."

Matthew begins by immediately spotlighting
Jesus' Jewishness (Abraham ancestry)
and his messiahship (Davidic ancestry).

Following this introduction, Matthew's genealogy
begins with Abraham and goes forward to Jesus.
Writing mainly for Jewish Christians,
Matthew wants to highlight Jesus' bond
with Abraham, the father of Israel.

Luke's genealogy, by contrast,
begins with Jesus and moves backwards to Adam.
Writing mainly for gentile Christians,
Luke wants to stress Jesus' bond with Adam,
the father of the entire human family.

Matthew's family record
has an especially interesting conclusion:

Thus, the total generation number is:
from Abraham to David,
fourteen generations;
from David to the Babylonian captivity,
fourteen generations;
from the Babylonian captivity to the Messiah,
fourteen generations.

MATTHEW 1:17

Matthew's ending returns the spotlight
to the names Abraham, David, and Jesus.

Abraham received God's promise that through
him all nations would be blessed. (Genesis 12:3)
David received God's promise that from his line
an eternal ruler would come. (2 Samuel 7:12–14)

Jesus is presented by Matthew
as the final fulfillment of both of these promises.

GOD WITH US

Matthew's theological intent manifests itself
also in his discussion of Mary's pregnancy:

Mary was engaged to Joseph,
but before they lived together,
she was found with child
through the power of the Holy Spirit.

Joseph her husband, an upright man
unwilling to expose her to the law,
decided to divorce her quietly.
Such was his intention when suddenly
an angel of the Lord appeared in a dream
and said to him:

Betrothal

Joseph went . . .
to register with Mary, his espoused wife,
who was with child.   LUKE 2:4–5

Jewish marriages came at an early age.
Rabbis held 18 suitable for men, 13 for women.
A period of betrothal preceded marriages.
It apparently stemmed from the custom
of having parents pick marriage partners.
Conceivably, 2 young people
did not know each other before betrothal.
Betrothal usually lasted about a year.

Betrothal had the force of marriage.
A groom-to-be could not renounce
his bride-to-be except by divorce.
If a young man died during this period,
his bride-to-be was considered his legal widow.
Similarly, if a bride-to-be was unfaithful,
she could be punished for adultery.

29

"Joseph, son of David,
have no fear about taking Mary as your wife.
It is by the Holy Spirit
that she has conceived this child.
She is to have a son
and you are to name him Jesus
because he will save his people
from their sins."
All this happened to fulfill
what the Lord has said through the prophet:

"The virgin shall be with child
and give birth to a son,
and they shall call him Emmanuel,"
a name which means "God with us."

When Joseph awoke he did as the angel of the Lord
directed him
and received Mary into his home as his wife.
He had no relations with her at any time
before she bore a son,
whom he named Jesus.

MATTHEW 1:18–25

Matthew's reference to the Emmanuel prophecy
underscores the identical point that Luke makes
in his annunciation narrative:
God is now "with us" *personally* in Jesus,
and no longer merely *symbolically* in the ark.

In keeping with the literary artist that he is,
Matthew returns to this important theme
in the "grand finale" of his gospel:
"And know that I am with you always,
until the end of the world." (28:20)

JESUS' BIRTH

Welcome all wonders in one sight!
Eternity shut in a span!
Summer in Winter, Day in Night!
Heaven in earth, and God in man!

This is how poet Richard Crashaw described
the birth of Jesus.
Poets, artists, and musicians try to portray
what is believed as well as what is seen.
They try to go beyond surface appearances
to deeper meanings.
The poet Luke painted such a portrait
of Jesus' birth.

That portrait has become a model
for every Christian artist since Luke's time.

In those days
Caesar Augustus published a decree
ordering a census of the whole world.
The first census took place
while Quirinus was governor of Syria.

Everyone went to register,
each to his own town.
And so Joseph went from the town of Nazareth
in Galilee to Judea to David's town
of Bethlehem—
because he was of the house
and lineage of David—
to register with Mary, his espoused wife,
who was with child.

While they were in Bethlehem
the days of her confinement were completed.
She gave birth to her firstborn son
and wrapped him in swaddling clothes
and laid him in a manger,
because there was no room for them
in the place where travelers lodged.

There were shepherds in that region
living in the fields and keeping night watch
by turns over their flocks.
The angel of the Lord appeared to them
as the glory of the Lord shone around them,
and they were very much afraid.

The angel said to them:
"You have nothing to fear!
I come to proclaim good news to you—tidings
of great joy to be shared by the whole people.
This day in David's city
a savior has been born to you,
the Messiah and Lord.
Let this be a sign to you:
in a manger you will find an infant
wrapped in swaddling clothes. . . ."

They went in haste
and found Mary and Joseph, and the baby
lying in the manger.

LUKE 2:8–16

THREE THREADS

Like a tapestry woven from 3 kinds of thread,
the story of Jesus' birth is woven from

3 different perspectives: prophecy, history,
and theology.

These 3 perspectives are so artistically
interlaced that it is almost impossible to say
where one starts and the other stops.
But the overall message that they communicate
is both eloquent and beautiful:

God has visited and ransomed his people.
He has raised a horn of saving strength for us
in the house of David his servant,
As he promised through the mouths
of his holy ones, the prophets of ancient times.

LUKE 1:68–70

Modern Bethlehem still
retains a biblical flavor.
Farmers terrace
hillsides for better
crop production.

31

Luke's reference to "those days" harks back
to "Herod's day." (1:15)
Thus, 3 "time" frames emerge for dating Jesus'
birth: Herod's rule (37–4 B.C.), Augustus' rule
(27 B.C.–A.D. 14), and the world census during
Quirinus' rule.

Scholars debate the census reference,
but all agree that Jesus was born before A.D. 1.
Our B.C.–A.D. calendar was designed in the
sixth century to the calculations of a Roman,
Dionysius Exiguus.
He erred by about 5 years in his figures.

Luke's "time" frame for Jesus' birth served
both historical and theological purposes.
Historically,
it pinpointed Jesus' arrival on the human scene.
Theologically, it dramatized
that the Son of God did take on flesh and blood.
Indeed, he was even numbered in a world census.

Luke's "place" frame of Jesus' birth
also served an important theological purpose.

The poverty-stricken surroundings,
and the visit from poor shepherds
previewed a theological theme
that Luke would develop later in his gospel:
Jesus' identification with society's poor and lowly.

Lastly, Luke's birth narrative is woven
with strands of prophecy.
Luke does not claim, explicitly,
that a prophecy has been fulfilled,
but there is no mistaking prophetic threads:

But you, Bethlehem-Ephrathah,
too small to be among the clans of Judah,
From you shall come forth for me
one who is to be the ruler of Israel. . . .
He shall stand firm and shepherd his flock. . . .
His greatness shall reach to the ends of the earth.

MICAH 5:1–3

Jesus' Birthplace

Bethlehem's Church of the Nativity
is built over the cave where tradition says
Jesus was born.
As far back as A.D. 150, Justin wrote:
"In line with the gospel story of Jesus' birth,
they still show the cave in Bethlehem."

Around A.D. 325, Helena,
mother of the Roman Emperor Constantine,
built a church over the cave.
Mosaics from its floor are still visible
in the present, reconstructed church.

A journalist describes a visit to the cave grotto:

"Where Jesus Walked"
HOWARD LaFAY

I followed the stairway
down below the main altar in the grotto. . . .
I came upon a lone woman—
apparently a pilgrim from England—
kneeling before the simple altar
that stands above Jesus' birthplace. . . .

The cave was absolutely still
save for the surration of her voice,
as she read quietly to herself
from the second chapter of St. Luke:

"And she brought forth her firstborn son,
and wrapped him in swaddling clothes,
and laid him in a manger. . . ."

The famous
dwarfed doorway
of Bethlehem's
Church of the Nativity.

32

Caves still pockmark Israel's countryside.
Perhaps a shelter similar to this
provided the setting for Jesus' birth.

Some think shepherds were "keeping night watch
in the fields" because it was the "lambing season."
Normally, flocks were herded into a cave
or some other shelter for the night.
This might also suggest why Joseph sought a cave.
He realized they would be empty in lambing time.

This huge star on the grotto floor marks the spot
where tradition says Jesus was born.

Water troughs, excavated at Meggido,
recall Luke's words:
"Mary wrapped Jesus in swaddling clothes
and laid him in a manger."

"Swaddling clothes" refer to a large cloth
to which a long band of cloth was attached.
After a child was put in the larger cloth,
the long band was wound around the child,
securing it snugly and safely.

6

Youth of Jesus

In his book, *Roots*, Alex Haley describes
the ancient rite by which his ancestors
in Africa were named.
It took place eight days after birth
and made the child a member of the tribe.
The highpoint in the ceremony came
when the father took the child in his arms.

Roots
ALEX HALEY

He lifted the infant, and as all watched,
whispered three times into his son's ear
the name he had chosen for him.
It was the first time the name
had ever been spoken as the child's name,
for Omorro's people felt that each human being
should be the first to know who he was.

That night the father completed the ceremony.

Out under the moon and the stars,
alone with his son that eighth night,
Omorro completed the naming ritual.
Carrying little Kunta in his strong arms,
he walked to the edge of the village,
lifted his baby up with his face to the heavens,
and said softly,
"Fend kiling dorong leh warrata ka iteh tee
(Behold—the only thing greater than yourself)."

This beautiful episode helps us to appreciate
better a similar rite in the youth of Jesus:

When
the eighth day arrived for his circumcision,
the name Jesus was given the child,
the name the angel had given him
before he was conceived.

When the time came to purify them
according to the law of Moses,
the couple brought Jesus up to Jerusalem
so that he could be presented to the Lord,
for it was written in the law of the Lord,
"Every firstborn male
shall be consecrated to the Lord."
They came to offer in sacrifice
"a pair of turtledoves or two young pigeons,"
in accord with the dictates of the law.

LUKE 2:21-24

INFANCY RITES

Three religious ceremonies
celebrated the birth of every firstborn male:

circumcision after 8 days,	Genesis 17:10
presentation after a month,	Exodus 13
purification after 40 days.	Leviticus 12

Circumcision initiated the child
into the covenant community of God's people.
Not to be circumcised, said the *Book of Jubilees*,
a religious document from the second century B.C.,
was to be counted among the
"children of doom, not the children of Yahweh."

Linked to this rite was the naming of the child.
Ancients regarded names as highly important.
They even believed the name affected
the child's character and future.

Balzac, a modern novelist, revived this idea
and named the characters of his novels
according to the roles they were to play.

Presentation of the child in the temple
consisted in consecrating the firstborn male
to God, in a spirit of thanksgiving for Yahweh's
protection of Israel's firstborn in Egypt.
It also recalls a tradition among ancients
that a child was never given to parents by God,
only lent to them.

Lastly, purification was a rite for the mother.
It welcomed her back to full participation again
in the worshiping community.

Jesus' presentation in the temple
occasions the prophetic witness of 2 aged Jews:
Simeon and Anna.
They are the idealized portrait of faithful Jews
awaiting the messiah's coming.
Seeing in Jesus the fulfillment of this dream,
Simeon took the child in his arms and prayed:

Now, Master,
you can dismiss your servant in peace;
you have fulfilled your word.
For my eyes have witnessed your saving deed
displayed for all the peoples to see:
A revealing light to the Gentiles,
the glory of your people Israel.

Turning to Mary, Simeon prophesied:

This child
is destined to be the downfall and the rise
of many in Israel, a sign that will be opposed—
and you yourself
shall be pierced with a sword—so that
the thoughts of many hearts may be laid bare.

LUKE 2:29-35

LIGHT TO THE GENTILES

NARRATOR *After Jesus' birth in Bethlehem . . .*
astrologers from the east
arrived one day in Jerusalem. . . .

VISITORS *Where is the newborn king of the Jews?*
We observed his star at its rising
and have come to pay him homage.

NARRATOR *At the news*
King Herod became greatly disturbed
and with him all Jerusalem.
Summoning all of the chief priests
and scribes of the people,
he inquired of them
where the Messiah was to be born.

PRIESTS *In Bethlehem of Judea . . .*
here is what the prophet has written:
"And you, Bethlehem, land of Judah,
are by no means least
among the princes of Judah,
since from you shall come a ruler
who is to shepherd my people Israel."

NARRATOR *Herod called the astrologers aside*
and found out from them the exact time
of the star's appearance.
Then he sent them to Bethlehem. . . .

HEROD *Go and get detailed information*
about the child.
When you have found him,
report to me so that I may go
and offer him homage too.

MATTHEW 2:1-8

Just as Luke's narrative of Jesus' birth
is like a tapestry woven from 3 different threads,
so Matthew's narrative of the astrologers
is woven from 3 different perspectives:
history, prophecy, and theology.

Star Controversy

Most scholars think it is pointless
to try to identify the star of Bethlehem.
But this hasn't kept a few scholars from trying.
A 17th-century astronomer, Johannes Kepler,
thought it could be the conjunction of planets
within the constellation of the Fishes,
which occurred in his lifetime
and which reoccurs about every 800 years.

Discovery of the *Star Almanac of Sippar*
has renewed interest in Kepler's theory.
The almanac lists star movements for 7 B.C.
Considering the mistake in our calendar,
7 B.C. could be a possible date for Jesus' birth.

*Principal movements and crossings of the year
are reckoned exactly to the month and day.
But the main theme is the conjunction
of Jupiter and Saturn in the Fishes,
which is noted in advance
about five times with exact dates. . . .*

*What did contemporary astrology
say about this heavenly phenomenon?
We know about this too today.
Jupiter was regarded
as the star of the world ruler,
and the constellation of the Fishes
as the sign of the last days;
the Planet Saturn was considered
in the east to be the star of Palestine.
When Jupiter meets Saturn
in the constellation of the Fishes, that signifies:
there will appear in Palestine in this year
a ruler of the last days.*

The 3 perspectives are so delicately interwoven
that it is hard to say when one stops
and the other starts.

Historically, the astrologers ("magi")
appear to have been learned priests in Persia.

<hr>
"The Birthday of the Unconquerable Sun"
JOHN M. SCOTT

The Magi were not kings . . .
they were the masters of kings.
The kings ruled the people,
but the wise men directed the kings.
They alone could
communicate with Ahuramazda,
the god of light.
No king began a war without consulting them.
In the name of science and religion,
they held first rank in the nation.

From the point of view of prophecy,
Matthew echoes 3 Old Testament references.

Micah refers to the messiah's birthplace:
"But you Bethlehem-Ephrathah,
too small to be among the clans of Judah,
From you shall come forth . . .
one who is to be the ruler of Israel." (5:1)

The psalmist sings of gifts:
"The kings . . . shall offer gifts . . .
all nations shall serve him." (72:10–11)

The Book of Numbers refers to a star:
"I see him, though not now;
I behold him, though not near:
A star shall advance from Jacob." (24:17)

Finally, there is the all-important theological
thread. It emerges from Matthew's narrative
eloquently and dramatically:
Jesus is the messiah-king,
recognized by the gentiles, but not by the Jews.

OUT OF EGYPT

NARRATOR *After the astrologers had left,*
the angel of the Lord suddenly
appeared to Joseph. . . .

ANGEL *Take the child and his mother*
and flee to Egypt. Stay there
until I tell you otherwise.
Herod is searching for the child. (2:13)

Only Matthew mentions this episode
and the massacre of infants that followed. (2:16)

<hr>
Everyday Life in Bible Times
HOWARD LaFAY

Herod's slaughter of the infant boys . . .
vividly reflects
the pathological character of the king.
He murdered members of his own family—
yet scrupulously observed Mosaic dietary laws
and would eat no pork.
This provoked his Roman master Augustus
into jesting:
"I would rather be Herod's pig than Herod's son."

DEATH OF HEROD

NARRATOR *Joseph stayed in Egypt*
until the death of Herod
to fulfill what the Lord has said
through the prophet:
"Out of Egypt I have called my son."
MATTHEW 2:15

The historian, Josephus,
describes the death of Herod at great length.
When Herod's health began to fail him rapidly,
he was moved to his winter capital in Jericho.
From there he was carried by stretcher
to the hot springs on the shores of the Dead Sea.
The springs did no good; Herod returned home.

Racked by despondency, Herod attempted suicide.
Rumors of the attempt
caused loud wailing throughout the palace.
Herod's son, imprisoned by his paranoid father,
mistook the cries to mean his father was dead.
Immediately, he tried to bribe his jailers,
who reported the bribery attempt to Herod.
The sick king ordered his son executed on the spot.

Now Herod plunged deeper into depression.
He was only days away from his own death—
and he knew it.
What pained him most was the knowledge
that his death would be met with joy in Judea.
To forestall this, he devised an incredible plan.

Having assembled
the most distinguished men from every village
from one end of Judea to the other,
he ordered them to be locked in the hippodrome
at Jericho.

Herod then gave the order to execute them
at the very moment he, himself, died.
His sick mind reasoned that their death
would dispel any joy in Judea over his own death.
The order was never carried out.

After Herod's death,
his body was carried in procession from Jericho
to the Herodium outside Bethlehem for burial.

Herodium

Looking like a volcano,
the Herodium is one of several fortress-palaces
built by Herod the Great.
It was artificially shaped, with everything placed
inside its protected craterlike top.
Josephus wrote of the Herodium:

Two hundred steps of purest white marble
led up to it.
Its top was crowned with circular towers;
its courtyard contained splendid structures.

In the 1960s archaeologists unearthed
the courtyard, fortification towers, and palace.
No trace of Herod's remains were found.

View into a section
of the Herodium's protected craterlike top.

Herod's body was adorned in purple,
a crown of gold rested on his head,
and a scepter of gold was placed in his hand.
The bier bearing his body was made of gold
and studded with jewels that sparkled
as it was carried along under the desert sun.

Following the bier was Herod's household
and hundreds of slaves, swinging censers.
Slowly, the procession inched its way
up the mountainside to the Herodium,
where it was laid to rest.

Today, the excavated ruins of the Herodium
stand out grandly against the clear blue sky—
reminding Bethlehem-bound tourists of the king
who sought to kill the child
whom they have come so far to honor.

ARCHELAUS

When Joseph learned that Herod was dead,
he took Jesus and Mary and returned to Israel.
Matthew portrays Joseph as intending to return
to Judea—in the Bethlehem area.

NARRATOR *Joseph heard, however, that Archelaus*
had succeeded his father Herod
as king of Judea,
and he was afraid to go back there.
Instead, because of a warning
received in a dream,
Joseph went to the region of Galilee.

MATTHEW 2:22

Herod's will decreed that his kingdom
should be divided among his 3 surviving sons.
The northern sector went to Philip;
the Galilean sector to Herod Antipas;
and the prize sector of Samaria and Judea
to Herod's favorite son, 18-year-old Archelaus.

Archelaus inherited all of his father's vices
but few of his father's abilities.
His reign ended in A.D. 6, after 10 short years,
when Jews and Samaritans carried to Rome
a damaging report of his gross mismanagement.

The Emperor Augustus called Archelaus to Rome
to allow him to explain his conduct.
It turned out to be so unconvincing
that Augustus stripped Archelaus of his throne
and exiled him to Gaul.

Augustus then established an office of prefect
to rule Archelaus' territory.
The most famous man to hold this position
was Pontius Pilate (A.D. 26–36).

HEROD ANTIPAS

NARRATOR *Joseph went to the region of Galilee.*
There he settled in a town called
Nazareth.
In this way what was said
through the prophets was fulfilled:
"He shall be called a Nazorean."
MATTHEW 2:22–23

Because Joseph feared Archelaus,
he took his family north to the hills of Galilee.
Thus, Jesus grew up under the jurisdiction
of Herod Antipas.
Excavated coins bearing his name
simply refer to him as Herod.

Ruling from 4 B.C. to A.D. 39,
Herod's reign paralleled the life of Jesus.

Herod knew about Jesus and was intrigued by him.
When Jesus was brought to trial, the bible says:

Herod was extremely pleased to see Jesus.
From the reports about him
he wanted for a long time to see him, and
he was hoping to see him work some miracle.
LUKE 23:8

Jesus had little respect for Herod.
He once referred to him as "that fox." (Luke 13:32)
The title fitted Antipas for several reasons.

For one, Herod served as a spy for Tiberius,
the Roman Emperor,
informing on certain Roman officials.
This probably accounts for Pilate's dislike
of Herod. (Luke 23:12)

Second, Herod courted the Emperor's favor
by building a city on the southwest shore
of the Sea of Galilee, naming it Tiberius.

JESUS' BOYHOOD

Little is known of Jesus' boyhood in Nazareth.
Luke dismisses it with a sentence:
"Jesus for his part progressed steadily in wisdom
and age and grace before God and men." (2:52)

No doubt, however, Jesus' life followed the pattern
of most Jewish boys.

Lord of History
VINCENT NOVAK

He probably climbed the nearby hills
and watched with fascination as an eagle
soared and circled overhead.

He would track down foxes, (Luke 9:58)
or make friends
with the neighboring shepherds. (John 10:1–4)

40

*He got to know the fishermen at the Sea of Galilee;
they probably showed him how to cast
the little handnet and how to set the huge dragnet
tied to two boats.*

*From the vantage point of a hill in Galilee,
Jesus must have let his eye wander. . . .
He caught a glimpse of the west
of white-sailed ships creeping up the
Mediterranean coast from Alexandria. . . .*

*A passing caravan on the road below
might disturb his thoughts.
Caravans often moved north to Damascus,
around the crescent to Mesopotamia,
or south to Egypt. . . .*

*He learned to recognize Roman legions kicking up
dust in the distance as they marched along
Galilean roads on their way to new assignments.
The flash of the sun on their armor
and the proud step of their horses
must have thrilled him.*

Jesus got to know the fishermen.
What he learned from them
was never forgotten.
Fishing images occurred
often in his later teaching.

But there was another aspect of Jesus' personality that was growing in a remarkable way.

"Hidden in Jesus Before the Father"
GEORGE A. ASCHENBRENNER

In the midst of the ordinariness
of his early life in Nazareth,
Jesus began to grow in religious experience.
As would be true for any young Hebrew boy,
Jesus was taught by his mother how to pray
and come in touch with
the revelation of the Old Testament.

We can imagine Jesus at an early age
able to mouth the human words and images
of Psalm 139.
But it was a special day, finally,
when Jesus' own heart was touched by its originality
and moved to pray on his own, Psalm 139. . . .
Now these human words are significative
of a sentiment in the heart of this young boy. . . .
A conscious personal relationship to Yahweh
begins to grow and mature.

SABBATH

The sabbath has always been special in Israel.
It began
each Friday at sunset with a loud trumpet blast.

Lord of History
VINCENT NOVAK

On sabbath morning
Jesus, Mary, and Joseph attended the synagogue.
Inside, the seating arrangements separated
the men and women;
Jesus sat in front of Joseph
while Mary stayed in the back behind a screen
with the other women of the town. . . .

Youth and the Elders

Wearing the *yarmulka* or skull cap,
a sign of God's presence, this boy reads
a selection from the Prophets and the Penteteuch
as part of the *Bar Mitzvah* service.

He also wears about his shoulders
the *tallith* or prayer shawl,
and the *tefillin* around his left arm and forehead.
These are donned
by all Jewish men during weekday prayer.

Attached to the *tefillin* are tiny boxes containing
inscriptions from Exodus and Deuteronomy.
Wearing these in this way
reminds the worshiper that his mind and his heart
should be united with Yahweh, in a special way,
during the time of prayer. (Deuteronomy 6:8)

42

A prayer and hymn opened the service.
Then the rabbi signaled for the first of seven
readings from the sacred text.
Any of the male worshipers could be asked
to read the chosen passages,
usually recounting God's gifts to Israel.

It is highly probable
that Joseph and Jesus took their turns. . . .
A final blessing and prayer concluded the service.
All then returned to their homes for a day
of rest and prayer.

TEMPLE EPISODE

The Talmud says of a Jewish boy:

At five he must begin sacred studies;
at ten he must set himself to learning the tradition;
at thirteen he must know the whole law of Yahweh
and practice its requirements. (Pirke Aboth)

Today, the religious rite of Bar Mitzvah
celebrates the 13-year-old's entry into adulthood,
making him a "son of the law."
One author says of Bar Mitzvah:

Daily Life in the Time of Jesus
HENRI DANIEL-ROPS

Even now in Israel
among the least practicing families
it has retained a quasi-religious character;
the boy is taken from the kibbutz to some point
on the frontier
where he takes his turn as one of the armed guards
of the Holy Land,
or else gives some of his blood
to be used in transfusions.
As it was two thousand years ago,
the child of Israel upon coming of age
must understand that he belongs to a community.

It is against this backdrop that we must read
Jesus' experience in the Jerusalem temple:

Jesus' parents used to go every year
to Jerusalem for the feast of the Passover,
and when he was twelve
they went up for the celebration. . . .
As they were returning at the end of the feast,
the child Jesus remained behind
unknown to his parents.
Thinking that he was in the party,
they continued their journey for a day,
looking for him
among their relatives and acquaintances.

Not finding him,
they returned to Jerusalem in search of him.
On the third day they came upon him in the temple
sitting in the midst of the teachers,
listening to them and asking them questions.
All who heard him
were amazed at his intelligence and his answers.

When his parents saw him
they were astonished, and his mother said to him:
"Son, why have you done this to us?
You see that your father and I
have been searching for you in sorrow."
He said to them.
"Why did you search for me? Did you not know
I had to be in my Father's house?"
But they did not grasp what he said to them.
LUKE 2:41-50

This episode came alive in a striking way
for a journalist when he visited Jerusalem.

In the Steps of the Master
H. V. MORTON

Early one Sabbath morning a young Jew
took me round the synagogues in the old city.
It was extraordinarily interesting.
We plunged straight into the Old Testament. . . .

43

In one obscure synagogue . . .
the morning service had just ended.
A lad of about twelve years of age was standing
before three bearded elders talking to them
in a precocious and animated manner.
Sometimes he pleased them,
and they smiled and patted him on the shoulder;
but sometimes he annoyed them, and the three
old men shook their beards in disagreement
and frowned at the lad over their spectacles.
But the little fellow stood his ground,
waiting respectfully to be spoken to;
then, his questions over, he gave a little bob
to the men and walked slowly away.

This, I thought,
must have been something like the sight
that met the eyes of Joseph and Mary when,
seeking Jesus,
"they found him in the Temple."

SIGNIFICANCE OF THE TEMPLE EPISODE

At the heart of the temple episode
is Jesus' statement: "Did you not know
I had to be in my Father's house?"

"Hidden in Jesus Before the Father"
GEORGE A. ASCHENBRENNER

It was a word about the religious experience
and identity of Jesus. . . .
This word of truth and identity . . .
revealed not only Jesus' identity,
but also the identity of Mary and Joseph
in relationship to him.

Perhaps Mary had to confront for the first time
the reality that, although she was mother,
her son did not in some real way belong to her.
One wonders also whether Jesus himself
did not have to ponder deeply the word of truth
and identity that had been given to him
there in his Father's house.

Another author says:

The Gospel of Luke
WILLIAM BARCLAY

At some time Jesus must have discovered
his own unique relationship to God.
He cannot have known it when he was a child
in the manger and a baby at his mother's breast
or he would be a monstrosity.
As the years went on he must have had thoughts
and then at this first Passover,
with manhood dawning, there came a sudden
blaze of realization the consciousness
that he was in a unique sense the Son of God.

Ancient documents
reproduce Jesus' name this way in Hebrew.
Jesus is the Greek for the Hebrew name, Joshua.
In New Testament times, however,
people spoke Aramaic in daily conversation.
Thus, Jesus would have answered to Jeshua.

Language of Jesus

Stepping off a tourist bus in Maalula in Syria
is like stepping off a time machine
and finding yourself in A.D. 30.
A smiling villager greets you and says:
"Here we still speak the language of Jesus. Listen:
*'Hodhe alotha tyiho logtha mahegbe machikba
katimoi bahar.'*"

A *Wall Street Journal* reporter visited
the Syrian village not long ago and filed this report:

"Language of Christ Still Buys
Loaves, Fishes in Maalula"
RAY VICKER

This little village . . .
is probably the last place where Aramaic,
the language of Jesus Christ and his disciples,
is still spoken as an everyday language. . . .

It became the official language
of the Persian Empire, spoken from Egypt to India,
and replaced Hebrew as the language of the Jews. . . .

Aramaic continued as the Mideast's dominant
language until Syria fell to the Arabs in A.D. 635.
It survived in its pure form only among Christians
who fled the Arabs
into mountain retreats such as Maalula.

Until modern times Maalula was reachable
only by mule trail.
This explains why it was left untouched by the years.
Now a modern highway links it with the world.

Mark's gospel preserves 7 Aramaic phrases.
Among these are:

Talitha, koum: "Little girl, get up"; (5:41)
Ephphatha: "Be opened"; (7:34)
Eloi, Eloi, lama sabachtani: "My God, my God,
why have you forsaken me?" (16:34)

Jesus may have traveled this ancient road.
The columns are remains of Samaria-Sebaste,
a city remodeled by Herod the Great (37–4 B.C.).

PART TWO

GALILEAN MINISTRY I

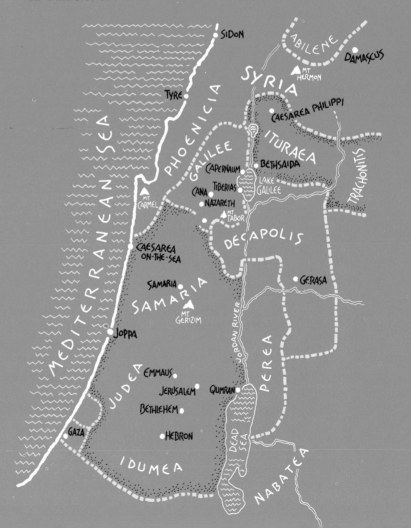

7

Baptism of Jesus

"The Years of Galilee"
HOWARD LaFAY

I was struck by the smallness of the Jordan.
Compared to rivers like the Mississippi,
the Rhine, or the St. Lawrence,
it seems puny indeed.
Then a rowboat moved into midstream.
In it stood a Greek Orthodox priest,
prayerbook in hand. With him was an elderly
woman in a white gown. . . .
The priest dipped the basil leaves into the water
and sprinkled her head and shoulders. . . .
She wept quietly.

Afterward, I talked to her.
She was indeed very old and had journeyed
from Australia to cleanse her soul
in the waters that had baptized her Redeemer.
Her pilgrim's gown would one day serve
as her shroud.
"Now I am at peace," she said.
A radiant smile lit her face.

JOHN THE BAPTIZER

The Jordan is where John made his appearance.
He came there from the desert.
Whether he lived in the desert alone
or was part of a larger group, like the Essenes,
is unknown.

Luke introduced John similar to the way
Greek writers introduced great events

and Hebrew writers introduced the prophets.
(Isaiah 1:1, Jeremiah 1:3)
He pinpoints the date of his appearance
in a variety of ways:

In the fifteenth year
of the rule of Tiberius Caesar,
when Pontius Pilate was procurator of Judea,
Herod tetrarch of Galilee,
Philip his brother tetrarch of the region
of Ituraea and Trachonitis,
and Lysanias tetrarch of Abilene,
during the high priesthood of Annas and Caiaphas,
the word of God
was spoken to John son of Zechariah
in the desert.
He went about the entire region of the Jordan
proclaiming a baptism of repentance
which led to the forgiveness of sins. . . .

"Make ready the way of the Lord,
Clear him a straight path."

LUKE 3:1–4

Tradition says that Jesus was baptized
at this site on the Jordan.

48

John's words echo Isaiah 40:3
and recall an ancient near-eastern practice.
When a king decided to visit his subjects,
he sent an "advance man" ahead of him
to tell the people how to prepare for his arrival.
John is portrayed as this advance man.
"Get ready!" John says. "Your king is coming!"

JOHN'S BAPTISM

The first step in getting ready is baptism.
Baptism was nothing new in Israel. In fact,
all converts to Judaism had to undergo it.

New Testament History
F. F. BRUCE

Members of the school of Hillel
went so far as to maintain . . .
that it was by baptism rather than circumcision
that a Gentile became a Jew. . . .

But John's baptism was distinctive. . . .
Ezekiel promised that, at the dawn of the new age,
the God of Israel would purify his people
from their defilement with clear water
and give them a new heart and a new spirit—
his own spirit.

EZEKIEL 36:25-29

John's baptism matched Ezekiel's prophecy.
It was not a baptism of initiation,
but a baptism of reformation.
John spotlighted this point dramatically:

JOHN   *Give some evidence*
that you mean to reform. . . .

CROWD   *What ought we to do?*

JOHN   *Let the man with two coats*
give to him who has none. . . .

TAX MEN   *Teacher, what are we to do?*

JOHN   *Exact nothing over and above*
your fixed amount.

SOLDIERS   *What about us?*

JOHN   *Don't bully anyone. . . .*
Be content with your pay.

LUKE 3:10-14

Mirroring his special concern for gentiles,
Luke portrays 3 different groups of people
reacting to John's preaching:

     crowds (Jews),
     tax collectors (Jews turned gentile),
     and soldiers (gentiles).

For each of these groups,
reform called for a unique personal response.

BAPTISM TO COME

Describing the person
for whom he is preparing the people, John says:

I am baptizing you in water,
but there is one to come who is mightier than I.
I am not fit to loosen his sandal strap.
He will baptize you in the Holy Spirit and fire.
His winnowing-fan is in his hand
to clear his threshing floor
and gather the wheat into his barn;
but the chaff he will burn in unquenchable fire.

LUKE 3:15-18

The phrase "the Holy Spirit and fire" is debated.
Some interpret it to mean the Spirit's coming
on Pentecost in fire-like tongues. (Acts 2:3)

Others interpret it to mean, primarily,
a fire-like judgment. (1 Corinthians 3:13)
In other words,
Jesus' invitation to be baptized into God's kingdom
constitutes a judgment. (John 3:5)
Depending on one's response to the invitation,
it leads to salvation or condemnation.

Winnowing

John chose this striking image to teach the people.
In effect, he told them:
"Jesus' invitation to you will be like the wind:
it will winnow the chaff from the wheat."

Winnowing was done on a "threshing floor,"
a smooth, clean surface.
Usually community-owned,
the floor was located in the open on a hill
where the strong west wind blew freely.

During harvest season,
owners sometimes slept on the threshing floor
to protect their grain from
night-prowling animals and thieves. (Ruth 3:7)

The poet put it this way: "The same fire
that purifies the gold, destroys the straw."

To concretize the idea,
John borrowed the image of "winnowing."
A farmer tosses threshed wheat into the air.
The solid kernels fall back into the pile,
while the straw-like chaff
blows to the edge of the threshing floor.
There it is swept up and burned.

John's point is this: People's response
to the baptism preached by Jesus
will winnow the "wheat" from the "chaff."
The wheat will be saved; the chaff burned.

JESUS' BAPTISM

Luke introduces Jesus' baptism so abruptly
that we are tempted to think that a paragraph
from the gospel text is missing:

When all the people were baptized
and Jesus was at prayer
after likewise being baptized,
the skies opened
and the Holy Spirit descended on him
in a visible form like a dove.
A voice from heaven was heard to say:
"You are my beloved Son.
On you my favor rests."

LUKE 3:21-22

Significantly, Luke portrays Jesus at prayer.
Luke also notes elsewhere that Jesus prayed
before other important events in his life.
For example, Jesus prayed before he:

chose his disciples,	6:12
asked them who he was,	9:18
taught them how to pray,	11:1
began his passion,	22:41
passed to the Father.	23:46

Luke also notes the presence of the Spirit.
Again, this is a typical observation of Luke.

For example,
he notes the Holy Spirit's presence at Jesus':

conception,	1:35
presentation,	2:27
baptism,	3:22
temptation,	4:1
ministry.	10:21

The presence of the Holy Spirit recalls
what the prophets had foretold:
an outpouring of the Holy Spirit would trumpet
the dawning of the messianic age. (Joel 3:1)

THREEFOLD EPISODE

Luke portrays the all-important episode
after Jesus' baptism in 3 stages:

the sky opens,
the Spirit descends,
a voice identifies Jesus.

First, the sky opens.
This striking image recalls Isaiah's prayer
to God:
"Oh, that you would rend the heavens
and come down." (Isaiah 63:19)

The same image
also occurs in a first-century document
that looks forward to the day of the messiah:

Then the heavens shall be opened . . .
and the glory of the Most High
shall be uttered over him;
and the spirit of understanding
shall rest upon him.
TESTAMENT OF LEVI

Following the opening of the sky,
the Spirit descends in a visible dove-like form.
This image echoes the beginning of creation:
"A mighty wind swept over the waters."
(Genesis 1:2)

Rabbis likened the wind above the water
to a dove hovering above its newborn.

The dove hovering above Jesus in the water
resembles the setting before creation.
Luke implies, perhaps, that Jesus' baptism
is the dawn of a new creation.
Paul himself called Jesus the "new Adam."
(1 Corinthians 15:45)
A fourth-century Christian wrote:

Oratio 39 in Sancta Lumina
GREGORY OF NYSSA

Jesus who is spirit and flesh
comes to begin a new creation
through Spirit and water.
Jesus rises from the water;
and the world rises with him.
The heavens . . .
once closed to Adam and his descendants
are now torn open.

The final stage of the event describes a voice
coming from the heaven and saying:
"You are my beloved Son.
On you my favor rests."

These words held a deep meaning for all Jews.
They echoed the wording and the spirit
of 2 important Old Testament prophecies.

The first prophecy
concerned the coming of a messiah-king.
The psalmist set the prophecy to music:
"The Lord said to me, 'You are my son;
this day I have begotten you.'" (Psalm 2:7)

The second prophecy
concerned the mission of a suffering servant.
He is described in Isaiah's Servant Songs:
"Here is my servant . . .
upon whom I have put my spirit." (Isaiah 42:1)
And again:
"Through his suffering my servant will justify
many, and their guilt he shall bear." (Isaiah 53:11)

Reed Image

"What did you go out to the desert to see—
a reed swayed by the wind?" (Luke 7:24)
Jesus used this image to praise John the Baptizer.

Reeds, like these along the Sea of Galilee,
reach heights up to 20 feet.
When fully grown, they serve as measuring rods
(Ezekiel 40:3) and walking sticks (Ezekiel 29:6).

"Reed images" abound in the bible.
Matthew applied Isaiah's reed image to Jesus:

The bruised reed he will not crush;
the smoldering wick he will not quench
until judgment is made victorious.
In his name, the Gentiles will find hope.

MATTHEW 12:20-21

THREEFOLD PERSPECTIVE

In brief, early Christians summed up the
meaning of Jesus' baptism in this threefold way:

an *anointing* of Jesus
to begin his messianic mission;

a *revelation* of God
as Trinity: Father, Son, and Holy Spirit;

a *preview* of Christian baptism:
the Christian's "anointing" and sharing
in the work begun by Jesus at the Jordan.

DEPARTURE OF JOHN

After Jesus' baptism,
John disappeared quickly from the picture.
The immediate cause of his disappearance
was his outspoken criticism of Herod.
Luke refers to it in passing:
Herod divorced his wife,
the daughter of the Nabataean King Aretas,
to marry his brother's wife, Herodias.

The affair shocked Herod's Jewish subjects
and angered King Aretas.
Later, the Nabataean king
used a border squabble to get even with Herod.
He attacked and crushed Herod's army.

Jewish Antiquities
FLAVIUS JOSEPHUS

Some Jews considered the defeat . . .
just punishment for what he did to John the Baptist.
Herod had ordered his death,
even though John was a good man
who encouraged the Jews to live uprightly. . . .

Herod feared that John's persuasive power
might spark a revolt among the people. . . .
Moved by this fear, he arrested John
and dispatched him in chains to the Machaerus. . . .
There, John was executed.

MARK 6:14-29

Today, Machaerus lies in a tangle of ruins
high up on the eastern cliffs of the Dead Sea.
Only a few twisting paths snake up to the site.
Still unexcavated by modern archaeologists,
the ancient fortress lives alone with its memories.

Among these memories,
of course, is John the Baptist.
Another is the sight of Zealots surrendering
the fortress to Romans around A.D. 72.
The surrender came after the Romans captured
the young Zealot leader
and were preparing to crucify him.
His comrades laid down their weapons
rather than see their hero die in this manner.

8

Temptation of Jesus

When winter comes to the South Pole,
the sun buries itself below the snowy horizon.
The polar night—days of 24 hours of darkness—
sets in.

In 1934 the Arctic explorer, Richard Byrd,
braved 4½ months of this total darkness alone.
Holed up in a 9-by-12-foot shelter,
he pushed the snow from the roof trapdoor
3 times daily to venture into the darkness
to record weather information.
At times, the temperature in his shelter
dipped to 50 degrees below zero.
Yet, Byrd chose to cope alone. Why?

He gives the answer in a book of his adventure:
"for experience's sake," to "be by myself,"
to "taste peace and quiet and solitude."

> Alone
> RICHARD BYRD

It was all that simple.
And it is something, I believe, that people
beset by the complexities of modern life
will understand instinctively.
We are caught up
in the winds that blow every which way. . . .
The thinking man is driven to ponder
where he is being blown

and to long desperately for some quiet place
where he can reason undisturbed
and take inventory. . . .

I wanted to sink my roots
into some replenishing philosophy.
And so it occurred to me . . .
that here was the opportunity. . . .
I should be able to live exactly as I chose,
obedient to no necessities
but those imposed by wind and night and cold,
and to no man's law but my own.

After the first month of solitude,
Byrd reported something "good" was happening:

I was learning
what the philosophers have long been harping on—
that a man can live profoundly
without masses of things. . . .
Freed from materialistic distractions,
my senses sharpened in new directions,
and the random or commonplace affairs
of sky and earth and spirit . . .
became exciting and portentous.

Byrd emerged from his months of solitude
a changed man. He concludes his book:

All this happened four years ago.
Civilization has not altered my ideas.
I live more simply now, and with more peace.

DESERT ENCOUNTER

Jesus underwent a similar experience
right after his baptism.

NARRATOR *Jesus was conducted by the Spirit*
into the desert for forty days
where he was tempted by the devil.
During that time he ate nothing
and at the end of it he was hungry.

DEVIL *If you are the Son of God,*
command this stone to turn into bread.

53

The "mountain of the 40 days" overlooks Jericho, the biblical "city of palms." (Joshua 1:18) Ancient Jericho nested in a sunken pocket, which gave it a Florida-like weather. Josephus wrote: "Jericho's climate is so mild that its inhabitants wear linen when the snow is falling throughout the rest of Judea." At Jericho, Herod built his palatial winter capital.

JESUS	*Scripture has it,* *"Not on bread alone shall man live."*
NARRATOR	*Then the devil took him higher* *and showed him all the kingdoms* *of the world in a single instant.*
DEVIL	*I will give you all the power and glory* *of these kingdoms. . . .* *Prostrate yourself in homage* *before me, and it shall all be yours.*
JESUS	*Scripture has it,* *"You shall do homage to the Lord* *your God; him alone shall you adore."*
NARRATOR	*Then the devil led him to Jerusalem,* *set him on the parapet of the temple,* *and said . . .*
DEVIL	*If you are the Son of God,* *throw yourself down from here,* *for Scripture has it,* *"He will bid his angels watch over you";* *and again,* *"With their hands they will support you,* *that you may never stumble on a stone."*
JESUS	*It also says, "You shall not put* *the Lord your God to the test."*
NARRATOR	*When the devil finished with* *all the tempting he left him.*

LUKE 4:1–13

Tradition locates Jesus' desert encounter on *Jebel Qarantal,* "the mountain of the 40 days." Carved into the mountain's face are scores of chalk caves dating from the third century. Hermits once occupied them, living lives of prayer and penance in imitation of Jesus.

Wrapping itself around the face of the mountain is a Greek monastery.
Tourists who visit the monastery are greeted at the door by a white-bearded monk. As he shows them around, he tells how thousands of monks once lived there.

It was on this desolate mountain site that tradition says Jesus lived for forty days.

TEMPTATION EXPERIENCE

The exact nature of Jesus' temptation encounter is often discussed.
For example, how did Satan show himself? Medieval artists used to depict Satan in a starkly literal way, often showing him in red tights and a grotesque humanoid body. Modern artists prefer a more symbolic approach showing him in clown's dress and grease paint, or in business suit, with briefcase and dark glasses.

A British television team, on assignment in Israel to film Jesus' life, tells how it solved the problem.

Hidden away in Wadi el Qilt,
not far from Jericho, is this Greek monastery.
Inspired by Jesus' desert austerities,
monks have prayed and performed penances here
since the 5th century.

*The location was easy enough—anywhere
in the stretch of desert
between Jerusalem and the Dead Sea.
The time, too . . .
when the shadows are longest and the jackal cries
shrillest: just before the sun
sinks below the horizon, to go out like a light,
leaving the burning sand suddenly cold and dead.
The difficulty was the Devil's appearance.
How should we show him . . . ?
Finally, it was decided that the Devil's presence
should be conveyed only by a black shadow
falling across the sand.*

The decision was a happy one,
for it bypassed the traditional questions
about Jesus' temptations: were they externally
presented or merely internally experienced?
Are they described metaphorically or literally?
It placed the focus precisely where it should be,
on Jesus.

This raises the all-important question:
What was the purpose of Jesus' desert encounter?

IDENTITY

Jesus' temptation experience served a purpose
similar to the "desert" experiences of men
like Byrd.
It gave Jesus the opportunity
to inquire more deeply into the mystery
of his own identity.

Like all of us, Jesus enjoyed moments in life
when he experienced a special awareness of
his identity and calling.
One such time was his early temple experience.
Another was right after his baptism.
A third was the desert experience.

55

The encounter with Satan
showed a unique power to be present in Jesus.
No person born of a woman
ever demonstrated such mastery over Satan.

In later years,
Jesus must have told his disciples of the event.
Knowing the traditions about the messiah,
they would have understood its significance.
It fitted popular belief
that one of the marks identifying the messiah
would be a head-on clash with Satan
in a great contest of power.
That clash began here in the desert;
it would continue throughout Jesus' life.

MISSION

Besides clarifying Jesus' identity as messiah,
the desert encounter also
clarified the nature of Jesus' messianic mission.

First of all, the experience defined this mission
as being that of a "new Adam."
To understand how it did this, we must recall
God's dealing with the "first Adam."

God said to the first Adam ("man"): "Be my son."
Adam said: "No!"
Jesus' job is to right Adam's wrong.
Jesus is the firstborn of the new creation.

Paul drew this parallel between Adam and Jesus:

Just as in Adam all die,
so in Christ all will come to life again. . . .
Adam, the first man, became a living soul;
the last Adam has become a life-giving spirit. . . .
Just as we resemble the man from earth,
so shall we bear the likeness
of the man from heaven.

1 CORINTHIANS 15:22–49

In other words, Satan tempted the first Adam,
and he fell.

Satan tempted Jesus, the new Adam,
and he remained firm.
Through Jesus' victory, all were restored to life.

Second, the experience defined Jesus' mission
further as being the "new Israel."
To understand how it did this, we must recall
Israel's 40-year desert experience.
During it, Israel fell into temptations of:

sensuality,	Deuteronomy 8:3
idolatry,	Deuteronomy 6:13
presumption.	Deuteronomy 6:16

Jesus relived Israel's desert experience,
undergoing the same series of temptations:

sensuality,	"turn this into bread"
idolatry,	"bow down before me"
presumption.	"throw yourself down"

After each temptation, Jesus cites Israel's fall,
as noted in the Book of Deuteronomy.
Jesus is the "new Israel,"
firstborn of the new people of God.

MEANS

Finally, the temptation experience clarified
the means Jesus would choose to carry out
his mission.
Commenting on these means, a writer
(following Matthew's temptation order) says:

Jesus of Nazareth
WILLIAM BARCLAY

There were alternative methods he could use,
and it would be fatally easy
to choose the wrong way.
He therefore went out into the wilderness
to reflect over the alternatives,
and reject alluring shortcuts. . . .

The first temptation arose when he was feeling
tired and hungry and very much alone. Stones
looking like small loaves covered the ground.

Search for Myself

Almost everyone
goes through some sort of a desert experience.
It brings temptations, but it also brings
a new understanding of life and one's self.
After such an experience, a young person wrote:

"I wished I were starting all over again on a
2,045-mile journey on the Appalachian Trail—
searching for myself."

"Why Drive When You Can Walk?"
DOUG ALDERSON

My journey began when . . .
I jetted from my home in Tallahassee, Florida
to Bangor, Maine, a five-hour flight,
but a five-month walk back home.

I had just graduated from high school.
I had many questions.
My goals in life? My future? Was there a God?
I thought the answers
might lie in the beautiful wilderness ahead.
There had to be more to life than money,
TV, parties and getting high.
In a sense, my hike was a search for inner peace,
a journey to find myself. . . .

As I gazed
upon Mt. Katahdin for the first time,
I wondered if I was ready to take on such a challenge.
I was a greenhorn.
My only previous hike was a five-day excursion
in the North Georgia mountains.
Was I prepared for a five-month hike?

The first section in Maine was the longest portion
of the trail free from man-made interference—
nine days of total wilderness. I saw beauty
I had seen only in movies and pictures.
My childhood dreams of walking the mountains
and forests as the early pioneers and Indians had
were coming true. . . .

The long hours of solitude in the forest
gave me time to really think back through my life
and help plan the future.
I got to know myself much better
for there was no one else to influence me. . . .

[But there were problems.]
I became very homesick. . . .
To keep from quitting I had to say to myself . . .
"Things will get better." They always did.
If I had quit I would have missed out
on many lessons and experiences.
Worse, I would have let myself down. . . .

[And there were other difficulties.]
For three more days, I climbed over steep mountains,
finding only a view of white mist in every direction
and a chilly rain hitting my face for my reward.
The trail was muddy and my boots wet,
I felt like quitting.

But when the rain finally cleared
there were days I wished would never end. . . .

When I came home, it seemed very strange. . . .
Even my own dog
looked at me strangely, as if asking,
"Where have you been? You look different.". . .

57

Conscious of his superhuman power, Jesus felt
an impulse to turn the stones into bread. . . .

The second temptation was more subtle.
"Look," whispered the Tempter,
"how can you expect anyone to believe in you?
You, an unknown carpenter from Nazareth!
Startle them into paying attention. . . ."

In the third temptation the inner voice said,
"Think of the poor, the enslaved, the deprived,
the suffering. They wait for your coming
and desperately need your help.
You will be unable to tackle a problem so vast
and bring them relief, unless you have power.
Follow my way and I will give you mastery
over the whole earth."

By rejecting all 3 of Satan's proposals,
Jesus previews how he will carry out his mission:

> not by evading suffering, but by embracing it;
> not by being served, but by serving;
> not by "dealing" with evil, but by destroying it.

Jesus of Nazareth
WILLIAM BARCLAY

Thus Jesus conquered the Tempter,
and when day broke and morning came,
he left the desert, his mind made up,
and returned to mingle again with men.

World of Jesus

Jesus' temptation experience closed the door
on one period of his life and opened it on another.

Jesus and His Times
HENRI DANIEL-ROPS

When Jesus came down from the mountain,
it would have been in early March . . .
warm during the day but cold at night:
"In Adar (March)," says a Jewish proverb,
"the ox shivers in the morning
but in the afternoon he seeks the shade
of a fig tree to cool his hide."

Once down the mountain,
Jesus returned to the site of his baptism.
At least this is the impression John 1:43 leaves.
In any event, soon Jesus went north to Galilee.
Luke says: "Jesus returned in the power of the
Spirit to Galilee." (4:14)
Matthew suggests why Jesus turned north.
Herod had arrested John the Baptizer
and ordered the crowds dispersed:
"When Jesus heard that John had been arrested
he withdrew to Galilee." (4:12)

POLITICAL PICTURE

What was the political picture in Israel
on the eve of Jesus' teaching ministry?
The far-northern section was ruled by Philip;
the southern by Pilate, the Roman prefect;
and the Galilee area by Herod Antipas.

Herod the Great built this magnificent structure at Hebron over the Cave of Machpelah, where tradition says Abraham and Sarah were buried. The minarets and crenelations are medieval additions, but the walls are Herodian. By a unique arrangement, the building serves both as a mosque and a synagogue.

Judging by Josephus, Pilate was a lackluster man.
He spent most of his time in Caesarea-on-the-Sea,
which Herod the Great had built
to honor his friend and patron, Augustus Caesar.
Pilate went to Jerusalem only on major festivals.
Then, he usually stayed in the Fortress Antonio,
which overlooked the great temple complex.

RELIGIOUS PICTURE

Religiously, the climate between Romans and Jews
was touch-and-go.
By their own admission, Romans found it hard
to understand the rigidity of Jewish tradition
and their worship of only one God.
Wisely, as far as possible, the Romans followed
a "hands-off" policy toward Jewish religion.
Nor did they meddle, unduly, in Jewish
government which was linked with their religion.

SYNAGOGUE

The focal point of Jewish worship in each town
was the synagogue.
Here the people gathered each sabbath to pray
and to hear the Scriptures read and explained.

Only One God

Hear, O Israel:
The Lord our God, the Lord is one.
Therefore, you shall love the Lord, your God,
with all your heart,
and with all your soul,
and with all your strength.

DEUTERONOMY 6:4–5

Man's Search For Meaning
VIKTOR FRANKL

I had to surrender my clothes and in turn
inherited the worn-out rags of an inmate
who had been sent to the gas chamber
immediately after his arrival
at the Auschwitz railway station. . . .
I found in a pocket of the newly-acquired coat
a single page torn out of a Hebrew prayer book.

Written on the page was the *Shema Israel.*
Quoted above,
it is the first prayer a Jewish child learns
and the last prayer a dying Jew utters.
The prayer excited in Viktor Frankl
a "challenge to live" and "to suffer bravely."

These Hebrew words read from right to left:
"Hear, O Israel;
The Lord our God,
the Lord is one."

Modern Synagogues

Synagogue services vary from place to place. Certain practices, however, remain common in all synagogues.

For example, prayers of blessing always begin with the Hebrew *Beraka:*
"Blessed are you, Lord, God of all creation." Similarly, the *Shema*, always said in Hebrew, remains the central prayer.

Today, a rabbi, assisted by a cantor, usually delivers sermons and leads the service. In ancient times, the rabbi was merely a highly respected scholar in the community to whom people turned for religious guidance. He worked in the fields like everyone else. Today, the title is reserved for those educated in rabbinical schools or seminaries.

The *Ner Tamid* ("eternal light") burns continuously before the curtain of the ark, compartment containing the Torah.
The 2 tablets above the curtain contain Hebrew letters, abbreviations of the 10 Commandments.

A Shorter Life of Christ
DONALD GUTHRIE

*The choice of reader and preacher
was left to the ruler of the synagogue,
who could invite anyone capable of doing it.
This accounts for the number of occasions
when Jesus addressed synagogue audiences.
The ruler of the synagogue exercised
a great deal of influence
and was regarded with respect by the people.
The local communities
were essentially religious communities.*

TEMPLE

Although the synagogue
was the focal point of local life and worship,
the temple of Jerusalem
was the focal point of national life and worship.
Israel's one and only temple
dramatized the fact that there was only one God.

Unlike the synagogue, chiefly a place of instruction,
the temple was mainly a place of sacrifice.
Jews in Palestine and Jews of the diaspora
(those living outside Palestine)
looked to the temple as the symbol of their unity.
Each year, Jews throughout the world
sent contributions to the temple;
and most Jews longed to visit the temple
at least once in their lifetime.

The temple courts were always crowded.
Temple worship included sacrificial offerings
each morning and evening,
as well as private offerings during the day.

Understanding the New Testament
KEE, YOUNG, FROEHLICH

*To officiate at the numerous sacrificial rites
there were multitudes of priests
from a long line of priestly families
whose genealogies were recorded in the Torah.*

A *Bar Mitzvah* service
at Jerusalem's famous Western Wall.
Among other things, *Bar Mitzvah* qualifies
a boy to be one of the 10 people (*minyan*)
required to hold a synagogue service.

The Temple Jesus Knew

The Western (Wailing) Wall
is all that remains of the Jerusalem temple
where Jesus taught and prayed.
This wall formed part of the plaza
upon which stood the remodeled temple
of Herod the Great.

Herod's vast remodeling project began in 19 B.C.,
and continued long after his death.
It was completed only 7 years
before the Romans destroyed the temple in A.D. 70.

When Israeli tanks rumbled into Jerusalem's
Old City in 1967, it was the first time,
except for a brief period in A.D. 135,
that Jews controlled the site since A.D. 70.

Hundreds visit the Western Wall each day,
many for *Bar Mitzvah* services.

Admission to the priesthood was carefully
controlled, since the Jews were determined
that worship
be conducted only by properly qualified men.
Only descendants
from the sons of Aaron could be priests,
although descendants from the line of Levi
could perform restricted functions. . . .

At the head of the priesthood
was the High Priest. . . .
As the titular head of the Jewish people,
the High Priest carried on negotiations
with the various governments to which the Jews
were subject.
From the beginning,
this meant that the High Priest, together with
the other priests whom he represented,
exercised unusual authority in the community.

We should not confuse the title "high priest"
with that of "chief priest."
The high priest was the head of temple worship.
A chief priest was the head of one of Israel's
many priestly families.

SANHEDRIN

Helping the high priest to govern was a central
council, called the Sanhedrin. (Acts 5:21)
Numbering 70 people, it drew its members from
the chief priests, retired high priests, scribes,
and elders of important families.

The council acted as a kind of national high court.
It had its own police and its own power of arrest.
It was this council that apprehended Jesus.

RABBINICAL SCHOOLS

Next in importance in Israel were the rabbis,
often called scribes or lawyers.
Since their role was to interpret the Torah,
their decisions affected every area of Jewish life.
They were, therefore, influential and powerful.

Jesus was widely known and accepted as a rabbi.
Rabbis attracted admiring disciples.
Naturally, rabbinical schools began to emerge.
Each school had its own style of interpretation,
which led to occasional clashes between schools.
The stricter Shammai school, for example,
permitted divorce only for infidelity, whereas
the Hillel school granted it for lesser reasons.

RELIGIOUS PARTIES

Paralleling the different religious points of view
were religious groups or parties.
Two major parties were Pharisees and Sadducees.
Two lesser ones were Essenes and Zealots.
Within the 4 groups were various subdivisions.

PHARISEES

Pharisees were mostly lay people, not priests.
They observed not merely the Torah, but also
certain other writings and "oral" traditions.
Oral traditions served as a kind of "fence"
around the "written" law.
By interpreting written laws more rigidly
than required, oral traditions protected them
against inadvertent or accidental violation.

Doctrinally, Pharisees believed in angels,
the resurrection, and a final judgment.
Pharisees numbered among their members
such outstanding men as Paul, Nicodemus,
and Gamaliel. (Acts 23:6, John 3:1, Acts 5:34)

SADDUCEES

The Sadducees were a smaller party.
But, since they drew heavily from the priestly
and the wealthy families, they were powerful.

Sadducees observed only the Torah as binding.
All other writings and traditions were relative.
If the Torah did not legislate on some point,
Sadducees exercised freedom.
This is why they accepted the Roman occupation
and adjusted their lives accordingly.

Doctrinally, Sadducees denied angels
and the resurrection of the dead. (Acts 23:8)

ESSENES

Most of our information about the Essenes
comes from Josephus and the Dead Sea Scrolls.
Essenes defected from conventional Judaism.
They shunned it as corrupt.
They even broke with temple worship.
Believing a Day of Judgment was at hand,
many withdrew into desert communities,
like Qumran, to await the end.

Essenes considered themselves the true Israel,
heirs of the new covenant of Jeremiah 31:31–34
and Ezekiel 36:22–28.
Doctrinally, Essenes believed the human heart
was the battleground of 2 conflicting spirits:
light and good, and darkness and evil.
Though they emphasized human sinfulness,
they also stressed divine forgiveness.

ZEALOTS

If any of the 4 religious groups got stirred up
when Jesus began to preach
about the kingdom of God, it was the Zealots.
Radical and militant in their religious views,
they could not stand Jews who prayed for
the coming of God's kingdom, but wouldn't
lift a finger against the kingdom of Rome.

The Zealots were convinced
that the first step toward the kingdom of God
was to drive the Romans out of Israel.
"God will help us," they said,
"just as he helped the Maccabees of old."

Zealots scorned the Sadducees,
who collaborated with Roman occupation forces.
Zealots merely tolerated the Pharisees,
who opposed the Romans, but only passively.
And Zealots completely ignored the Essenes,
who separated themselves from Jewish society
and buried their heads in the desert sand.

Essenes

Called by some the "City of Salt,"
these ruins were left unstudied by archaeologists
who thought them to be the remains
of a minor Roman fort.

Then came the famous discovery of scrolls in nearby
Dead Sea Caves between 1947 and 1956.
Suddenly, archaeologists became interested in the site.

Subsequent excavations
turned up a spectacular complex of buildings—
the exciting remains of a once-thriving community
of desert-dwelling Essenes.
Elaborate baptismal facilities, a scriptorium
with dried ink still in containers, a lecture hall,
and a cemetery of over 1,100 graves were unearthed.

Essene occupation of Qumran ended
with Roman invasion of the area in A.D. 70,
at which time the scroll library was taken away
and hidden in nearby caves.

A cable car lifts thousands of tourists, daily,
to the top of Masada.
Student volunteers from all over the world
helped in its excavation between 1963–65.

Masada

"I can't believe it!" gasped a modern tourist.
Ancient peoples were amazed by it, also.
Josephus says it looked spectacular from below.

Its gleaming white walls framed sharply
against the clear blue, desert sky.
An incredible network of cisterns
captured and stored the winter rains.
Vast warehouses of food and weapons
insured long-term supply in case of siege.

Herod's own private villa was here, too.
Built on 3 rock terraces,
it jutted in tiers from the northen slope.
The villa included a Roman bath, royal suites,
a circular dining lounge, and hidden stairways.
Painted plaster and mosaics gave it class.
There was nothing else like it in the Roman world.

<hr>

Dictionary of the Bible
JOHN L. McKENZIE

Zealot tactics
were those of the modern political terrorists;
they raided and killed frequently,
attacking both foreigners and Jews
whom they suspected of "collaboration". . . .
The Romans called them sicarii _("stabbers")_
from the practice of concealing a dagger
beneath their garments for stealthy use.

PARABLE OF THE GROWING SEED

When Jesus began to talk about God's kingdom,
Zealots flocked to hear what he had to say.
(Simon the Zealot eventually followed Jesus.)

It is interesting to note
that one of the first parables Mark records
seems to be addressed to Zealots. Jesus said:

"This is how it is with the reign of God.
A man scatters seed on the ground.
He goes to bed and gets up day after day.
Through it all the seed sprouts and grows
without his knowing how it happens.
The soil produces of itself first the blade,
then the ear, finally the ripe wheat in the ear.
When the crop is ready he 'wields the sickle,
for the time is ripe for the harvest.'"

MARK 4:26–29

The Zealots would have gotten the point.
"He's a dreamer!" they would have said.

This synagogue atop Masada dates from A.D. 70. Two badly damaged scrolls of Deuteronomy and Ezekiel were found buried beneath the floor.

These excavated storerooms still contained food supplies, some in a remarkable state of preservation.

"He claims God's kingdom is out of human control.
At least that's what he implies when he says
the seed grows 'without our knowing how'
and the 'soil produces of itself.'"

And so Jesus and the Zealots parted company,
but not before Jesus had made his point:
God's kingdom is a gift from God;
you can't hasten it with swords and daggers,
nor can you stop it with such force.

ZEALOT FATE

Decades after Jesus' death,
Zealots engineered a revolt against Rome.
The uprising was brutally stamped out
and ended with Jerusalem's destruction in A.D. 70.

Survivors fled to Masada,
a fortress built by Herod near the Dead Sea.
Today, the excavated remains of Masada
have become a national symbol for all Israelis.

Am I Free?
CATHERINE FLETCHER

A steep narrow trail called the Snake's Path
winds its way to the top.
When you reach the bared summit
and look out in the burning bright sunlight,
you are overwhelmed
by the loneliness of the place.
It is a formidable site
cut off on all sides by steep valleys.
Here 2,000 years ago Herod the Great
built a powerful fortress and a luxurious palace

65

as a refuge from his enemies.
The wall surrounding the mountain top
had 37 defense towers.

After Herod's death Masada was occupied
for 70 years by a Roman garrison. Then in A.D. *66*
came the Great Revolt of the Zealots.
A party of them captured Masada
and to this remote place gathered multitudes
of refugees, men, women, and children.

Here 900 Zealots held out until the year 73.
Then, the inevitable day came
when 15,000 Roman troops breached its walls.
Since it was late in the day,
the Romans delayed the final attack until dawn.
That night the survivors met
and voted for suicide, rather than for capture.

Jewish Wars
FLAVIUS JOSEPHUS

The survivors chose, by lot, 10 men
to slay all the rest.
Each man lay down on the ground with his wife
and children and embraced them.
Together, they awaited the blow
from the men chosen to deliver it.

When the 10 executioners had, unflinchingly,
completed their task,
they drew lots again to see who would kill
the other 9 and, then, take his own life.

At dawn,
the Romans poured through the breached walls.
Fires burned quietly everywhere.
A ghostly stillness hung over the air.
Finally, 2 old women and 3 small children
came out of hiding to tell the story.

Josephus concludes his report of Masada
with these striking words:

When the Romans saw the mass of slain,
they were unable to take pleasure in the sight,
even though the people were their enemies.

10

Message of Jesus

Everything seemed to stop for a split second.
Neil Armstrong was about to make world history
by becoming the first man to walk on the moon.
As he paused on the bottom step of the spacecraft,
everyone sensed he was going to say something.
He spoke:

"One small step for man;
one giant leap for mankind."

Then astronaut Armstrong placed his booted foot
onto the powdery surface of the moon.
As he did, people around TV sets everywhere
began to hail the "new age" in history
that began with Armstrong's "one small step."

Many who watched this history-making event
may no longer recall Armstrong's exact words,
but they do remember the spirit behind them.

JESUS' FIRST WORDS

The same is true of Jesus' first words.
They may or may not be his exact words,
but they do preserve the spirit of what he said:

"This is the time of fulfillment.
The reign of God is at hand!
Reform your lives and believe in the Gospel."
MARK 1:15

After Jesus' desert experience, he went north
to Galilee to the lakeside town of Capernaum.

In teaching the people,
Jesus twice referred to a mill or millstone.
(Matthew 18:6, 24:41)
This one, unearthed near the Capernaum synagogue,
is made up of an upper stone (moveable)
and a lower stone (permanent).
Two people operated the mill.
Grain, poured in at the top,
slipped down between the 2 stones
and was ground into flour as the upper stone turned.

Where Jesus Taught?

This excavated synagogue at Capernaum
dates from shortly after Jesus' time.
But, because of ancient building customs,
it is probably built on the spot
of the destroyed synagogue where Jesus taught.

Some stone carvings in the excavated synagogue
may be from Jesus' synagogue.
Ancients often reused sculptured pieces.
Two carvings, especially, stir the imagination:
an emblem of the Tenth Roman Legion,
and a manna bowl.

Take the Roman army emblem. People ask:
"Could it be linked with the Roman army officer
who sent elders to ask Jesus to heal his servant?"

Recall that the elders told Jesus:

*"The centurion deserves this favor from us,
because he loves our people
and even built our synagogue."* LUKE 7:4–5

A similar fascination surrounds the carving
of the manna bowl. As you read Jesus' sermon
on the Eucharist at Capernaum,
you can almost see him point to the bowl and say:

*"Your ancestors ate manna in the desert,
but they died. . . . The bread I give
is my flesh for the life of the world. . . .
The man who feeds on this bread
shall live forever."* JOHN 6:49–59

67

There he proclaimed God's kingdom was at hand
and invited people to open their hearts to it.
Jesus also performed works of healing
that created excitement and talk.
Soon people from nearby towns came
to invite Jesus to preach in their synagogues.

Then, one day Jesus went to Nazareth
to preach in the synagogue
which he had attended since he was a boy:

Jesus stood up to do the reading.
When the book of the prophet Isaiah
was handed to him, he unrolled the scroll
and found the passage where it was written:

"The spirit of the Lord is upon me;
therefore, he has anointed me.

He has sent me to bring glad tidings to the poor,
to proclaim liberty to captives,
recovery of sight to the blind,
and release to prisoners,
to announce a year of favor from the Lord."

Rolling up the scroll
he gave it back to the assistant and sat down.
All in the synagogue had their eyes fixed on him.
Then he began by saying to them.
"Today this Scripture passage
is fulfilled in your hearing."

All who were present spoke favorably of him;
they marveled at the appealing discourse
which came from his lips.
They also asked, "Is not this Joseph's son?"

LUKE 4:16–22

Voice from the Past

"Can any good come out of Nazareth?"
quipped Nathaniel, speaking of Jesus. (John 1:46)
His remark was, apparently, well-founded.
The Old Testament never mentions the town,
as such.
Nor is it listed among the 63 Galilean towns
in the *Talmud*, a book of Jewish traditions.

The first ancient reference to Nazareth,
found outside the New Testament writings,
turned up in 1962.
Digging near Caesarea-on-the-Sea,
archaeologists unearthed these 2 inscribed tablets.

The 2 stone fragments were once part of a wall panel
of a third-century synagogue,
which listed the current residences
of the 24 priestly classes who once served the temple.
(1 Chronicles 24:7–18, Luke 1:15)

The name "Nazareth" appears on the left stone,
in the second of the four lines.

TIME OF FULFILLMENT

For centuries, people had gathered each sabbath
in their synagogues to read the Scriptures
and to pray for the coming of God's kingdom.
One of the traditional prayers read:

Sanctified be his great name. . . .
May he establish his kingdom in your lifetime.

Now, Jesus was telling his fellow townsmen
that their prayers have been heard.
What the prophets foretold is now at hand:

The God of heaven will set up a kingdom
that shall never be destroyed . . .
and it shall stand forever.

DANIEL 2:44

For Jews the phrase "kingdom or reign of God"
did not designate, primarily, a place or people.
Rather, its main emphasis was an action by God.
By this action God would arrest the tide of evil
and begin the long process
of bringing all things into conformity with his will.
Three things, therefore, need emphasis:

the kingdom is not, primarily, a place or people;
the kingdom's coming depends on God's power;
the kingdom's coming will not be an event,
but a process,
because the forces of evil will not collapse
without a struggle.

Jesus proclaims
that God is now beginning this long process.
The old world order, the kingdom of Satan,
is about to be challenged by the kingdom of God.
One age begins its birth; another its death.
Later, the author of the letter to the Hebrews
would say of the new age:

In times past,
God spoke in fragmentary and varied ways
to our fathers through the prophets;
in this final age,
he has spoken to us through his Son. . . .
This Son is the reflection of the Father's glory.

HEBREWS 1:1–3

REACTION

Suddenly, the full impact of Jesus' teaching
struck the synagogue congregation.
A wave of whispering broke:
"Is this not Joseph's son?
Is he not one of us, a poor villager of Nazareth?
Is he now pretending to be a prophet?
What has come over him?
What credentials has he to prove that he is
God-appointed—and not self-appointed?"

Jesus sensed the sudden mood of hostility.
He motioned for silence:

"You will doubtless quote me the proverb,
'Physician, heal yourself,' and say,
'Do here in your own country
the things we have heard you have done
in Capernaum.'
But in fact," Jesus went on,
"no prophet gains acceptance in his native place.

"Indeed, let me remind you,
there were many widows in Israel
in the days of Elijah when the heavens
remained closed for three and a half years
and a great famine spread over the land.
It was to none of these that Elijah was sent,
but to a widow of Zarephath near Sidon.

"Recall, too, the many lepers in Israel
in the time of Elisha the prophet;
yet not one was cured except Naaman the Syrian."

At these words
the whole audience in the synagogue
was filled with indignation.

How Did Jesus Look?

A black artist, Murray De Pillars,
says in *Ebony* magazine:

If we are to believe the life Jesus lived,
the pictures that were painted of him
just didn't fit the man.

The question arises: What did Jesus look like?
What kind of personality did he have?
Though the bible is silent about these questions,
it does leave some fascinating clues.

For example,
Jesus held crowds spellbound. (Mark 6:34–36)
Children liked him. (Luke 18:15–16)
People had a deep affection for him. (John 11:1–6)
These clues suggest that Jesus possessed
an attractive appearance and a warm personality.

Furthermore, Jesus lived a rugged life.
He walked miles at a stretch. (John 4:1–6)
He spent whole nights in prayer. (Luke 6:12)
He often slept out under the stars. (Luke 9:58)
These facts suggest
that Jesus was physically fit and strong.

For these reasons, some experts conclude
that Jesus was, indeed, attractive and strong.
But the fact is that we are not sure of either.

The important thing about Jesus
is not his appearance,
but the significance of what he said and did.

They rose up and expelled him from the town,
leading him to the brow of the hill . . .
and intending to hurl him over the edge.
But he went straight through their midst
and walked away.

LUKE 4:23–30

The reaction to Jesus' teaching swung swiftly
from that of "marveling" at his words
to that of being "filled with indignation."

So swiftly does the reaction reverse itself
that some wonder if Luke, for brevity's sake,
has perhaps telescoped into one single account
a series of teachings Jesus gave in Nazareth.
Others note the abrupt switch in mood
but feel the situation justifies it.

REJECTION

Luke's report brings the starry-eyed Christian
down to earth with a thud.

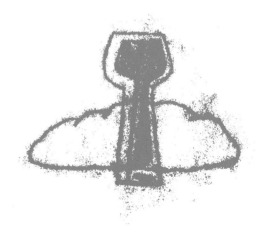

It previews something
that will take place often in Jesus' lifetime:
his words will fall on deaf ears.

Nor is rejection of Jesus' message
a phenomenon peculiar to his day alone.
Many centuries later, Thomas Carlyle wrote:

11

Miracles of Jesus

If Jesus were to come today,
people would not crucify him.
They would ask him to dinner,
hear what he had to say,
and make fun of him.

Why haven't 2,000 years changed things?
A high-school boy volunteered his own answer:

Why don't I take Jesus' words more seriously?
I guess it's because if I did,
most of my friends would reject me,
just as many of Jesus' friends rejected him.
And I guess I couldn't take that just now.

Jesus left Nazareth with a deeper awareness of
not only what lay ahead for him,
but also what it meant to be a prophet.
To be a prophet meant to expose himself
to rejection—even death.

Pianist Marta Korwin-Rhodes was in Warsaw
when the city was besieged.
She stayed on to help care for the wounded.

"The Magic of Touch"
SMILEY BLANTON, MD

"Late one night," she wrote,
"going through the wards, I noticed a soldier
whose face was buried in a pillow.
In his agony, he was sobbing and moaning. . . .
How could I help him? I looked at my hands.
If I could translate vibrations in harmony
through a piano, why could I not transmit harmony
directly without an instrument?

"When I took the boy's head in my hands,
he grabbed them with such force
I thought his nails would be embedded in my flesh.
I prayed that the harmony of the world
would come to alleviate his pain.
His sobs quieted.
Then his hands released their grip,
and he fell asleep."

Today, the healing power of touch
is receiving growing attention.
Jesus himself often touched people to heal them.

Some people brought Jesus a deaf man,
who had a speech impediment
and begged him to lay his hands on him.
Jesus took him off by himself
away from the crowd.

Jesus healed the deaf-mute
"in the district of the Ten Cities."
These cities were built between 64–4 B.C.
to protect Roman trade routes.
Gerasa (ruins partially shown here)
was one of the ten. (Mark 7:31)

He put his finger into the man's ears
and, spitting, touched his tongue;
then he looked up to heaven and emitted a groan.
He said to him,
"Ephphatha!" (that is, "Be opened!").
At once the man's ears were opened;
he was freed from the impediment,
and began to speak plainly.

MARK 7:31–35

MIRACLES

It is said that medieval Christians
believed because of Jesus' miracles,
while modern ones believe in spite of them.
Not everyone agrees with this statement,
but most agree with the point underlying it.
We moderns are products of our scientific age.
And one of our unspoken laws seems to be this:
we can explain everything.
By definition we tend to rule out the mysterious.

But, when it comes to the life of Jesus,
we must confront the mysterious head on.
We cannot rule it out or ignore it.

"Aspects of New Testament Thought"
DAVID STANLEY & RAYMOND BROWN

To start with the presupposition
that miracles are impossible . . .
is to forget the unique character
of the divine intervention in history of Jesus.

The whole Gospel conviction is
that the kingdom (or dominion) of God
was making its presence felt
in an extraordinary way in the ministry of Jesus;
and any attempt to set boundaries
as to what was possible at this unique moment
on the basis of our ordinary experience
is very risky.

MIRACLES AS SIGNS

We used to think nature followed fixed laws.
A disruption of these laws was thought a miracle.
Now, we are slower to assume nature is fixed.
While it seems to follow a set pattern,
this could be more apparent than real.

The older notion of a miracle,
as being a disruption of the laws of nature,
is totally opposed to the biblical notion.

"Towards Understanding
Miracles in the Bible"
JOHN J. PILCH

For biblical man, miracles were signs
of the immediate activity of God in his creation.
He didn't ask, "How did it happen?" so much as
"Who is responsible?"

A modern echo of this mentality can be heard
in Fiddler on the Roof, *when Motel the Tailor*
wins as his wife Tevye's daughter who had
already been "matched" with another. He sings:

"But of all God's miracles large and small
  The most miraculous one of all
Is the one I thought could never be—
  God has given you to me!"

Miracle Controversy

People attacked Jesus' miracles from the start.
Some denied he healed people. (John 9:18)
Others admitted his power to heal,
but charged it came from Satan. (Luke 11:15)

People still challenge Jesus' miracles.
Some treat miracle accounts almost as parables.

A blind beggar in Jerusalem's Old City.

The Gospels Without Myth
LOUIS EVELY

*The true miracle of the loaves and fishes
is this: Jesus persuaded one man to risk
sharing what he had, and that man's example
led others to put into a common pot
the food they had been hiding for their own use.
And thus the crowd gained a blessing
greater than that which a full stomach could
confer; they learned the joy of brotherhood.*

Similarly, some suggest Jesus' exorcisms
were cures of insanity or epilepsy. (Mark 9:18)
Others suggest Jesus raised the widow's son
from a coma, not death.

Christians respond to such theories in 2 ways:
by not taking them seriously (loaves and fishes),
or by weighing each proposal separately.
Take the case of the widow's son.

The Gospel of Luke
WILLIAM BARCLAY

*It may well be
that here we have a miracle of diagnosis;
that Jesus with those keen eyes of his
saw that the lad was in a cataleptic trance
and saved him from being buried alive,
as so many were in Palestine.
It does not matter;
the fact remains that Jesus claimed for life
a lad who had been marked for death.*

Take, also, the exorcisms of Jesus.
Were these really cures of insanity or epilepsy?

"Possession and Exorcism"
JOHN NAVONE

*The texts seem to indicate more than that. . . .
This is implied by the unnatural signs
of violence (Mark 5:4–5, 9:22, Luke 4:25),
and the religious knowledge exhibited
by the expelled demons (Mark 1:24). . . .*

*Furthermore, were the belief in demons
a fact based on religious error, it would seem
that Jesus would have to correct it. . . .*

*What is primary in the New Testament accounts
is that Jesus overcomes evil;
the material conception of this power,
manifested in the action of personal evil spirits,
is secondary, yet seems required.*

73

Morals on the Book of Job
GREGORY THE GREAT

All men wonder to see water turned into wine.
Every day the earth's moisture,
being drawn into the root of a vine,
is turned by the grape into wine,
and no man wonders.

Ancient peoples never viewed nature as fixed.
Rather, they viewed it under God's control.
He could direct it as he wished.
But sometimes God seemed to direct it
in a more extraordinary way than usual.
When this happened, biblical writers
used a special Hebrew word for the event,
such as *ot*, something that attracted attention,
or *pala*, something beyond the expected.

New Testament evangelists
held the same view of nature and miracles.
When John spoke of Jesus' miracles,
he often used the Greek word for "sign."
For John, the miracles of Jesus had 2 levels:
a *sense* level and a *sign* level.

The *sense* level was the level everyone saw:
a deaf man regaining his hearing,
a blind person being restored to sight.

The *sign* level was the deeper, faith meaning
that Jesus intended these miracles to have.
They were *signs* of something more.

COMPASSION SIGNS

Miracles were, first of all,
signs of Jesus' concern for the sick and disabled.
Sometimes the people in these groups
were treated as outcasts. Consider lepers:

The one who bears the sore of leprosy
shall keep his garments rent
and his head bare. . . .
He shall cry out, "Unclean, unclean!"
As long as the sore is on him
he shall declare himself unclean. . . .
He shall dwell apart,
making his abode outside the camp.

LEVITICUS 14:45–46

Concerning one who seemed healed of leprosy, the law of Moses said:

He shall be brought to the priest,
who is to go outside the camp to examine him.
If the priest finds that the sore of leprosy
has healed in the leper,
he shall order the man purified. . . .
Only when he is thus made clean
may he come inside the camp.

LEVITICUS 14:2–8

It is within this context
that Luke describes the following episode:

On Jesus' journey to Jerusalem . . .
ten lepers met him.
Keeping their distance,
they raised their voices and said,
"Jesus, Master, have pity on us!"
When Jesus saw them, he responded,
"Go and show yourselves to the priests."
On their way there they were cured.

LUKE 17:11–17

The ways of the ancient world
come as a shock to the modern mind.
Hospitals and clinics were unheard of.
Pain and suffering were like floods and storms—
people's companions from cradle to grave.

Jesus' reaction to all this was one of compassion.
Mark's gospel shows him beginning his ministry
with a burst of healing:

a shrieking man is restored to peace,	1:23
a woman is cured of a fever,	1:29
possessed people are freed,	1:34
a leper is healed,	1:40
a paralytic is restored body and soul.	2:12

Jesus' miracles are signs of his compassion
for his brothers and sisters.

Jesus
DONALD SENIOR

The Gospels leave little doubt that compassion
was the motivation behind Jesus' healing ministry.
Compassion urges Jesus to touch the leper
and cure him (Mark 1:41).
Compassion for the crowd's hunger
moves him to feed them (Matthew 14:14).
Compassion for their aimlessness and affliction
causes him to enlist the disciples
in the same healing ministry (Matthew 9:36).
Compassion for the widow of Naim
leads Jesus to restore her son to life (Luke 7:13).
Quite simply,
Jesus cures because people are sick.

SIGN OF GOD'S POWER

A second sign-function of miracles is this:
they show God's power to be present in Jesus.
One of the more dramatic manifestations
of this power is the so-called nature miracle:
stilling a storm, walking on water.

The Sea of Galilee is 600 feet below sea level.
It is completely encircled by hilly land masses.
Over the ages, streams have cut deep ravines
into these land masses.
The ravines now act as natural wind funnels.
As warm air rises, especially around sunset,
cool air rushes in from the ravines to replace it.
The result is amazing.

Within minutes, a tranquil lake is whipped into
a white-capped sea of angry 6-foot waves.
One traveler wrote in his journal:

The sun had scarcely set
when the wind began to rush upon the lake.
It continued all night long with stepped-up violence.
When we reached shore next morning,
the lake face was like a huge boiling cauldron.

"He hushed the storm
to a gentle breeze,
and the
billows of the sea
were stilled." (Psalm 107:29)

This description tallies exactly with the account in Mark's gospel:

As evening drew on Jesus said to his disciples,
"Let us cross over to the farther shore."
Leaving the crowd, they took him away
in the boat in which he was sitting,
while the other boats accompanied him.

It happened that a bad squall blew up.
The waves were breaking over the boat
and it began to ship water badly.
Jesus was in the stern through it all,
sound asleep on a cushion.

They finally woke him and said to him,
"Teacher, does it not matter to you
that we are going to drown?"
He awoke and rebuked the wind
and said to the sea: "Quiet! Be still!"
Then he said to them, "Why are you so terrified?
Why are you lacking faith?"

A great awe overcame them at this.
They kept saying to one another,
"Who can this be that the wind and sea obey him?"

MARK 4:35–41

Mark shows Jesus performing the same feats that Yahweh was praised for performing in Old Testament times:

God our savior . . .
You still the roaring seas,
the roaring of the waves.

PSALM 65:8

He hushed the storm to a gentle breeze,
and the billows of the sea were stilled.

PSALM 107:29

Mark's point is this: Jesus demonstrates the same power over nature that Yahweh did. He, too, is "Lord of the waves and the winds."

Some suggest, further, that Mark intended Jesus' power over the storm to be a sign also of his power over demons.

The Gospel According to Luke
CARROLL STUHLMUELLER

In the Old Testament
the sea was often presented as the abode
of such powers. . . .
In calming the lake, Jesus appears as conqueror
of the demonic forces of the world of nature.

This observation leads
to a further sign-function of Jesus' miracles.

76

KINGDOM SIGN

The gospel portrays demonic forces
operating not only in the world of nature,
but also in people.
A contemporary film and novel, *The Exorcist*,
deals with the latter phenomenon.
It is based on an actual case that took place
in 1949 and involved a 14-year-old boy
from Mt. Rainier, Maryland.

"The Exorcism Frenzy"
NEWSWEEK

*Without apparent cause, pictures, chairs
and the boy's bed would suddenly move about.
At night, he could barely sleep.
After he was admitted to Georgetown University
Hospital, according to one newspaper account,
the boy began to mouth fierce curses
in ancient languages and at one point,
while strapped helplessly to his bed,
long red scratches appeared on his body.*

The boy survived an exorcism
and now lives in the Washington, D.C. area.

"What's the purpose of demonic possession?"
Fr. Karras asked old Fr. Merrin in *The Exorcist*.
"Who can know?" answered Merrin.
"Who can really hope to know?"

The gospel portrays Jesus as involving himself
frequently in cases of demonic possession.
Mark writes:

*Shortly afterward they came to Capernaum,
and on the Sabbath
Jesus entered the synagogue and began to teach.
The people were spellbound by his teaching
because he taught with authority,
and not like the scribes.*

*There appeared in their synagogue
a man with an unclean spirit that shrieked:
"What do you want of us, Jesus of Nazareth?*

*Have you come to destroy us?
I know who you are—the holy One of God!"
Jesus rebuked him sharply:
"Be quiet! Come out of the man!"
At that the unclean spirit convulsed the man
violently and with a loud shriek came out of him.
All who looked on were amazed.
They began to ask one another:
"What does this mean?"*

MARK 1:23-27

Later, Jesus himself
answered the question: "What does this mean?"

One day he was casting out a devil.
When his opponents accused him of doing it
by the power of Satan, Jesus responded:

*"If Satan is divided against himself,
how can his kingdom last? . . .
But if it is by the finger of God
that I cast out devils,
then the reign of God is upon you."*

LUKE 11:18-20

The evangelists present Jesus' power over devils
as a sign of the decline of Satan's kingdom
and the rise of God's kingdom.

Jesus' miracles marked the end of Satan's reign
and the arrival of God's reign in another way.
They showed Jesus' power over sin, sickness,
and death.
These 3 evils characterized Satan's kingdom
and had entered the world when Adam sinned.

One day Jesus was teaching.
Present were Pharisees and teachers of the law
from various parts of Galilee and Judea.

NARRATOR *Some men came along
carrying a paralytic on a mat.
They were trying to bring him in*

and lay him before Jesus;
but they found no way of getting him
through because of the crowd,
so they went up on the roof.
There they let him down with his mat
through the tiles into the middle
of the crowd before Jesus. . . .

JESUS   *My friend, your sins are forgiven you.*

NARRATOR   *The scribes and Pharisees*
began a discussion, saying:
"Who is this man who utters
blasphemies? Who can forgive sins
but God alone?"

JESUS   *Why do you harbor these thoughts?*
Which is easier:
to say "Your sins are forgiven you,"
or to say, "Get up and walk"?
In any case, to make clear to you
that the Son of Man has authority·
on earth to forgive sins—
(he then addressed the paralyzed man):
"I say to you, get up!"

NARRATOR   *At once the man stood erect. . . .*
Full of awe, the people gave praise
to God saying,
"We have seen incredible things today."
LUKE 5:17–26

The people would see something
even more incredible than this.
But first, consider this scene:

    "Jerusalem and the Last Days"
        JOHN PUTMAN

As I left the Dome of the Rock
a group of Arabs moved swiftly across the Haram,
led by a tall man who bore in his arms
a bundle wrapped in a carpet. . . .

The doorkeeper answered my unspoken question.
"It is a small dead boy.

When a boy dies,
they wash his body and wrap him in white
and bring him here for prayers."
Then they take him outside the walls and bury him.

I asked who carried him.
"An uncle or close family friend.
Not the father. It would hurt too much."

Jesus came upon a similar sight one day
as he and his disciples entered Naim.

NARRATOR   *As they approached the gate of the town*
a dead man was being carried out,
the only son of a widowed mother.
A considerable crowd of townsfolk
were with her.

The Moslem Dome of the Rock marks a site
precious to Jews, Christians, and Moslems.
Here, says tradition,
Abraham brought Isaac to be sacrificed,
and Mohammed departed for heaven.
Here Solomon built the great Jewish temple.
Here Jesus taught and prayed.

The Lord was moved with pity. . . .
He stepped forward and touched
the litter; at this the bearers halted.

JESUS   *Young man, I bid you get up.*

NARRATOR *The young man*
sat up and began to speak.
Then Jesus gave him back to his mother.
Fear seized them all
and they began to praise God.
LUKE 7:12–16

The significance of Jesus' power
over sin, sickness (paralytic's forgiveness/cure)
and death (restoration of life to widow's son)
is clear.

These 3 evils—sin, sickness, and death—
entered the world with Adam's sin.
They were the signs of Satan's kingdom on earth.
Jesus' power over these 3 evils
is a sign that Satan's kingdom is about to end
and God's kingdom is at hand.

Jesus' miracles heralded God's kingdom
in a final way.
Old Testament prophets foretold that certain
signs would precede the kingdom's arrival:

Then will the eyes of the blind be opened,
the ears of the deaf will be cleared;
then will the lame leap like a stag;
then the tongue of the dumb will sing.
ISAIAH 35:5–6

Jesus offered his miracles
as the fulfillment of these prophecies.
When John the Baptist sent his disciples
to ask Jesus if he were "the one to come,"
Jesus answered:

"Go and report to John
what you have seen and heard.

One artist's conception
of how the site referred to in John 5:1
may have looked in Jesus' day.

Striking Verification

Now in Jerusalem by the Sheep Pool
there is a place with the Hebrew name Bethesda.
Its 5 porticoes were crowded with sick people
lying there blind, lame or disabled. . . .
Jesus said to one of the sick,
"Pick up your mat and walk!"
The man was immediately cured;
he picked up his mat and began to walk.
JOHN 5:1–9

The historicity of this report was once questioned.
Scholars, like Alfred Loisy,
claimed the detail of the 5 porticoes was invented.
They said John made it up to stand for the 5 books
of the Torah, which Jesus came to fulfill.

In 1956, archaeologists upheld John's report fully.
Digging at the ancient biblical site of Bethesda,
they unearthed a rectangular pool
with a portico on each side and a fifth one
dividing the pool into 2 separate compartments.

Pool of Siloam

Today, small boys bathe
in the same pool where the blind man washed.

Built 8 centuries before Jesus,
the pool was designed
to insure Jerusalem of water in case of siege.

A 600-yard-long tunnel, cut through solid rock,
linked it with the hidden Gihon Spring
outside the fortified walls.
The tunnel is mentioned in the bible
in 3 different places: 2 Kings 20:20, Sirach 48:17,
and 2 Chronicles 32:3, 30.

The blind recover their sight, cripples walk,
lepers are cured, the deaf hear,
dead men are raised to life, and the poor
have the good news preached to them."
LUKE 7:22

CONVERSION SIGN

Finally, Jesus used miracles to call men
to conversion—that is, to invite them
to open their hearts to God's kingdom.

Bruce Marshall has written a delightful novel
called *Father Malachy's Miracle.*
It centers around a naive priest in Scotland.
He gets the idea of praying for a miracle
that will be so striking
as to leave no doubt about God and religion.

"One spectacular miracle," he tells a friend,
"and we shall prove to the world . . .
that we have the Light and the Truth."
The miracle he chooses is to have a nightclub
transported to an island off Scotland's coast.

The next night the priest kneels in deep prayer.
Suddenly, the nightclub rises up, floats away
and comes to rest on the coastal island.
When panic within the nightclub subsides,
lifeboats come to carry the frightened patrons
back to the mainland.

Instead of convincing people of the truth,
the miracle has the opposite effect.
People miss—or close their eyes to—the point.
The crushing blow comes when a female vocalist
sings a sultry ballad about the miracle.
She ends her act by raffling off the silk stockings
she was wearing during the famous flight.

A defeated Father Malachy asks God
to put an end to the whole affair.

Suddenly, the nightclub goes airborne again
and returns to its original site.

A much wiser Father Malachy now realizes
that it was foolish of him to ever think
that a miracle was all that was needed
to bring people to belief.

The point
that *Father Malachy's Miracle* illustrates
is also illustrated in Jesus' cure of a blind man:

Jesus smeared the man's eyes with mud.
Then he told him,
"Go wash in the pool of Siloam". . . .
So the man went off and washed
and came back able to see. . . .

The Jews refused to believe
that he had really been born blind
and had begun to see. . . .

Then Jesus said:
"I came into this world to divide it,
to make the sightless see and the seeing blind."
Some of the Pharisees around him
picked this up, saying,
"You are not calling us blind, are you?"

JOHN 9:1–7, 39–40

No one, not even Jesus, can compel belief.
Believing involves more
than hearing words and seeing signs.
It involves an openness of one's heart
to what one hears and sees—
a readiness to view the world in a new way.

To those whose hearts remained closed,
Jesus repeated Isaiah's words:

Sluggish indeed is this people's heart.
They have scarcely heard with their ears,
they have firmly closed their eyes,
otherwise they might see with their eyes,
and hear with their ears,
and understand with their hearts.

MATTHEW 13:15

Jesus' miracles—
the healing of the blind man,
the curing of the deaf person,
the raising to life of the widow's son—
these were marvelous deeds.

But it is also true
that the blind man's sight would dim again with age,
the deaf man's hearing would fade again,
and the widow's son, eventually die.

What then was the deeper, long-range significance
of these miracles?

Jesus healed the blind.
But behind this miracle was a deeper meaning.
It was a sign to all people to open their eyes
to the bright light of a new day.

Jesus unplugged the ears of the deaf.
It, too, was a sign to all people to open their ears
to what he had to say.

Jesus raised the dead.
Again, this was a sign to all people to be reborn—
to begin to live new lives in God's kingdom—
here and now.

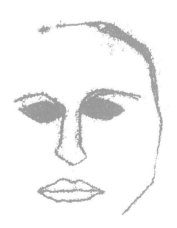

Modern Miracles

In 1858 a French girl reported apparitions
of the mother of Jesus at a hillside in Lourdes.
As a result,
sick people visited the site and were cured.
Today, the Medical Bureau of Lourdes
has on file the records of over 1,200 cures.

The Miracle of Lourdes
RUTH CRANSTON

A Medical Commission
of twenty distinguished physicians and surgeons
of various countries passes upon these records
before a cure is finally and officially declared.

In the 1930s Dr. Alexis Carrel,
New York surgeon and Nobel Prize winner,
went to the shrine to check out its claims.
While en route by train,
he was called several times to the bedside
of a sick girl going to Lourdes, too.
"If such a case as hers were cured,"
he told a friend, "it would indeed be a miracle.
I would never doubt again."

Dr. Carrel accompanied the girl to the shrine.
He described the episode in a published report.
For professional reasons, he changed all names
and called himself Lerrac.

The Voyage to Lourdes
ALEXIS CARREL

Suddenly, Lerrac felt himself turning pale.
The blanket which covered Marie Ferrand's
distended abdomen was gradually
flattening out. . . .

Standing beside Marie Ferrand,
he watched the intake of her breath
and the pulsing of her throat. . . .
"How do you feel?" he asked her. . . .
"I feel I am cured."

Lerrac stood in silence, his mind a blank.
Later, he and two other doctors
examined Marie at the Bureau of Medical Records.
Their conclusion was unanimous: cured.

That night,
Lerrac went for a long walk to think things out.
He ended up in the back of a church.

For a long time he sat there motionless,
his hands over his face. . . .
This was the prayer he found himself saying:

"I am still blind . . . I still doubt. . . .
Beneath the deep, harsh warnings
of my intellectual pride
a smothered dream persists. . . .
It is the dream of believing. . . ."

Back at his hotel . . .
he took the big green notebook from his bag
and sat down to write his observations. . . .
By now it was three o'clock. . . .
A new coolness penetrated the open window.
He felt the serenity of nature
enter his soul with gentle calm. . . .
All intellectual doubts had vanished.

82

12

Parables of Jesus

Two pots were lying on a river bank.
One was brass, the other clay.
One day the river flooded over.
The 2 pots went floating downstream.
As they drifted along, the brass pot saw
the clay pot was staying a safe distance behind.
"Fear not," said the brass pot, "I won't bump you."
The clay pot answered:
"Whether you strike me or I strike you,
the result will be the same."

This famous story by a Greek slave
reminds us that the telling of a story
is one of the world's oldest teaching techniques.
Even today, whether in book or film,
the story form is still an effective way to teach.
Film director Alfred Hitchcock tells why:

"Meeting the Master of Suspense"
ROBERTA OSTROFF

*To make a suspense film that works
you must involve your audience.
You do this by giving them information.
You get them into the film. They know something.
If you go out and make a whodunit
where they don't know anything
until the last few minutes of the film,
well then they feel cheated.
They're never really involved in the story
because you've given them nothing to think about.
So you must always keep them informed. . . .*

*For example,
let us say that you have several people
sitting around a table talking about fishing—
a meaningless, really boring talk.
Suddenly you see that under that very table
there is a bomb that is going to go off.
Aha, suddenly this conversation becomes
very important. You hang on every word.
You as the audience are becoming very nervous
because you know
there's a bomb getting ready to explode
and these people are talking about something silly.*

The suspense film, like every good story,
involves the audience.

PARABLES

Jesus made wide use of stories called parables.
A parable is a simile drawn from life or nature,
designed to arrest the hearer's attention
and to prod the hearer's imagination.

Parables were ideally suited
to handle some of the problems Jesus faced
in teaching the people.

First of all, many people thought
that God's kingdom was to be a worldly one
which would give Israel great worldly power,
wealth, and prestige.
They also thought that the messiah
would be a great warrior-king.

Jesus had to correct these false ideas
before revealing his identity fully
and before revealing the nature of God's kingdom.

This explains why,
in the early portion of his teaching ministry,
Jesus guarded against anything that reinforced
popular false ideas about God's kingdom
and the messiah.
Thus, after healing a leper, Jesus said to him:
"Not a word to anyone now!" (Mark 2:44)

Similarly, when "unclean spirits"
kept calling out, "You are the Son of God,"
Jesus "kept ordering them sternly not to reveal
who he was." (Mark 3:12)
So, too, when Jesus fed the people miraculously
and they wanted to acclaim him as a king,
Jesus "fled back to the mountain alone." (John 6:15)

Jesus had to reeducate the masses of people
concerning God's kingdom and the messiah.
This required tact and great care.
It had to be done slowly and by degrees.
Parables were ideally suited to do just this.
They made their point subtly and delicately,
without crushing or disillusioning the people.

Second, the true nature of God's kingdom
was so beyond people's everyday experience
that there was no way to speak about it directly.
Paul said of the kingdom's final form:

"Eye has not seen, ear has not heard,
nor has it so much as dawned on man
what God has prepared for those who love him."
1 CORINTHIANS 2:9

Parables taught about God's kingdom
by using simple comparisons familiar to all.
They helped people move slowly but surely
from the known to the unknown.
Parables helped people
to prod their imaginations and stretch their minds
to embrace ideas and possibilities bigger
than those to which
they were normally accustomed.

Finally, besides revealing
the nature of God's kingdom and the messiah,
parables revealed the status of people's hearts.
Parables invited people to discover themselves
as they really were: open or closed to truth.

Since a parable did not make its point directly,
it gave people the option of accepting or rejecting
the deeper meaning to which it pointed.

Hearers were free to acknowledge the point
or to close their ears and their eyes to it.
Thus, parables acted as a kind of test
to see if a person's heart was open or closed.
Concerning people with closed hearts,
Jesus remarked to his disciples:

"They listen but do not hear or understand.
Isaiah's prophecy is fulfilled in them
which says . . .

'Sluggish indeed is this people's heart. . . .'

"But blest are your eyes because they see
and blest are your ears because they hear."
MATTHEW 13:13–16

PARABLE OF THE BUILDERS

One April morning,
2 groups of pilgrims headed for the Siq.
The Siq is a narrow gorge south of Palestine
that links ancient Petra with the outside world.
Each year, thousands of tourists
snake through the 3-mile-long, narrow pass
to view the ruins of this unusual city.

"Cloudburst at Petra"
TIME

The French party gaily entered the Siq gorge
just as a sprinkle of rain began to fall.
Four were traveling in a Land Rover,
the rest on foot.

Suddenly, the light rain became a cloudburst—
the worst in arid Petra's recorded history.
Within half an hour,
torrential floods were streaming down the hills
and pouring into the Siq as into a tunnel.
One Italian pilgrim said,
"We heard shrieks and cries within the ravine,
as the muddy cascade of water rushed by us.
We saw
the little car with the four women and driver
swept along by the torrent and then submerged.
In an instant

Figures in front of "The Treasury" in Petra give some idea of its size.

Siq means "pass."
The Siq's walls tower upwards
sometimes reaching heights of nearly 300 feet.

Petra owes much of its beauty to King Aretas whose daughter was divorced by Herod Antipas.

Petra

Lost for centuries,
Petra was rediscovered in 1812
by Swiss adventurer, Johann Burckhardt,
who gained admission disguised as a bedouin.

Many of Petra's exquisite buildings
were chiseled by stonecutters
directly from the sandstone canyon walls.

The Nabataean kingdom, of which Petra was a part,
disappeared from the pages of history
shortly after the Romans took control in A.D. 106.

they all disappeared in the floodwaters
raging along at perhaps 60 miles an hour."

This report of the raging torrent in the Siq
and the tragedy that resulted
helps us to appreciate the impact
that Jesus' Parable of the Two Housebuilders
must have had upon Palestinian audiences.
People were familiar with the images Jesus used
and could relate to them perfectly.

Both Matthew and Luke record the parable.
We reprint their 2 versions in parallel columns.

Matthew 7:24–27	Luke 6:47–49
Jesus said:	*Jesus said:*
"Anyone who	*"Any man who desires*
hears my words and	*to come to me will*
puts them into practice	*hear my words and put*
is like the man	*them into practice. . . .*
who built his house	*He may be likened to*
on rock."	*the man who,*
	in building his house,
	dug deeply and laid
	the foundation on rock.
"When the rainy season	*"When the floods came*
set in, the torrents came	*the torrents rushed in*
and the winds blew	*on that house,*
and buffeted the house.	*but failed to shake it*
It did not collapse;	*because of its solid*
it had been solidly set	*foundation. . . .*
on rock.	
"Anyone who hears	*"Anyone who has heard*
my words but does not	*my words but not put*
put them into practice	*them into practice*
is like the foolish man	*is like the man*
who built his house	*who built his house*
on sandy ground.	*on the ground*
	without any foundation.

"The rains fell,
the torrents came and
lashed against his house.
It collapsed."

"When the torrents
rushed in upon it,
it immediately fell in."

Comparing these 2 versions,
we notice slight but interesting variations.
Some readers explain these variations,
saying Jesus probably told the same parable
to different groups on 2 different occasions.

Others note that Matthew's version reflects
a Palestinian setting: "building on rock,"
"a rainy season," and "high winds."
The foolish man builds his house on the edge
of a wadi, which is dry during summer months
but flowing with water during the rainy season.

Luke's version, on the other hand,
seems to reflect conditions more in keeping
with a Greek setting.
Luke speaks of "digging and laying a foundation,"
according to Greek building practices.
He also makes explicit references to floods.
Lastly, Luke drops references to "winds"
and a "rainy season."

Luke's differences do not change the meaning
of Jesus' parable.
The same point emerges: to listen to the words
of Jesus and to admire his deeds is not enough.
You must put them into practice in your life.

PARABLE OF THE LOST SHEEP

An Arab goatherd counted his flock at 11 A.M.
He did it at this unusual hour,
because he suddenly remembered not counting it
the night before.
When one goat turned up missing,
the goatherd entrusted his flock to 2 companions
and set off in search of the lost animal.
The young Arab ended up
discovering the first of the Dead Sea Scrolls.

Roof Detail

Details surrounding the paralytic's cure in Mark
fit mud roof construction, common in Palestine.
Details in Luke
fit tile roof construction, common in Greece.

Mark 2:3–4

The four who carried
the paralytic
were unable to bring him
to Jesus
because of the crowd,

so they began to open up
the roof over the spot
where Jesus was.
When they had
made a hole,
they let down the mat
on which the paralytic
was lying.

Luke 5:19

They found no way
of getting
the paralytic through
because of
the crowd,

so they
went up to the roof.
They let him down
with his mat
through the tiles
in the middle
of the crowd
before Jesus.

Our point in recalling this story
is not to dramatize the odd set of circumstances
that led to the finding of the Dead Sea Scrolls,
but to dramatize
the herder's perennial problem: a lost animal.
This problem became the focal point
of one of Jesus' best-known parables.
It appears in different versions and settings
in Matthew and Luke.

Matthew 18:2, 10–14

Jesus . . .
said to his disciples . . .
"See that you
never despise
one of these little ones.
I assure you,
their angels in heaven
constantly behold my
heavenly Father's face.

"What is your thought
on this: A man owns
a hundred sheep

Luke 15:1–7

Pharisees and scribes
murmured,
"This man welcomes
sinners
and eats with them."
Then Jesus addressed
this parable to them:

"Who among you,
if he has
a hundred sheep

and one of them
wanders away;
will he not leave
the ninety-nine
out in the hills and go
in search of the stray?
"If he succeeds
in finding it,
believe me
he will be happier
about this one
than
about the ninety-nine
that did not
wander away.

"Just so,
it is no part of your
heavenly Father's plan
that a single one
of these little ones
shall ever come
to grief."

and loses one of them,
does not leave
the ninety-nine
in the wasteland
and follow the lost one
until he finds it?
"And when he finds it,
he puts it on his
shoulders in jubilation.
Once arrived home,
he invites his friends
and neighbors in
and says to them,
'Rejoice with me
because I have found
my lost sheep.'

"I tell you, there will be
more joy in heaven over
one repentant sinner
than over ninety-nine
righteous people who
have no need to repent."

Some readers think this is one case
where Jesus did use the same parable
to illustrate different points to different groups.

Others think it is an example of how
the apostles sometimes adapted Jesus' parables
to situations in their own lives.

Luke seems to preserve the original context:
to explain Jesus' concern for sinners.
Matthew seems to report the adapted context:
to charge Jesus' disciples with special concern
for the "least members" of the community.

Luke stresses the Father's great joy
over the return of one sinner.
Matthew stresses the pastor's obligation
to be solicitous of the needy of the community.

Jesus' concern for the downtrodden in Luke
is enjoined upon Jesus' disciples in Matthew.

Flocks munching grass
on the slopes of the Mount of Olives
recall the image of Psalm 100:
"The Lord is God;
he made us; his we are . . .
the flock he tends."

Shepherd Image

The shepherd still goes about his work
much as he did in Jesus' day.
He still walks at the head of his flock
often talking to them in a singsong way.

In the Steps of the Master
H. V. MORTON

Early one morning I saw an extraordinary sight
not far from Bethlehem.
Two shepherds had evidently spent the night
with their flocks in a cave.
The sheep were all mixed together
and the time had come
for the shepherds to go in different directions.

One of the shepherds stood some distance
from the sheep and began to call.
First one, then another,
then four or five animals ran toward him;
and so on until he had counted his whole flock.

Jesus said:
"The shepherd calls his own by name
and leads them out . . .
he walks in front of them,
and the sheep follow him
because they recognize his voice." (John 10:3–4)

PARABLE OF THE SOWER

Sometimes early Christians
allegorized the parables of Jesus.
That is, they developed the parable
beyond the *one* explicit point that Jesus gave it.
For example, Augustine interpreted the meaning
of the Parable of the Good Samaritan this way:

Jerusalem	heaven
Jericho	world
robber band	Satan and bad angels
wounded man	Adam
priest	Torah
levite	prophets
Samaritan	Jesus
inn	church
Samaritan's return	Jesus' second coming.

Referring to Augustine and teachers like him,
one modern scholar said this:

The Parables of the Gospels
RAYMOND BROWN

They recognized
that the parables were stories with a point
but they sought significance
in all the details of the parables. . . .

This method of allegorizing
has to be understood sympathetically against
the background of the patristic use of the Bible.
The Scriptures
were the basic catechism of the Church,
and all theology was taught from the Bible.

In the case above
Augustine wished to teach his audience
about original sin and redemption,
and the parable was his catechetical tool.

Some bible readers think the evangelists
may have allegorized a few of Jesus' parables.
In other words,
they dotted the "i's" and crossed the "t's"
of what Jesus meant.
They spelled out details in Jesus' parables
to let them speak to new situations
that arose in the young church after Pentecost.
Consider the Parable of the Sower.

A farmer went out to sow some seed.
In the sowing, some fell on the footpath . . .
and the birds of the air ate it up.
Some fell on rocky ground, sprouted up,
then withered through lack of moisture.
Some fell among briers,
but the thorns . . . stifled it.
But some fell on good soil, grew up,
and yielded grain a hundredfold.

LUKE 8:5–8

Jesus told the parable
to explain why God's word was not having
its intended effect in the lives of some people.
The problem lies
not with God's word, but with people's hearts.
Stated simply, the parable's single point is this:
the seed's fruitfulness (God's word)
depends upon the soil's openness (human heart).

Some people think this *single* point of the parable
was allegorized by the apostles
in their preaching to the people after Pentecost.

In other words,
just as Augustine developed the various details
of the Parable of the Good Samaritan,

perhaps the evangelists developed the details
of the Parable of the Sower. Luke writes:

This is the meaning of the parable.
The seed is the word of God.
Those on the footpath are people who hear,
but the devil comes and takes the word out of
their hearts lest they believe and be saved.

Those on rocky ground are the ones who,
when they hear the word, receive it with joy.
They have no root; they believe it for a while
but fall away in time of temptation.

The seed fallen among briers
are those who hear but their progress is stifled
by the cares and riches and pleasures of life
and they do not mature.

The seed on good ground are those
who hear the word in a spirit of openness,
retain it, and bear fruit through perseverance.

LUKE 8:9-15

One reason why some people tend to think
that this explanation derives from the preaching
of the apostles after Pentecost
is that it seems to presuppose a situation
that developed after Pentecost.

This is especially evident in Matthew's
explanation of the same parable.
He uses the word "persecution" in place of
Luke's "temptation." (Matthew 13:21)
Formal persecution of Jesus' followers
didn't begin until after Pentecost.

This reason, along with more complex ones,
leads some to think the apostles spelled out
what was implicit in Jesus' parable,
applying it to the situation of their own day.

Spelling out the parable's details, they say,
deepens our appreciation of the total parable.

"Gathering the Fragments:
Of Fear and Scholarship"
BARNABAS AHERN

A penetrating study of this passage shows
that our understanding of Jesus' full message
is greatly enriched. . . .
This is what Jesus promised would happen
after the coming of the Holy Spirit.
(John 14:26, 16:12–13)

In the Parable of the Sower, therefore,
we hear not only what Jesus said
to his immediate audience,
but also what he meant for Christians of all time.

Describing how the Parable of the Sower
gave her a whole new outlook on life, a girl said:

I got this really strange feeling
when we were discussing the parable's meaning.
It was like Jesus was speaking right to me.
Let me explain.

At the end of last year, I had a great talk
with my counselor. The first ever.
I made several resolutions for this year.
Then, yesterday, it dawned on me:
I hadn't followed through on a single resolution.
Maybe this was why my life had not changed.
I had let my resolutions get lost
by a lot of other things that weren't important.

The Parable of the Sower
helped me to see myself in a whole new way.

PARABLE THEMES

As with his miracles,
Jesus' parables operated at 2 different levels:
the *sense* level and the *sign* level.
The sense level
of Jesus' miracles was what everyone saw:
a blind man seeing again, a deaf person hearing,
a lame person walking again.
The sign level

was the deeper significance Jesus intended his miracles to have. In general, they were signs:

> proclaiming God's kingdom, and
> inviting people's conversion.

The sense level of the parables
was the literal meaning of the story Jesus told:
2 men built different houses for their families,
a shepherd lost a sheep and went in search of it,
a farmer planted some seed and got mixed results.

The sign level
was the deeper meaning that Jesus meant
his parables to communicate.
They, too, followed 2 general themes, namely:

> explaining God's kingdom, and
> explaining people's conversion.

In many cases,
the same parable contains both of these themes.

A parable that explains God's kingdom
is sometimes called a *window* parable.
That is, it acts as a kind of window
through which we can look
to get a better understanding of God's kingdom.

A parable that explains how people should
open their hearts to God's kingdom
is sometimes called a *mirror* parable.
That is, it acts as a kind of mirror
into which we can look
to get a better understanding of ourselves.

Seed Image

This field outside modern Jerusalem illustrates the imagery of Jesus' Parable of the Sower:

Some seed fell to the footpath . . .
some fell on rocky ground . . .
some fell among briers . . .
some fell on good ground.

LUKE 8:5-8

The fate of the seed that fell on the footpath recalls the fate of seeds in a similar situation, described in the *Book of Jubilees*.

New Testament Essays
RAYMOND BROWN

Mastema
sent ravens and birds to devour the seed
which was sown in the land. . . .
Before they could plow in the seed, the ravens
picked (it) from the surface of the ground.

Not only do we have here
the same type of farming (sowing before plowing)
as in the gospels, but also the birds
are the instruments of Satan or Mastema.

91

MIRROR PARABLES

An unforgettable scene in *Hamlet* has the young prince confront his mother, the Queen:

HAMLET *Come,*
come and sit down.
You shall not budge,
You go not
till I set you up a glass
Where you may see
the inmost part of you.

QUEEN *O Hamlet, speak no more.*
Thou turn'st mine eyes
into my very soul.
And there I see such black
and grained spots
As will not leave their tinct.

What Hamlet asked his mother to look into
was not a glass mirror, but a word mirror.
She saw reflected in it
her own ugly part in his father's tragic murder.

Jesus' parables also acted as word mirrors.
Jesus frequently composed them
so that people in the parable
mirrored persons in his listening audience.

For example, the Parable of the Two Builders
involved 2 builders: a wise one and a foolish one.
Jesus likened them to 2 hearers of God's word:
one who lived the word and one who did not.
Jesus let each hearer decide which situation
mirrored his or her own situation.

Likewise,
Jesus' Parable of the Sower acted as a mirror.
It concerned 4 kinds of soil into which seed fell.
Jesus likened the soils to the 4 kinds of hearts
into which God's word falls.
Jesus let each hearer decide which of the soils
best reflected his or her own openness
to the word of God.

Jesus Christ
YVES CONGAR

The parables, then, are like a collection
of mirrors
in which I am invited to see myself. . . .
They lead me to put to myself this question:
is it not I who received the seed of the Word
as though on rocks,
I who let it be choked by thorns? Is it not I
who buried the talent, leaving it unproductive?
Is it not I
who am the priest or levite who passed by,
without bothering myself about the man
who lay wounded by the road. . . ?

When I ask myself questions like these,
the parables reveal me to myself. . . .
They lead me to see myself as I am. . . .
By means of them,
I am, as it were, driven to make the decision
and to give the answer I had been evading.
I am personally summoned,
brought back to the heart . . .
where man can no longer try to avoid the issue.

WINDOW PARABLES

The novel, *The Heart Is a Lonely Hunter*,
contains a moving scene.

A teenage girl is listening to recorded music.
As she does, she tries to explain to Mr. Singer,
a deaf and dumb man, what music is like.
To do this, she stands in front of him
so that he can read her lips.
She also gestures with her hands and face.

Finally, both laugh and give it up.
They realize that trying to describe sound
to a deaf person is like trying to describe color
to a blind person.

Jesus faced a similar challenge when he tried
to explain to people what God's kingdom was like.

It was like describing sound to a deaf person.
It was something beyond their experience.
At best, Jesus could convey to his audience
only a vague idea of what it was actually like.

Some of Jesus' parables acted as *windows*,
through which people could glimpse, vaguely,
what the kingdom of God was like.
The Parable of the Lost Sheep is an example.
It allowed people to glimpse God's concern
for every single person.
In God's kingdom, even the most insignificant
individual has great value.
God does not measure as the world measures.

PARABLE OF THE TREASURE

The Arab goatherd's discovery of the first
Dead Sea Scrolls led to further discoveries.
Eventually, 11 caves yielded nearly 600 scrolls.
About one-third were biblical writings.
One nonbiblical writing was a surprise.

"The Qumran Story"
ROLAND DE VAUX

It contained a list of about sixty treasures
supposedly hidden in all parts of Palestine,
many around Jerusalem, a few around Qumran.
There were also
directions on how to find those treasures.

Someone in England decided to do something
about it and organized an expedition to search
for the treasures. Nothing was found.

The "treasure" scroll gave many biblical readers
a renewed appreciation
of one of Jesus' better-known *window* parables.
Jesus said:

"The reign of God is like a buried treasure
which a man found in a field.
He hid it again, and rejoicing at his find
went and sold all he had and bought that field."

MATTHEW 13:44

Traditionally, Palestine has been a battlefield
and a corridor for armies.
Any day a town might become a battleground.
The only safe place for valuables was in the soil.

In modern times, German Jews buried valuables.
In his book, *Night*, Elie Wiesel relates
how his dying father pressed his lips to Elie's ear
to whisper where he had buried family valuables.

The point of the Parable of the Buried Treasure
is not the price one must pay to buy the field.
Rather, it is the overwhelming joy of the finder.
Selling everything is not a sacrifice, but a joy.

What is the kingdom of God like?
Jesus said: "Think of it as a buried treasure—
something beyond your fondest dreams!"

PARABLE OF THE PEARL

Mel Ellis recalls the exciting summer
when he learned where to find clam shells
on the bottom of Wisconsin's Rock River
and how to check inside the shells for pearls.

"More Precious Than Pearl"
MEL ELLIS

The next day
I felt the first nubbin beneath my thumb
and brought my first seed pearl to light.
It was almost as big as a perch's eye,
and though it wasn't completely round,
its color took my breath away. . . .
I found two small ones that day.
Even my family was excited by my discovery.
We sat around the kerosene lamp
until way past my bedtime,
admiring and talking about pearls.

After that there was no time for anything else.
Buck, my dog, had a droopy, sad look in his eye
because I had no time to hunt and swim with him,
and the fishermen who saw me feeling for clams
with my feet asked what that crazy kid was up to.

When I got back into my shoes to go to school,
I had a small wineglass full of the most beautiful
pearls a man could ever want to see.
None was round enough to be worth much.
I knew that, but it made no difference,
because I didn't want to sell them anyway.

Hunting pearls was not merely a popular art
among the river folk in the 1920s.
It dates back to biblical times and before.
Jesus said:

"The kingdom of heaven
is like a merchant's search for fine pearls.
When he found one really valuable pearl,
he went back and put up for sale
all that he had and bought it."

                        MATTHEW 13:45–46

Jesus' point is identical to the one
that he makes in the Parable of the Treasure.
God's kingdom is unlike anything
within the realm of human experience.
All else pales in significance before it.
No price can compare to its true worth.
Giving up all to gain the kingdom
is not sacrifice, but a privilege beyond belief.

The point of Jesus' *window* parables was
to free people from their limited human ideas
and to open their minds to bigger possibilities:

"Eye has not seen, ear has not heard,
nor has it so much as dawned on man
what God has prepared for those who love him."

                    1 CORINTHIANS 2:9

GOD'S KINGDOM

A final clarification is in order.
We may approach it this way.

The musical, *Man of La Mancha,*
was inspired by the tragic life of Cervantes,
the 16th-century author.

A "catalogue of catastrophe,"
Cervantes' life began in a poor Spanish family.
As a young soldier,
he was wounded seriously at Lepanto, captured,
and sentenced to 5 years of slavery in Africa.

Back in Spain, he failed to fit into society.
He served 3 terms in prison on various charges.
Broken in body, if not spirit, he died in 1616
after completing his great work, *Don Quixote.*

A moving scene from *Man of La Mancha*
occurs shortly after the play-stopping song,
"The Impossible Dream."
Cervantes stands before his accusers.

	Man of La Mancha
	DALE WASSERMAN and JOE DARION

THE DUKE   *Why are you poets so fascinated*
                    by madmen?

CERVANTES   *I suppose . . .*
                    we have much in common.

THE DUKE   *You both turn your backs on life.*

CERVANTES   *We both*
                    select from life what pleases us.

THE DUKE   *A man must come to terms with life*
                    as it is.

CERVANTES   *I have lived nearly fifty years,*
                    and I have seen life as it is.
                    Pain, misery, hunger . . .
                    cruelty beyond belief.
                    I have heard the singing
                    from the taverns
                    and the moans from bundles of filth
                    in the streets.
                    I have been a soldier and seen
                    my comrades fall in battle . . .
                    or die more slowly
                    under the lash in Africa.
                    I have held them in my arms
                    at the final moment.

"I will order the harvesters,
First collect the weeds
and bundle them up to burn." (Matthew 13:30)

Unchanging Images

The Tales Christ Told
APRIL OURSLER ARMSTRONG

Christ told his parables
in terms of things that never change,
in the barest fundamentals of living.
And we can claim them for our own
if we will make the effort
to pierce the years with a little study,
to breathe the clean air of the countryside
and lift our eyes to the stars. . . .

In a city park in London,
in the sprawling mechanized farms
of the American Middle West,
in a backyard garden or a window box
there is still a seed and a sower.

These were men
who saw life as it is,
yet they died despairing.
No glory, no gallant last words . . .
only their eyes filled with confusion,
whimpering the question: "Why?"
I do not think they asked
why they were dying,
but why they had lived.
When life itself seems lunatic,
who knows where madness lies?
Perhaps to be too practical
is madness.
To surrender dreams—
this may be madness.
And maddest of all,
to see life as it is
and not as it should be.

Cervantes' words are not those of a madman,
but of every person who has thought about life.
They give voice to a question
that puzzles young Christians especially.
"If Jesus set in motion the kingdom of God,
why is evil still widespread 2,000 years later?"
Insight into the dilemma comes
when we look more closely at Jesus' words.
Teaching his disciples about prayer, he said:

*"When you pray, say:
'Father, hallowed be your name,
your kingdom come. . . .'"*

LUKE 11:2

Jesus' words raised eyebrows.
They referred to God's kingdom as "coming."
Didn't this contradict what Jesus said elsewhere?

*Once on being asked by the Pharisees
when the reign of God would come,
Jesus replied . . .
"The reign of God is already in your midst."*

LUKE 17:21–22

95

What did Jesus mean?
Is the kingdom of God already on earth,
or is it something that is still to come?
And, if the new order is already present,
why is evil still so widespread?

Invitation to the New Testament
W. D. DAVIES

The new order has come,
but the old order has not yet fully passed away. . . .
This is why the Lord's Prayer
prays for the coming of the Kingdom,
even though it is already present in Jesus.

In other words, the kingdom of God is not
an instant happening, but a gradual process.
It is not a static event, but a dynamic movement,
which Jesus set in motion.
The kingdom of God is like a plant
that is growing, but not yet fully grown.
Negatively,
the kingdom of Satan has not yet come to an end;
it is only under the sentence of death.

PARABLE OF THE WEEDS AND WHEAT

To dramatize the present situation of the world,
Jesus told this parable:

NARRATOR *The reign of God*
may be likened to a man
who sowed good seed in his field.
While everyone was asleep,
his enemy came and sowed weeds
through his wheat and made off.
When the crop began to mature
and yield grain, the weeds
made their appearance as well.

WORKER *Sir, did you not sow good seed*
in your field?
Where are the weeds coming from?

OWNER *I see an enemy's hand in this.*

WORKER *Do you want us to . . . pull them up?*

OWNER *Let them grow together until harvest,*
then at harvest time
I will order the harvesters:
First collect the weeds
and bundle them up to burn,
then gather the wheat into my barns.

MATTHEW 13:24-30

Sowing another's field with weeds or salt
was a horrendous practice among ancients.
Roman law punished it as a crime.
The Old Testament also cites the practice.
After a battle, an enemy's fields were salted
to render them unfit for cultivation. (Judges 9:45)

Later, Jesus explained his parable:

"The farmer sowing good seed is the Son of Man;
the field is the world,
the good seed the citizens of the kingdom.
The weeds are the followers of the evil one
and the enemy who sowed them is the devil.
The harvest is the end of the world,
while the harvesters are the angels.

"Just as weeds are collected and burned,
so will it be at the end of the world."

MATTHEW 13:37-40

A dragnet collects all sorts of things—
debris as well as fish.
Not until the net is ashore can the sorting start.
First the debris is separated from the fish;
then the fish are separated into 2 batches:
"clean" and "unclean." (Leviticus 11:9–12)

Net Image

The reign of God
is like a dragnet thrown into the lake,
which collected all sorts of things.
When it was full they hauled it ashore
and sat down to put what was worthwhile
into containers.
What was useless they threw away.
That is how it will be at the end of the world.
                    MATTHEW 13:47–49

The dragnet is still used by Galilean fishermen.
Over 10 feet deep and over 100 feet long,
it is usually towed between 2 large boats.

Another net
still used by Galilean fishermen is the handnet.
Released by a swift overhand motion,
it swishes through the air and hits the water
like a ballet dancer's skirt.

Dozens of tiny metal weights pull the handnet
down into the water, trapping all fish in the area.
A fish commonly caught this way is the *musht*,
also called "Peter's Fish."
Matthew writes that Jesus said to Peter:

"Go to the lake, throw in a line,
and take out the first fish you catch.
Open its mouth and you will discover there
a coin worth twice the temple tax.
Take it and give it to them for you and me."
                    MATTHEW 17:27

Tradition says the fish Peter caught was a *musht*,
hence the name "Peter's Fish." Daniel-Rops says:

The musht, like the tilapia of Siam,
keeps its young in its mouth:
when the little fishes grow too big it expels them,
taking a pebble in their place—
though indeed it may be a coin instead of a stone.

97

This narrow street
is not too unlike those through which Jesus walked.

PART THREE

GALILEAN MINISTRY II

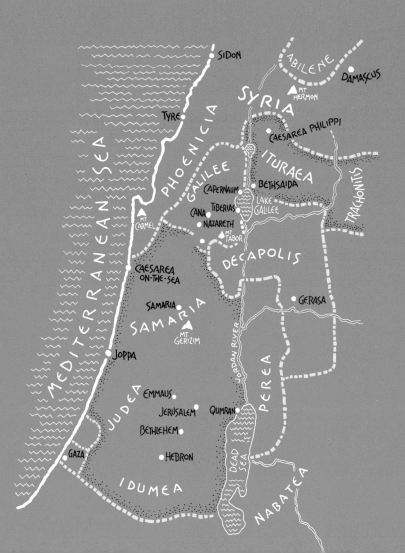

13

Challenge of Jesus

There are mothers
who want to enjoy their daughters more.
But the days are short and the hours few.

There are fathers
who plan to spend more time with their sons.
But work keeps pressing and sons keep growing.

There are wives and husbands
who would like to share more time with each other.
But days pass and so do opportunities.

"When in the world," asks Richard Evans,
"are we going to begin to live
as if we understood that this is life?
This is our time, our day . . . and it is passing.
What are we waiting for?"

DECISION TIME

Jesus ran into similar problems with people
when he proclaimed God's kingdom
and invited them to open their hearts to it.

Jesus said, "Come to me."
The man replied,
"Let me bury my father first."
Jesus said to him,
"Let the dead bury their dead."
LUKE 9:59-60

At first, these words of Jesus sound harsh.
But, given an eastern context, they are not.
The story is told of a young Arab
who refused a college scholarship saying:
"I will take it only after I bury my father."
The father was healthy and still under fifty.
The boy wanted to postpone leaving home
until his father's death;
perhaps his father might need him in old age.

Jesus' point is that not even the noblest reason
qualifies as an excuse to postpone one's response
to God's kingdom. "Not to decide is to decide."

But Jesus makes something else clear.
Just as a person should not postpone decision,
so one should not fail to calculate the cost.

"If one of you decides to build a tower,
will he not first sit down and calculate the outlay
to see if he has enough money. . . .

"Or if a king is about to . . . do battle . . .
will he not sit down first and consider whether,
with ten thousand men, he can withstand an enemy
coming against him with twenty thousand. . . .

"In the same way, none of you can be my disciple
if he does not renounce all his possessions."
LUKE 14:28-33

Jesus repeatedly cautioned enthusiasts:

"If anyone comes to me without turning his back
on his father and mother, his wife, and his children,
his brothers and sisters, indeed his very self,
he cannot be my follower."
LUKE 14:26

Some idea of the kind of commitment
Jesus was asking of his disciples
is suggested in an unforgettable scene
in Joseph Stein's play, *Fiddler On the Roof.*

These sepulchers, on the Mount of Olives,
lie not far away from the Garden of Gethsemani.
Placing a stone on a loved one's sepulcher
is a sign of mourning and sharing in the burial.

Bury the Dead

In the Steps of the Master
H. V. MORTON

One night,
when the full moon burned above Jerusalem,
I went down and stood . . .
looking towards the Garden of Gethsemani.
Every limestone path was clear and white
on the dark mass of the hill.
The thousands of whited sepulchers
that lie in the heights and in the hollows
gleamed in the moonlight
like companies of sheeted ghosts. . . .
The whole Mount
slept in the green downpour of the moon.

The play is set in Russia in 1905.
The plot centers around a man named Tevye,
the father of a poor, orthodox Jewish family.
Tevye has 5 daughters and no sons.

As the play develops,
the eldest daughter marries a poor tailor
who was not chosen for her by the traditional
matchmaker. Tevye accepts the marriage,
but only after a struggle with his conscience.

Tevye's next daughter marries a young student
who has broken with many Jewish traditions.
After another painful conscience struggle,
Tevye accepts this marriage, too.

Finally, the third daughter, Chava,
marries a gentile, a young Russian soldier.
Tevye's wife, Golde,
breaks the news to her husband in the fields:

Fiddler On the Roof
JOSEPH STEIN

TEVYE   *Married!* (She nods.) *Go home, Golde.*
       We have other children at home.
       Go home, Golde. You have work to do.
       I have work to do.

GOLDE   *But, Chava—*

TEVYE   *Chava is dead to us! We will forget her.*
       Go home. (Golde exits. Tevye sings.)

       ("Chavaleh")

       Little bird, little Chavaleh,
       I don't understand
       what's happening today.
       Everything is all a blur.
       All I can see is a happy child.
       The sweet little bird you were.
       Chavaleh, Chavaleh,
       You were always
       such a pretty little thing.
       Everybody's fav'rite child,

Gentle and kind and affectionate,
What a sweet little bird you were,
Chavaleh, Chavaleh.

(Chava enters.)

CHAVA   *Papa, I want to talk with you.*
Papa, stop. At least listen to me.
Papa, I beg you to accept us.

TEVYE   (to heaven) *Accept them?*
How can I accept them?
Can I deny everything I believe in?
On the other hand,
can I deny my own child?
On the other hand,

*how can I turn my back on my faith,
my people?*
If I try to bend that far, I will break.
On the other hand . . .
there is no other hand. No Chava.

CHAVA   *Papa. Papa.*

When Jesus invited people to follow him,
he realized what he was asking of them.
For some,
the choice was like the one Chava had to make.
It was almost like dying—or being born again.

For some people
this kind of total commitment was too much.

Decision Times

Julius Caesar
WILLIAM SHAKESPEARE

There is a tide in the affairs of men,
Which taken at the flood, leads on to fortune;
Omitted, all the voyage of life
Is bound in shallows and in miseries;
And we must take the current when it serves,
Or lose our ventures.

THE RICH YOUNG MAN

YOUTH   *Teacher, what good must I do*
         to possess everlasting life?

JESUS   *Why do you question me*
         about what is good?
         There is One who is good.
         If you wish to enter into life,
         keep the commandments.

YOUTH   *Which ones?*

JESUS   *"You shall not kill;*
         You shall not commit adultery;
         You shall not bear false witness;
         Honor your father and your mother;
         and love your neighbor as yourself."

YOUTH   *I have kept all these;*
         what do I need to do further?

JESUS   *If you seek perfection,*
         go, sell your possessions,
         and give to the poor.
         You will then have treasure in heaven.
         Afterward, come back and follow me.

NARRATOR *Hearing these words,*
         the young man went away sad,
         for his possessions were many.

                    MATTHEW 19:16–22

The youth's question gave Jesus the opportunity
to warn his disciples of the tyranny
that wealth can exercise over human freedom:

"I assure you, only with difficulty
will a rich man enter into the kingdom of God.
I repeat what I said: it is easier for a camel
to pass through a needle's eye
than for a rich man to enter the kingdom of God."

When the disciples heard this
they were completely overwhelmed and exclaimed,

"Then who can be saved?"
Jesus looked at them and said,
"For man it is impossible;
but for God all things are possible."

                    MATTHEW 19:23–26

Some people try to soften Jesus' words,
suggesting a "needle's eye" was a narrow gate
through which a camel could barely squeeze.
Others suggest the Greek word *kamilon* (cable),
not *kamelon* (camel), is what Jesus meant.
Most think Jesus' imagery fits with oriental
practice of exaggerating to make a point.

Some also try to soften Jesus' invitation
to "sell your possessions and give to the poor."
They say Jesus meant it only for those
who wish to follow him as closely as possible.
Facts suggest otherwise.

The community of believers
were of one heart and one mind. . . .
Nor was there anyone needy among them,
for all who owned property or houses
sold them and donated the proceeds . . .
to be distributed to everyone
according to his needs.

                    ACTS 4:32–35

The New Testament shows also
that rich communities shared with poor ones.
(Acts 11:27–30, Romans 15:22–23)

Why did Christians discontinue sharing goods?
Perhaps they realized
that they had begun it for the wrong reason:
thinking Jesus' "second coming" was near.
Or perhaps they embraced it prematurely,
before they were spiritually mature enough
to espouse the ideal.

Unfit Plowman

"Lord, my task is the red, the green is yours.
We plow, but it is you who give the crop."

Daniel-Rops says Palestinian farmers began plowing
with this prayer.
The reddish soil was rock-infested.
Plowers had to keep looking ahead lest they wreck
the plow on protruding rocks.
Jesus applied this image to the kingdom of God:

Someone said to Jesus,
"I will be your follower, Lord,
but first let me take leave of my people at home."
Jesus answered him,
"Whoever puts his hand to the plow
but keeps looking back
is unfit for the reign of God."

LUKE 9:61–62

When the larger Christian community
postponed the ideal, smaller ones (monastic)
continued to witness to it.

Today, many Christians pray for the day
when the larger community will again
bear witness to the ideal
of brotherhood and sisterhood in its fullness.
Until then, Christians follow it to the extent
that the Holy Spirit guides each one personally.

Wealth, as an obstacle to discipleship,
is a prominent gospel theme.

FOOLISH FARMER

One day a young man appealed to Jesus:
"Teacher, tell my brother to give me my share
of our inheritance." Jesus refused, saying:

"There was a rich man who had a good harvest.
'What shall I do?' he asked himself.
'I have no place to store my harvest.
I know!' he said, 'I will pull down
my grain bins and build larger ones.
All my grain and my goods will go there.
Then I will say to myself: You have blessings
in reserve for years to come. Relax!
Eat heartily, drink well. Enjoy yourself.'
But God said to him, 'You fool!
This very night your life shall be required of you.
To whom will all this piled-up wealth of yours go?'

"That is the way it works
with the man who grows rich for himself
instead of growing rich in the sight of God."

LUKE 12:13–21

Growing rich for one's self
is also the subject of another striking parable.

LAZARUS AND THE RICH MAN

NARRATOR *Once there was a rich man*
who dressed in purple and linen
and feasted splendidly every day.
At his gate lay a beggar named Lazarus
who was covered with sores.
Lazarus longed to eat the scraps
that fell from the rich man's table.
Even the dogs came
and licked his sores.

Eventually
the beggar died and was buried.
The rich man likewise died
and was buried.
From the abode of the dead
where he was in torment
he raised his eyes and saw Abraham
afar off,
and Lazarus resting in his bosom.

RICH MAN *Father Abraham, have pity on me.*
Send Lazarus to dip the tip of his
finger in water to refresh my tongue,
for I am tortured in these flames.

ABRAHAM *My child, remember*
that you were well off in your lifetime,
while Lazarus was in misery.
Now he has found consolation here,
but you have found torment.
And that is not all. Between you and us
there is fixed a great abyss,
so that those who might wish to cross
from here to you cannot do so,
nor can anyone cross over
from your side to us.

RICH MAN *Father, I ask you, then,*
send Lazarus to my father's house
where I have five brothers.

Let him be a warning to them
so that they may not end up
in this place of torment.

ABRAHAM *They have Moses and the prophets.*
Let them hear them.

RICH MAN *No, Father Abraham.*
But if someone would only go to them
from the dead, then they would repent.

ABRAHAM *If they do not listen to Moses*
and the prophets,
they will not be convinced even if
one should rise from the dead.
LUKE 16:19-31

This parable is sometimes called
a double-edged parable. (16:19–26, 27–31)
Three other parables fit this same category:

The Prodigal Son,   Luke 15:11–24, 25–32
The Vineyard Workers, Matthew 20:1–10, 11–16
The Wedding Banquet.   Matthew 22:1–10, 11–14

Each of these parables is really a twin parable,
and each twin makes its own point.

The Parables of Jesus
JOACHIM JEREMIAS

Like all other double-edged parables,
this one also has its stress on the second point.
That means that Jesus
does not want to comment on a social problem,
nor does he intend
to give teaching about afterlife,
but he relates the parable to warn men
who resemble the brothers of the rich man.

The rich man's brothers are men of the world,
like their dead brother was.
They live in luxury while others live in need.

In Jesus' day
there was not too much of a middle class.
People, in general, were divided into 2 groups:
the very rich and the very poor.

The gap between the 2 groups
stands out dramatically in Jesus' parable.
The rich man is covered with linen,
while poor Lazarus is "covered with sores."
The rich man "feasts splendidly,"
while poor Lazarus "longs for scraps."

The rich man lives in utter disregard
of Leviticus 25:23,
which reminds wealthy landowners:
"The land is mine and you are my tenants."
Thus, rich landowners were expected to pay
to God a kind of "rent" in the form of:

Sharing your bread with the hungry,
sheltering the oppressed and the homeless;
Clothing the naked when you see them.

ISAIAH 58:7

The deaths of the 2 men reverse their situations
remarkably.
Lazarus rests in the "bosom of Abraham,"
a symbol of ultimate contentment and intimacy.
The rich man, on the other hand,
is now "licked by flames" in contrast to Lazarus
who was once "licked by dogs."

When the rich man asks
to return to earth to warn his brothers
to reform their lives, Abraham refuses:
"If they do not listen to Moses and the prophets,
they will not be convinced
even if one should rise from the dead."

Abraham was right.
Later, a man did rise from the dead.
Ironically, his name was Lazarus also;
and many people were unconvinced. (John 14)
Interestingly, Albert Schweitzer
said it was this parable that made him decide
to pass up a brilliant career in music in Europe
to become a missionary doctor in Africa.
He reasoned that he was the rich man
and that his African brother was Lazarus:

"How can I enjoy applause
while Lazarus endures pain?"

The danger of material possessions
was the topic of a memorable "Peanuts" cartoon.
It showed Charlie Brown in his house
all bundled up to go skiing on a very cold day.
He was so bundled up
that he couldn't open the door to get outside.
Frustrated, he screamed:
"Well! Who's going to open the door?"

The Parables of Peanuts
ROBERT SHORT

"Who's going to open the door?"...
God has opened the door,
and the door . . . is Christ [John 10:9].

But what makes us angry as we stand
before the door is the same thing
that made Charlie Brown angry:
there is no getting through the door
while still wrapped up in our false securities.
All of us must first be completely stripped
of all false gods or false securities
before we can get through that narrow door
called "Jesus."

Another writer puts it this way:

The Cost of Discipleship
DIETRICH BONHOEFFER

If the heart
is devoted to the mirage of the world,
to the creature instead of the creator,
the disciple is lost. . . .
However urgently Jesus may call us,
his call fails to find access to our hearts.
Our hearts are closed,
for they have already been given over to another.

Following Jesus involves risk and uncertainty.
Jesus said:
"Foxes have lairs [holes for sleeping],
the birds of the sky have nests,
but the Son of Man has nowhere to lay his head."
                                        Luke 9:58

"Blest are you who are weeping . . ."
"Blest are you when men hate you. . . ."

The key stress in each set of beatitudes is clear.

"The Beatitudes According to St. Luke"
RAYMOND E. BROWN

In the spirituality of Matthew's beatitudes,
Christianity has place
for those who are comfortable in this world
if they preserve a spirit of detachment
in relation to their goods
and do not allow their wealth to choke off
the vitality of God's word. [Matthew 13:22]

Luke, on the other hand, is concerned about
economic poverty, not spiritual poverty.
He has in mind the real have-nots of society.

"The Beatitudes According to St. Luke"
RAYMOND E. BROWN

No one could suggest that Jesus is praising
poverty as a social phenomenon
without religious overtones.
The poor or hungry who blame God
for their suffering
would not be included in Luke's beatitudes.
The poverty that is blest is one which leads men
to place their whole trust in God. . . .

Karl Marx is called a revolutionary
because the Communist Manifesto
urged the workers of the world to unite
since they had nothing to lose but their chains.
This was not revolutionary,
but simply the age-old incitement of the poor
against the rich. . . .
The genuine revolutionary stood on a plain
in Galilee and dared to proclaim,
"Blest are you poor."

Rich and Poor

Each evangelist wrote for
different communities with different concerns.
Thus, each stressed
different aspects of Jesus' teaching.
This is notably clear in the beatitudes ("Blest
are you") with which both Luke and Matthew
begin the Sermon on the Mount.

The beatitudes that Matthew chooses,
along with the format he gives the sermon,
reflect the concern of Jewish Christians
to know how Jesus' teaching relates to Moses'.

"How blest are the poor in spirit . . ."
"Blest are they who hunger for holiness . . ."
"Blest too are the sorrowing . . ."
"Blest are those persecuted for holiness' sake. . . ."

Jesus' litany of beatitudes
recalls Moses' litany of the commandments.
The instruction after them is even more striking.
Repeated, Jesus says:
"You have heard . . . but I say." (5:21–43)
Matthew portrays the Sermon on the Mount
as being the fulfillment of the Law of Moses.
Jesus is the new Moses;
Jesus' followers are the new people of God.

Luke's beatitudes reflect the concern
of economically deprived gentile Christians.
His 4 counterparts to Matthew's beatitudes are:

"Blest are you poor . . ."
"Blest are you who hunger . . ."

14

Followers of Jesus

What kind of person answered Jesus' challenge?
Was it the kind who dreams things
other people don't dream—
the kind G. B. Shaw had in mind when he wrote:

You see things as they are;
and you ask "Why?"
But I dream things that never were;
and I ask "Why not?"

Or were they people who heard voices
that other people do not hear—the kind Shaw
again referred to in his play, *St. Joan:*

DAUPHIN (annoyed)
    Oh, your voices, your voices.
    Why don't the voices come to me?
    I am king, not you.

JOAN *They do come to you,*
    but you do not hear them.
    You have not sat in the field
    in the evening listening to them.
    When the angelus rings you cross
    yourself and have done with it;
    but if you prayed from your heart,
    and listened to the trilling of the bells
    in the air after they stopped ringing,
    you would hear the voices
    as well as I do.

What were the first disciples of Jesus like?

The disciples
do not come off as recruitment-poster models—
flawless, handsome, bigger than life.
In fact, one of the most amazing aspects
of the Gospel Story is that it avoids
building the disciples into bronzed heroes.
Any attempt to idealize them
would have been understandable. After all,
these were the first to be chosen by Jesus.

The gospels, however, paint a different picture.
Luke describes this episode.
One day the crowds by the sea were so large

This Sea of Galilee scene
recalls Luke's words
about Jesus' first disciples:
"With that they brought
their boats to land,
left everything
and became his followers."

that Jesus taught them from a boat.

When he had finished speaking
he said to Simon,
"Put out into deep water and lower your nets. . . ."
Simon answered, "Master, we have been hard at it
all night long and have caught nothing;
but if you say so, I will lower the nets."

Upon doing this,
they caught such a great number of fish
that their nets were at the breaking point.
They signaled to their mates in the other boat
to come and help them.
These came and together they filled two boats
until they nearly sank.

At the sight of this,
Simon Peter fell at the knees of Jesus saying,
"Leave me, Lord, I am a sinful man."
For indeed,
amazement at the catch they had made
seized him and all his shipmates,
as well as James and John, Zebedee's sons,
who were partners with Simon.
Jesus said to Simon, "Do not be afraid.
From now on you will be catching men."

With that they brought their boats to land,
left everything and became his followers.

LUKE 5:1–11

Jesus' first followers are not described
as having unusual gifts
that mark them as extraordinary people.
If they had any special talent at all,
perhaps it was their openness to Jesus' call.

THE UNNUMBERED CROWD

The gospels speak of Jesus' followers
in terms of 3 groups: the unnumbered crowd,
the disciples, and the Twelve.

The unnumbered crowd was that vast throng
who followed Jesus wherever he went:

Great crowds followed him.

MATTHEW 8:1

*The great crowds that followed Jesus
came from Galilee, the Ten Cities, Jerusalem
and Judea, and from across the Jordan.*

MATTHEW 4:25

*The Pharisees remarked . . .
"The whole world has run after him."*

JOHN 12:19

THE DISCIPLES

Besides the crowds, there were the disciples.
Meaning "learner," the word disciple appears
about 250 times in the New Testament.
Most often it refers to Jesus' disciples.
Sometimes it refers to the disciples of others,
like John the Baptizer. (Luke 5:33)

Every rabbi in New Testament times
had his disciples or "learners."
The situation between Jesus and his disciples,
however, was unique.

First, Jesus taught his disciples differently.
Other rabbis relied heavily upon the teaching
of previous rabbis to interpret the Scriptures.
Jesus relied largely on his own authority.
Matthew ends the Sermon on the Mount saying:

*Jesus finished his discourse
and left the crowds spellbound at his teaching.
The reason was that he taught with authority
and not like their scribes.*

MATTHEW 7:28-29

Second, Jesus related to his disciples differently.
The relationship between other rabbis
and their disciples was temporary.
After a learning period, other disciples "graduated"
and received the title of "rabbi" themselves.
Not so with Jesus' disciples. Jesus said:

*"One among you is your teacher,
the rest are learners. . . .
Avoid being called teacher.
Only one is your teacher, the Messiah."*

MATTHEW 23:8-10

Finally, Jesus shared with his disciples differently.
Other rabbis shared their wisdom and learning.
Jesus shared himself:

*"I am the true vine
and my Father is the vinegrower. . . .
Live on in me, as I do in you.
No more than a branch can bear fruit of itself
apart from the vine,
can you bear fruit apart from me. . . .
A man who does not live in me
is like a withered, rejected branch
picked up to be thrown in the fire and burnt."*

JOHN 15:1, 4-6

Thus, when Jesus' disciples were ready to share
with others what they had learned,
they went forth in Jesus' name with Jesus' power:

The Lord appointed a further seventy-two
and sent them in pairs before him
to every town and place he intended to visit.
He said to them . . .
"Into whatever city you go . . .
cure the sick there.
Say to them, 'The reign of God is at hand.'
If the people of any town you enter
do not welcome you, go into its streets and say,
'We shake the dust of this town from our feet
as a testimony against you.
But know that the reign of God is near.'"

LUKE 10:1–11

Later on, Luke says:

The seventy-two returned in jubilation saying,
"Master, even the demons
are subject to us in your name."

LUKE 10:17

The role and function of Jesus' disciples
is clear.

The Founder of Christianity
C. H. DODD

The disciples are recruiting agents
for the new people of God,
but their function as such
is simply to confront men with the reality
of God coming in his kingdom,
and leave it to them. . . .
Those who accept his kingdom "like a child"
enter in. . . .

Jesus did not contemplate a reformed Judaism.
Yet he recognized the need for some vehicle
to the new life which was emerging.
There is a hint of this in the parable:

"No one puts new wine into old wineskins;
if he does, the wine will burst the skins
and then wine and skins are both lost.
Fresh skins for new wine!"

The fresh vehicle
was in fact beginning to take shape.

THE TWELVE

Finally, there was an inner core of disciples
called the "Twelve."
Usually referred to as the 12 apostles,
they were consistently at Jesus' side.
Of them, Jesus himself said clearly:
"It was not you who chose me,
but it was I who chose you." (John 15:16)

Describing the choice of the "Twelve," Luke says:

Then Jesus went out to the mountain to pray,
spending the night in communion with God.
At daybreak he called his disciples
and selected twelve of them to be his apostles.

Simon, to whom he gave the name Peter,
and Andrew his brother,
James and John,

Philip and Bartholomew,
Matthew and Thomas,

James son of Alphaeus,
and Simon called the Zealot,
Judas son of James,
and Judas Iscariot, who turned traitor.

LUKE 6:12–16

Why did Jesus choose 12 apostles, no more
or no less?

The Founder of Christianity
C. H. DODD

It seems clear that Jesus himself fixed it so,
and, almost certainly,
to symbolize the people of Israel
with its traditional twelve tribes. (Luke 22:30)
In a very bold figure
they are represented as "sitting on twelve thrones
as judges of the twelve tribes. . . ."

The Twelve

"The Twelve Men"
G. K. CHESTERTON

Whenever our civilization
wants a library to be catalogued,
or a solar system to be discovered,
or any other trifle of this kind,
it uses up its specialists.
But when it wishes anything done
which is really serious,
it collects twelve of the ordinary men
standing around.

So reads an unusual tribute
to the 12-person jury system in Great Britain.
Jesus also
collected twelve of the ordinary men standing around
to carry out the most important undertaking
in the history of the world.

The full scope of the demand made on the Twelve
as the nucleus of the new community
comes into view at the point
when Jesus decided to lead them to Jerusalem.

The key moment came at the Last Supper:

At the close of the meal
Jesus passed round the cup of wine
with the words,
"This is the new covenant
sealed with my blood. . . ."
It was a postulate of the Jewish religion
that the status of Israel as the people of God
was founded upon a "covenant"
which bound them to his service.

When complete collapse
came in the sixth century B.C.,
a prophet had spoken of a 'new covenant'
as the basis of the new Israel
that was to arise from the ruins of the old.
(Jeremiah 31:31–34)

In the time of Jesus the sectaries of Qumran
regarded themselves
as the people of the new covenant.
The idea, therefore,
of a covenant as the foundation charter
(so to speak) of the new people of God
was very much alive at the time,
and there can be no doubt
what Jesus had in mind
when he invited his followers
to drink of the cup of the covenant:
he was formally installing them as the
foundation members of the new people of God.

Luke's list of the 12 "foundation members"
divides into 3 groups of 4 apostles each.

FIRST GROUP

Peter leads the list, just as he led the Twelve.
Nowhere is this leadership clearer

than in Matthew's gospel. For example,
Peter speaks for the others when Jesus:

is transfigured,	17:4
pays the tax,	17:25
discusses the kingdom.	18:21

More importantly, it is Peter who is appointed
by Jesus to be the church's:

foundation,	16:18
key-keeper,	16:19
shepherd.	John 21:17

Andrew, Peter's brother, appears next.
He is mentioned 3 times in John's gospel,
each time introducing someone to Jesus:

his brother,	1:41
a boy,	6:8
some Greeks.	12:22

James and John round out the first group.
Jesus called these Zebedee brothers *boanerges,*
that is "sons of thunder" or "hotheads."
The name dates, posssibly, from the flare-up
when some Samaritans block Jesus' way. (Luke 9:54)
With Simon Peter, they alone witness Jesus':

transfiguration,	Mark 9:2
agony,	Mark 14:32
raising of a girl.	Mark 5:37

SECOND GROUP

The second group begins with the third pair
of brothers in the apostles: Philip and Bartholomew.

Philip appears 4 times in John's gospel.
Each time he is conversing with Jesus:

at the Jordan,	1:43
in Galilee,	6:5
in Jerusalem,	12:21
at the Last Supper.	14:8

Bartholomew, which means "son of Tolmai,"
is generally identified as Nathaniel.
When Jesus first met Nathaniel,
he called him a true Israelite without guile.
Nathaniel was baffled: "How do you know me?"

Jesus answered: "Before Philip called you,
I saw you under the fig tree." (John 1:48)

13 Men Who Changed the World
H. S. VIGEVENO

You were sitting there, meditating,
thinking of God, gazing at the clouds.
The eyes of Jesus followed you
where no natural eye could see.
The eyes of Jesus penetrated your inner being. . . .
He saw your heart.

Matthew, the tax collector, comes next.
We can imagine the look on Peter's face
when Jesus called Matthew.
Possibly the 2 men had haggled on occasion
over the tax Peter owed on his fish.

Thomas completes the second group.
Strong-willed and frank, Thomas refused
to believe that Jesus had risen.
When Jesus appeared, he confessed:
"My Lord and my God!" (John 20:24–28)

Thomas also refused to be intimidated.
(John 11:6)
At the Last Supper, when Jesus said:
"You know the way that leads where I go,"
Thomas interrupted him, saying:
"We do not know where you are going.
How can we know the way?" (John 14:1–6)
Jesus replied:
"I am the way, the truth, and the life;
no one comes to the Father but through me."

THIRD GROUP

James, son of Alphaeus, heads the last group.
His name appears nowhere else in the gospels.
Because of this some call him the patron
of "dungeon Christians,"
those martyrs whose lives ended in silence
with the slam of a prison door.
Perhaps such a fate came to James.

Simon the Zealot appears next.
Belonging to a party of Jewish militants,
he probably had some interesting talks
with Matthew, a former Roman collaborator.

Completing the final group
are 2 men who bore the name Judas.

Judas son of James is usually equated with Jude,
the author of one of the New Testament letters.
Similarly, he is identified with Thaddaeus.
(Matthew 10:1, Mark 3:13)
Beyond this, little else is known of him.

Judas Iscariot completes the list of apostles.
He is one of the bible's great tragic figures.
The poet Dante locates him in the lowest hell.
The rock opera, *Jesus Christ Superstar*,
casts him in the role of a disillusioned idealist.
Judas sings of Jesus:

I don't understand
why you let the things you did
get so out of hand.
You'd have managed better
if you'd had it planned. . . .
Don't you get me wrong—
I only want to know.

In her play, *The Man Born To Be King*,
Dorothy Sayers takes issue with people
who write off Judas as a crook.
"To choose an obvious crook as one's follower,"
she says, "would be the act of a fool;
and Jesus of Nazareth was no fool."

It was to these 12 men
that Jesus entrusted his Father's kingdom.
They were the mustard seed
from which grew the great tree,
now called the church.

The foreground waters are on their way
to the Sea of Galilee and the Jordan River
to begin their 70-mile trip down to the Dead Sea.

On This Rock

These cliffs in the Golan Heights house a shrine
that Jesus was familiar with.
It was dedicated to the Greek shepherd god, Pan,
who had goat ears, horns, and played a flute.
The site lay in the neighborhood of Caesarea Philippi:

When Jesus came
to the neighborhood of Caesarea Philippi,
he asked his disciples this question . . .
"Who do you say I am?"
"You are the Messiah," Simon Peter answered.
Jesus replied,
"Blest are you, Simon son of Jonah!
No mere man has revealed this to you,
but my heavenly Father.

These niches once housed statues.
Formerly at a higher level,
an earthquake raised the land in front of them.

I for my part declare to you,
you are 'Rock,' and on this rock
I will build my church. . . .
I will entrust to you the keys
of the kingdom of heaven;
whatever you declare loosed on earth
shall be loosed in heaven."

MATTHEW 16:13–19

Josephus also mentions Caesarea Philippi.
The Roman general, Titus, set up his camp here
after he destroyed Jerusalem in A.D. 70.

Jewish Wars
FLAVIUS JOSEPHUS

Titus exhibited all sorts of shows here
and destroyed a great number of Jewish captives.
Some were thrown to the wild animals;
others were forced to kill one another,
as if they were enemies.

15

Love of Jesus

A man paused at the top of the subway stairs.
He took a few deep breaths,
descended, and boarded his train.
A boy of about 18 stood holding the center post.
Across from him, an attractive young lady
sat reading a book.

At 50th Street, the train lurched to a stop,
and the young lady got up to walk to the door.
Suddenly, she whirled and screamed at the boy.

"Why Should I Get Involved?"
SAL F. LAZZAROTTI

"You fresh punk! Don't look so innocent!
I know you touched me!". . .

She began flailing the astonished boy,
who in defense,
threw his arms up and tried to push her away.
In doing so he must have hit her in the face,
because suddenly her mouth was all bloody.

At last the boy broke free and made a dash
down the platform. The girl pursued. . . .

"Police, police!" she shrieked.

With the sound of her voice and the noise of
her shoes still echoing through the station . . .
we continued on our way. . . .

Inside the car, passengers smiled . . .
shrugged their shoulders
and returned to papers and books. . . .

I had seen that boy standing,
and had detected no move to touch the girl.
I wondered what would happen to the boy
if he were caught. . . .

At the office, I got some coffee, made a couple
of phone calls and worked on a rough sketch,
but I could not forget the sound
of that girl's voice and those high heels
echoing through the subway.

It took four calls
to locate the police precinct.
The desk sergeant listened to my story.
"You saw it all, huh? Well, the boy has been
sent to Juvenile Court, downtown."

I called Juvenile Court and obtained
the boy's name, Steven Larson. . . .
Through a girl in our office I learned of a lawyer
named George Fleary. He was contacted and
agreed to represent the boy without charge.

When I arrived Monday at the courtroom,
Mr. Fleary took me aside and briefed me. . . .
Steve had been in trouble once before when he
was 15. Police picked him up on suspicion
of stealing a car with some other boys,
but he had not been charged. . . .

Then the judge questioned the girl. . . .
I shook my head in disbelief. . . .
At one point the judge interrupted,
asking her to be more specific:
"There is a witness to this incident. . . ."

She started fumbling with words . . .
contradicting herself. Within five minutes
the judge called the two lawyers forward.
They huddled, whispered, nodded.
Then Mr. Fleary came back . . .
and said: "The case has been dismissed. . . ."

Steve grabbed my hand firmly . . .
he was too choked to speak. . . .

On the way home that night,
I thought how close I had come to saying,
"It's none of my business."

CHRISTIAN LOVE

Making my neighbor's need "my business"
is what Christianity is all about. Jesus said:
"This is how all will know you are my disciples:
your love for one another." (John 13:35)

Concerning Jesus' invitation to love, a woman
said: "I don't want to seem disrespectful,
but what is so new about that?
Other religions taught it before Jesus did."

BUDDHISM	*"Hurt not others in ways that you yourself would find hurtful."*
HINDUISM	*"This is the sum of duty: do not to others what would cause pain if done to you."*
CONFUCIANISM	*"Do not to others what you would not have them do to you."*
JUDAISM	*"What is hateful to you, do not do to your fellow man."*

Some people say Jesus stressed the positive;
other religions stressed the negative.
But this would hardly be a major innovation.
Jesus' teaching about love was not merely
"to love others as one loves one's self."
It was to love others as he himself loved us:

"As the Father loved me so I have loved you.
Live on in my love. You will live in my love
if you keep my commandments,
even as I have kept my Father's commandments.

"All this I tell you that my joy may be yours
and your joy may be complete.
This is my commandment:
love one another as I have loved you.

"There is no greater love than this:
to lay down one's life for one's friends.
You are my friends. . . ."

JOHN 15:9–14

Love is both the *sign* and the *power*
of God's kingdom.
As sign, it proclaims God's kingdom on earth.
As power, it brings God's kingdom to fulfillment.

Christianity and the Social Crisis
WALTER RAUSCHENBUSCH

Jesus
was not a Greek philosopher or Hindu pundit
teaching the individual the way of emancipation
from the world and its passions,
but a Hebrew prophet
preparing men for the righteous social order. . . .

Love with Jesus
was not a flickering and wayward emotion,
but the highest and most steadfast energy of will
bent on creating fellowship.

The priority and importance of Christian love
is the theme of one of Jesus' best-known parables.

GOOD SAMARITAN

The road from Jerusalem to Jericho
rolls and twists downward.
Sometimes it threads through rocky cliffs,
making its travelers especially vulnerable
to bands of outlaws.

A letter from A.D. 171 contains a complaint
to authorities about banditry along this road.
There are also historical records
of travelers having to pay protection money
to local thugs for safe passage over the road.

This ancient road
provided Jesus with a realistic setting
for his Parable of the Good Samaritan.

LAWYER   *Teacher, what must I do to inherit*
everlasting life?

JESUS   *What is written in the law?*
How do you read it?

LAWYER   *You shall love the Lord your God*
with all your heart,
with all your soul,
with all your strength,
with all your mind;
and your neighbor as yourself.

JESUS   *You have answered correctly.*
Do this and you shall live. . . .

LAWYER   *And who is my neighbor?*

JESUS   *There was a man going down*
from Jerusalem to Jericho
who fell prey to robbers.
They stripped him, beat him,
and then went off
leaving him half dead.

A priest happened to be going down
the same road;
he saw him and continued on.
Likewise there was a levite
who came the same way;
he saw him and went on.
But a Samaritan who was journeying
along came on him
and was moved to pity by the sight.
He approached him and dressed his
wounds, pouring in oil and wine.
He then hoisted him on his own beast
and brought him to an inn,
where he cared for him.
The next day
he took out two silver pieces
and gave them to the innkeeper
with the request: "Look after him,
and if there is further expense
I will repay you on my way back."

Which of these three, in your opinion,
was neighbor to the man
who fell in with robbers?

LAWYER   *The one*
who treated him with compassion.

JESUS   *Then go and do the same.*

LUKE 10:25–37

Jesus painted portraits of 3 different people:
a priest, a levite, and a Samaritan.

The priest apparently feared the man was dead.
To touch a dead man would make him unclean
and ban him temporarily from temple worship.
The priest's priority was worship before charity.

Then there was the portrait of the levite.
A levite was somewhat like a modern deacon.
He assisted the priests. (1 Chronicles 23:3–5)
But the levite was under a different cleanliness
code than priests; he could touch dead bodies.

Possibly, the levite's concern was different.
Outlaws frequently used set-ups in their trade.
One member played the victim, while others
waited for some passerby to take the bait.
If the levite had some such concern in mind,
he apparently opted for discretion.
His priority was safety before charity.

Finally, there was the Samaritan.
Making the Samaritan the hero of his parable
would have certainly shocked Jesus' hearers.
Jews regarded Samaritans as heretics.

The rift between the 2 groups had its roots
in Assyria's conquest of northern Israel
(Samaria) in 722 B.C.
Those northerners who survived the disaster
intermarried with foreigners
brought in by the Assyrian conquerors.
This shocked Jerusalem Jews.
The rift continued to widen with time.

In Jesus' day, Samaritans were banned
from the temple and from all synagogues.
Their religious contributions were refused,
and their testimony in courts was unacceptable.

Samaritans were also hostile to Jews.
They made common cause with Jewish enemies,
often not letting Jews into their towns. (Luke 9:52)

Jesus chose a Samaritan as his hero
to teach the people that love has no boundaries.
Neighborliness was not limited to neighborhoods.
This is why Jesus reworded the lawyer's question:
"Which of the 3 was neighbor to the man?"

Jesus shifted the discussion from "defining"
a neighbor to "being" a neighbor.
A neighbor was not the object of one's love,
but the one who loves.

Furthermore, a neighbor never considers love
an obligation, but only a privilege.
Morality in the kingdom of God
cannot be guided by a law inscribed in stone,
but only by a spirit alive in the heart.
Jesus echoed what the prophets had taught:
morality can't be written on tablets of stone,
only on tablets of flesh. (Jeremiah 31:33)

LOVE OF ENEMY

Raising his eyes to his disciples,
Jesus said . . . "Love your enemies,
do good to those who hate you;
bless those who curse you
and pray for those who maltreat you. . . .
If you do good to those who do good to you
how can you claim any credit?
Sinners do as much. . . . Be compassionate,
as your Father is compassionate. . . .
For the measure you measure with
will be answered back to you."

LUKE 6:27–38

"There was a man going from Jerusalem
to Jericho who fell prey to robbers."

Walk In Their Skins

In the novel, *To Kill a Mockingbird*,
Atticus Finch says
the only way to understand people
is to crawl inside their skins and walk around.

This is true of the gospel, also.
You will never understand it just by reading it.
You must meditate it: crawl inside the skin
of its characters and walk around.
For example, become the man attacked by robbers.
Prayerfully, replay what he experienced.

It was really stupid of me!
I should have waited for the caravan.

But I was greedy.
I wanted to beat the other merchants to Jericho.

I still don't know how it happened.
Suddenly, my donkey got really jumpy.
Then a shower of rocks hit me from all sides.
They grabbed my pack and ripped off my clothes
to see if I was carrying money on my body.

I must have lain there for hours—bleeding badly.
Finally, someone approached. Thank God!
I could make out the robes of a priest.
But then—I couldn't believe it—he kept on going.
I know he saw me! I know he did!
Why didn't he stop to help me? Why?

Prayer for Enemies

This prayer was found in Ravensbruck concentration camp:

"Take Up Your Cross"
MARY CRAIG

O Lord remember
not only the men and women of goodwill,
but also those of ill will.

Do not remember
all the suffering they have inflicted on us;
remember the fruits we have bought
thanks to this suffering—
our comradeship, our loyalty,
our humility, our courage,
our generosity, the greatness of heart
which has grown out of all this,
and when they come to judgment
let all the fruits
that they have borne be their forgiveness.

An eloquent commentary
on this difficult teaching of Jesus is the following.

"This Was Left Behind"
NEWSWEEK

When Gerald Lipke awakened that morning,
the first thing he did was turn on the radio.
Jerry, who is 11, likes to listen to the news
while he is dressing for school. That morning
the news was bad: United Air Lines Flight 629
with 44 persons aboard had exploded
and crashed the night before in Colorado.

Jerry
finished dressing and clattered down the stairs.
At the foot of the stairs,
he saw his grandmother, Mrs. William Wright,
talking with the parish priest. . . .

"My mother and father were on the plane
that crashed, weren't they?" Jerry asked them.

Someone had placed a bomb on Flight 629.
Later, students at St. Gabriel's School
(where Jerry goes with his 2 younger brothers)
asked their pastor for a prayer service.

Privately, the pastor asked Jerry whether
that would be alright with him and his brothers.
Jerry said that it would be.
And then Jerry asked the priest:

"Could they also say a prayer for the man
who killed my mother and father?"

Jesus taught compassion and forgiveness also
by his actions.
One day, some leaders brought Jesus a woman
who had just been caught in adultery.

LEADERS   *Moses ordered such a woman*
to be stoned. What do you
have to say about the case?

NARRATOR *They were posing this question*
to trap Jesus, so they could

have something to accuse him of.
Jesus bent down and started tracing
on the ground with his finger.
When they persisted in their
questioning, he straightened up. . . .

JESUS   *Let the man among you who has no sin*
be the first to cast a stone at her.

NARRATOR   *A second time Jesus bent down*
and wrote on the ground.
Then the audience drifted away
one by one,
beginning with the elders. . . .

JESUS   *Has no one condemned you?*

WOMAN   *No one, sir.*

JESUS   *Nor do I condemn you. You may go.*
But from now on, avoid this sin.
JOHN 8:5–11

A short story writer
might have created that dramatic touch
of having Jesus bend down and write in the dust.
But he would have certainly told us
what Jesus wrote.

Now I See
ARNOLD LUNN

It is contrary to the canons of fiction
to arouse the reader's expectation
without easing his curiosity.
Had Tolstoy invented this touch,
Christ would have written something very telling
in the dust, something very telling indeed,
but nothing half so telling as the silence of John.

Jesus' dramatic encounter with the leaders
is sometimes described as an "action" parable:
a story that makes its point
more by what is done than by what is said.

But Jesus also used "word" parables to teach
compassionate forgiveness.

Turn the Other Cheek

"The kingdom is the world upside down,"
says the Talmud.
And that is certainly the impression Jesus gave:

"You have heard the commandment,
'An eye for an eye, a tooth for a tooth.'
But what I say to you is:
offer no resistance to injury.
When a person strikes you on the right cheek,
turn and offer him the other."
MATTHEW 5:38–39

Jesus' point is clear.
His followers can no longer be satisfied
with a program for peace
that has the "threat of retaliation"
as its operating principle.
Christians are brothers and sisters,
and brothers and sisters don't live that way.

A creative response to Jesus' invitation
to "turn the other cheek"
received wide press coverage not long ago.
Four young men were caught
breaking into a construction contractor's office.
Instead of pressing charges,
the contractor literally turned the other cheek
and offered the unemployed youths jobs.

121

PHARISEE AND TAX COLLECTOR

Tax collectors were Jews who worked for Rome.
They acquired the right to collect taxes
by bidding for the job.
Once they got their assignment, it was up to them
to get their investment back and make a profit.
Because tax collectors worked for Rome,
they could count on Roman cooperation.

The Gospel of Luke
WILLIAM BARCLAY

A tax collector could bid a man
stop on the road and unpack his bundles
and charge him well nigh what he liked.
If a man could not pay,
sometimes the tax collector would offer to lend
him money at an exorbitant rate of interest,
and so get him further into his clutches. . . .

A Roman writer tells that he saw
a monument to an honest tax collector.
An honest specimen of this renegade profession
was so rare that he received a monument.

Against this background,
Jesus told this parable:

"Two men went to the temple to pray;
one was a Pharisee, the other a tax collector.
The Pharisee with head unbowed
prayed in this fashion:

'I give thanks, O God,
that I am not like the rest of men—
grasping, crooked, adulterous—
even like this tax collector.
I fast twice a week.
I pay tithes on all I possess.'

"The other man, however, kept his distance,
not even daring to raise his eyes to heaven.
All he did was beat his breast and say,
'O God, be merciful to me, a sinner.'"

LUKE 18:10-13

The Pharisee's posture
is one of praise: head raised and arms uplifted.
His prayer is a recital of vices he avoids
and virtues he practices.

The tax collector's posture is one of repentance:
head bowed with arms crossed on chest.
His prayer is a request for mercy,
probably in the words of Psalm 51:

Have mercy on me, O God . . .
in the greatness of your compassion
wipe out my offense. . . .
Wash me and I will be whiter than snow. . . .
A heart contrite and humble, O God,
you will not spurn.

Jesus ended the parable saying:

"Believe me, the tax collector
went home from the temple justified,
but the Pharisee did not."

Jesus' point is clear:

The Parables of Jesus
JOACHIM JEREMIAS

The character of God, says Jesus,
is such as is described in Psalm 51.
He welcomes the despairing, hopeless sinner,
and rejects the self-righteous.
He is the God of the despairing,
and for the broken heart his mercy is boundless.
That is what God is like.

Jesus' parable is a mirror by which
the self-righteous see themselves as they are;
it is also a window by which
they see what the Father invites them to become.
This same twofold instruction is the point
of still another parable.

GOOD EMPLOYER

Last summer I spent a sleepless night
in a Nazareth hotel.
Around 5:30 A.M. I got up and walked outside.

How God Behaves?

Apologetics and the Biblical Christ
AVERY DULLES

Jesus
constantly does the most unexpected things,
revolutionizing the accepted norms of conduct.

He praises pagans and prostitutes,
draws near to Samaritans and lepers.
He attacks the most respected classes,
and insults his hosts at dinner.

In the midst of his intense labors
he finds time to welcome little children. . . .
He rebukes the wind and the waves
and falls silent before his accusers.

Men would never have fabricated such a . . .
religious leader,
and precisely for this reason the gospels
have undying power to convert humble hearts.

This spendthrift charity is properly divine.
This is what God must really be,
and if he were to become man,
this is how he would behave.

"Will he not leave the ninety-nine on the hills
and go in search of the stray?" (Matthew 18:12)

Already, workers were gathering
in large numbers on the sidewalks.
As I stood there, a steady flow of vehicles
soon began to pick up the workers.
I thought of one of Jesus' parables:

"The reign of God
is like the case of the owner of an estate
who went out at dawn to hire workmen
for his vineyard.
After reaching an agreement with them
for the usual daily wage,
he sent them out to his vineyard."

MATTHEW 20:1–2

Again, at midmorning, noon, midafternoon,
and evening, the owner went to the market.
Each time he recruited more workers.
When night came, he paid all the same wage.
At this, a spokesman for the dawn workers
complained to the owner. The owner responded:

"My friend . . . I am free to do as I please
with my money, am I not?
Or are you envious because I am generous?"

MATTHEW 20:13–15

If the owner seems arbitrary, or even unfair,
Jesus' parable has achieved its purpose.
That's the effect that Jesus wanted it to have.
The parable is a double-edged one.
The stress, therefore, is on the second point.

The Four Gospels, II
_____
BRUCE VAWTER

It shows how the last becomes first
through a divine mercy
that men find incomprehensible,
yet with the preservation of justice for all.

Jesus very likely intended it
to be a cautionary story for the Pharisees,
but its message is perennial.

It applies also, as its context shows,
to people who have worked a whole lifetime
to enter God's kingdom,
only to find others entering it
after but a short time of effort.

Jesus' parable reminds us again
that God's kingdom is a gift.
No one has a right to it.
Thus, when we see another receive it,
we should not complain as did the workers,
but rejoice.

"Isn't it strange!" a high-school girl said.
"Had the dawn workers not known
what wage the owner gave the others,
they would have gone home happy and content.
Why is our happiness often dependent upon
whether or not we think we are better off
than other people?"

FORGIVING FATHER

Jesus' invitation to people
to be compassionate toward others
reached a new fullness in another parable.

On Christmas Eve, during the Vietnam War,
the commander of Hoa Loa prison camp
passed out bibles to American prisoners.
He told them they could have the bibles
for Christmas Day only.
The prisoners resolved
to make the best possible use of the opportunity.

Using toilet paper for writing pads,
fence wire for pens,
and a mixture of toothpaste and ashes for ink,
they began to copy.

One of the parables they copied
was the story of the young son who demanded
his inheritance money in advance.

When he received it,
he left home and squandered it foolishly.

NARRATOR *After he had spent everything,*
a great famine broke out . . .
and he was in dire need.
So he attached himself to one of the
propertied class of that place,
who sent him to his farm
to take care of pigs.
He longed to fill his belly with husks
that were fodder for the pigs
but no one made a move
to give him anything.

SON *How many hired hands*
at my father's place
have more than enough to eat,
while here I am starving!
I will break away and return
to my father, and say to him,
"Father, I have sinned against God
and against you; I no longer deserve
to be called your son. Treat me
like one of your hired hands."

NARRATOR *With that*
he set off for his father's house.
While he was still a long way off,
his father caught sight of him,
and was deeply moved.
He ran out to meet him,
threw his arms about his neck,
and kissed him. . . .

FATHER (to servants)
Quick! Bring out the finest robe
and put it on him;
put a ring on his finger
and shoes on his feet.
Take the fatted calf and kill it.
Let us eat and celebrate
because this son of mine was dead
and has come back to life.
He was lost and is found.

NARRATOR *Then the celebration began.*
Meanwhile the elder son . . .
heard the sound of music and dancing.
He called one of the servants
and asked him the reason. . . .

SERVANT *Your brother is home and your father*
has killed the fatted calf because
he has him back in good health.

NARRATOR *The son grew angry at this*
and would not go;
but his father came out
and began to plead with him.

ELDER SON *For years now I have slaved for you.*
I never disobeyed one of your orders,
yet you never gave me so much as a
kid goat to celebrate with my friends.
Then,
when this son of yours returns . . .
you kill the fatted calf for him.

FATHER *My son, you are always with me,*
and everything I have is yours.
But we had to celebrate and rejoice!
This brother of yours
was dead, and has come back to life.
He was lost, and is found.

LUKE 15:11–32

The parable is a double-edged one.
The first concerns
the father's attitude toward the returning son;
the second concerns the elder brother's attitude.

FATHER'S ATTITUDE

The father's attitude is portrayed graphically
in 3 beautiful details of the story.
The first is the warm welcome he gives the boy.
He runs out to meet him
and embraces him with deep, warm affection.

This sandal-shod foot of Zeus
was unearthed on the Palestinian coast.
Rich biblical symbolism surrounded sandals.
Voluntarily removing one's sandals
was a sign of respect or mourning. (Exodus 3:5,
2 Samuel 15:30)
Having one's sandals forcefully removed
was a sign of humiliation. (Deuteronomy 25:9)
Handing over one's sandals
signaled the transfer of a legal right. (Ruth 4:7)

"The Magic of Touch"
SMILEY BLANTON, MD

I once heard a family-court judge say
that although hundreds of juvenile offenders
and their parents had been brought before him,
he never once had seen a parent
put a protective arm
around the youngster's shoulder.

How differently the father in Jesus' parable acts.
He literally enfolds the boy in forgiveness.

The second detail that portrays the father's attitude
is his order to place shoes on the boy's feet.
The boy was willing to return home as a slave:
"I no longer deserve to be called your son."
Shoes were a sign of sonship, not slaveship.
Only free people wore shoes; slaves did not.
This was true also in American slave days.
A Negro Spiritual rejoices that, in heaven,
all of God's children will wear shoes.

The final detail that portrays the father's attitude
is his order to place a ring on the boy's finger.
A signet ring, which this probably was,
was a sign of authority.
It contained the family seal used for
authenticating legal and commercial papers.
To possess the ring was to have the power
to act in the name of the person or family
to whom the seal belonged:

Pharoah said to Joseph . . .
"You shall be in charge of my palace. . . ."
With that, he took off his signet ring
and put it on Joseph's finger.

GENESIS 40:39–41

The father extends to his younger son
not only a total welcome (embrace),
but also total forgiveness (shoes)
and total restoration (ring)
to the status he had before he left home.

BROTHER'S ATTITUDE

The second half of Jesus' parable
deals with the attitude of the elder brother
toward his returning younger brother.
Why did Jesus add it?

The Parables of Jesus
JOACHIM JEREMIAS

There can be only one answer
because of the actual situation.
The parable was addressed to men
who were offended at the gospel. . . .
To them Jesus says:
"Behold the greatness of God's love . . .
and contrast it with your own joyless,
loveless, thankless, self-righteous lives.
Cease then from your loveless ways."

Jesus left unanswered the question:
What did the elder brother do?
Did he persist in his unforgiving resentment,
or did he change his heart and join the dancing?
Jesus deliberately left the question unanswered.
Each listener had to answer it individually.

Jesus' invitation
to love, compassion, and forgiveness

challenged both the lawless and the law-abiding.
It invited the lawless to follow the example
of the younger brother and return home.
It invited the law-abiding (Pharisees) to follow
the father's example and welcome back sinners.

JESUS INVITES YOU

Why did Jesus stress
love, compassion, and forgiveness so much?
The answer lies in the new order,
God's kingdom, that dawned with Jesus' coming.

Invitation to the New Testament
W. D. DAVIES

*The marks of this new order
are seen in the activity of Jesus himself;
he casts out demons,
he forgives sins,
he breaks down barriers . . .
in short, the marks of the rule of God are,
above all, grace and forgiveness.
And this grace and forgiveness
which men encounter in Jesus
are the result of no merit in men.*

This undeserved love and forgiveness
carries with it an invitation:
as you have been forgiven by God,
so forgive others;
likewise, as you have been loved by God,
so love in return—
especially those who seem least deserving.

If you wait for people
to become loveable before loving them,
you will wait forever.
Rather, it is by loving them that they become
loveable and capable of loving in return.

Love
is not only a sign of the kingdom's presence,
but also the power by which it reaches completion.

Forgive As You Have Been Forgiven

Dag Hammarskjold,
second secretary-general of the United Nations,
was killed in a plane crash in 1961.
He was en route trying to negotiate a cease-fire
between UN forces and Katanga in the Congo.

Shortly after his death,
a diary-like journal and an undated letter
were found in his New York house.
The letter explained that the journal
"was begun without the thought of anyone else
reading it . . . as a sort of *white book*,
concerning my negotiations with myself—
and with God."

One revealing entry was dated Easter, 1960:

Markings
DAG HAMMARSKJOLD

*Forgiveness breaks the chain of causality,
because he who "forgives" you—out of love—
takes upon himself the consequences
of what you have done.
Forgiveness, therefore, always entails sacrifice.
The price you must pay for your own liberation
through another's sacrifice is that you in turn
must be willing to liberate in the same way
irrespective of the consequences to yourself.*

RESPONDING TO JESUS

In view of what Jesus was inviting his hearers to do
is it any wonder
that not a few of them turned the other way?

The Outline of History
H. G. WELLS

Even his disciples cried out
when he would not spare them the light. . . .
Is it any wonder that the Roman soldiers,

confronted and amazed
by something soaring over their comprehension
and threatening their disciplines,
should take refuge in wild laughter
and crown him with thorns
and robe him in purple
and make a mock Caesar of him?
For to take him seriously was to enter upon
a strange and alarming life. . . .

Is it any wonder that to this day
this Galilean is too much for our small hearts?

Walk a Second Mile

Like thunder after lightning,
signs of Roman oppression were taken for granted
in Jesus' day.
This inscribed Roman milestone, for example, was
used to count the miles along all major roads.

Roman law gave a Roman soldier the right
to order a Jew to carry his baggage for him
one mile under the hot desert sun.
This is the background for Jesus' instruction:
"Should anyone press you into service one mile,
go with him two miles." (Matthew 5:38–41)

Perhaps Jesus was saying in effect:
"Show the soldier that you live by love, not hate.
Show the state that you still retain the freedom
to choose whether or not to 'walk a second mile.'"

16

Prayer of Jesus

An unforgettable painting
shows George Washington kneeling in snow
at Valley Forge, praying for his men.
"They lacked everything," wrote LaFayette.
"They had neither coats, hats, shoes . . .
their feet and legs froze until they turned black,
and it was often necessary to amputate them."

"I have been driven many times to my knees,"
wrote President Lincoln,
"by the overwhelming conviction
that there was nowhere else to go;
my own wisdom and that of all around me
seemed insufficient for the day."

Nearer to our own day, Martin Luther King, Jr.
described his recourse in prayer.

Stride Toward Freedom
MARTIN LUTHER KING, JR.

*One night toward the end of January
I settled into bed after a strenuous day.
Coretta had already fallen asleep
and just as I was about to doze off
the telephone rang.*

*An angry voice said, "Listen, nigger,
we've taken all we want from you;
before next week
you'll be sorry you ever came to Montgomery."
I hung up, but could not sleep.
It seemed that all my fears*

*had come down on me at once.
I had reached the saturation point.*

*I got out of bed and began to walk the floor.
Finally,
I went to the kitchen and heated a pot of coffee.
I was ready to give up.
With my cup of coffee sitting untouched before me
I tried to think of a way to move out
of the picture without appearing a coward.*

*In this state of exhaustion,
when my courage had all but gone,
I decided to take my problem to God.
With my head in my hands,
I bowed over the kitchen table and prayed aloud.
The words I spoke to God that midnight
are still vivid in my memory.*

*"I am here taking a stand
for what I believe is right.
But now I am afraid.
The people are looking to me for leadership,
and if I stand before them
without strength and courage, they too will falter.
I am at the end of my powers. I have nothing left.
I've come to the point where I can't face it alone."*

*At that moment,
I experienced the presence of the Divine
as I have never experienced him before.*

JESUS AND PRAYER

Jesus often turned to prayer.
In fact, every important event in his life
seems to have been preceded by prayer.

Describing Jesus' baptism, Luke writes:
"Jesus was at prayer . . . the skies opened
and the Holy Spirit descended on him." (3:21)

Before starting his teaching career, Jesus rose
early and went "to a lonely place in the desert;
there he was absorbed in prayer." (Mark 1:35)

Christians at Prayer

Not a single sparrow falls to the ground
without your Father's consent. . . .
So do not be afraid of anything.
You are worth more than an entire flock
of sparrows.

MATTHEW 10:29–31

In God's Underground
RICHARD WURMBRAND

Martin Luther
used to raise his hat to the birds and say,
"Good morning, theologians—
you wake and sing,
but I, old fool, know less than you
and worry about everything,
instead of simply trusting
in the heavenly Father's care."

Report to Greco
NIKOS KAZANTZAKIS

There are
three kinds of souls, three kinds of prayers.

> *One:* *I am a bow in your hands, Lord.*
> *Draw me lest I rot.*
>
> *Two:* *Do not overdraw me, Lord.*
> *I shall break.*
>
> *Three:* *Overdraw me,*
> *and who cares if I break!*

Before choosing his 12 apostles,
"Jesus went out to the mountain to pray,
spending the night in communion with God."
(Luke 6:12)

Before asking his disciples the big question:
"Who do you say I am?" Jesus prayed. (Luke 9:18)

On the mountain,
"while Jesus was praying, his face changed
and his clothes became dazzling white."
(Luke 9:29)

Before teaching his disciples to pray,
Jesus was "praying in a certain place." (Luke 11:1)

On the eve of his passion,
Jesus withdrew from his disciples, knelt down
and prayed. (Luke 22:41)

While on the cross, Jesus prayed. (Luke 23:34)

In short, every important event in Jesus' life
seems to have found him in prayer.

LORD'S PRAYER

One day Jesus was praying in a certain place.
When he had finished,
one of his disciples asked him,
"Lord teach us to pray,
as John taught his disciples."
Jesus said to them, "When you pray, say:

'Father,
hallowed be thy name,
your kingdom come.
Give us this day our daily bread.
Forgive us our sins
for we too forgive all who do us wrong;
and subject us not to the trial.'"

LUKE 11:1–4

Matthew's *Lord's Prayer*, however,
is the one most people are familiar with:

Our Father in heaven,
hallowed be your name,
your kingdom come,
your will be done on earth as it is in heaven.
Give us today our daily bread,
and forgive us the wrong we have done
as we forgive those who wrong us.
Subject us not to the trial
but deliver us from the evil one.

MATTHEW 6:9-13

In Jesus' time,
no Jew ever dared to utter Yahweh's name.
Moreover, no rabbi ever dreamed of teaching
his disciples to address Yahweh as *Abba*,
as Jesus did.
It is important to grasp the full significance
of the title *Abba* ("Father").

"When You Pray Say: Abba!"
DOROTHY DAWES

A traveler
along the shore of the Sea of Galilee
may discover, after some diligent searching,
an area where "Bathing is permitted."
Here in the midday sun on a summer sabbath,
swarms of . . . Israeli children . . .
can be seen splashing and surfing. . . .

The author will not soon forget
a diminutive Sabra (native Israeli) . . .
who upon being asked his name,
identified himself . . . as "Eliezer."

Moments later, Eliezer
had made it to the top of a makeshift highdive
and was calling at the top of his voice
to his father to watch: "Ab-ba! Ab-ba!"

Abba is the word Palestinian children use
to address their fathers.
It is a title of warm and intimate affection,

somewhat like our word "daddy" or "papa."
This was the title
that Jesus taught his followers to use
in addressing God.

PRAYER MODEL

The 2 versions of the *Lord's Prayer* make us ask:
Did Jesus intend to give us a fixed formula
similar to other Jewish formula prayers?

New Testament Essays
RAYMOND BROWN

All that Jesus may have intended
was that the Lord's Prayer,
with its brevity and complete dependence on God,
serve as a model
for the spirit of Christian prayer. . . .

What is interesting is the fact that the disciples
felt the need of asking Jesus how to pray,
or that Jesus gave them a model of prayer.
This indicates a realization
that traditional Jewish prayer formulas
were no longer adequate for the followers of Jesus.

From the time of his introduction
by John the Baptist, Jesus stood for a certain
newness of religion. . . .
Thus, while many phrases of the Lord's Prayer
may be found in contemporary Jewish prayers,
there is a new spirit that invests
the Lord's Prayer. . . .

In the New Testament, God's Fatherhood
is not put on the basis of a national covenant,
but on the basis of union with Jesus,
who is God's Son in a special way.
He alone can call God "my Father"
in the proper sense;
those who unite themselves to him
share his power to do so through God's gift.

Fader Oure

An early translation of the *Lord's Prayer*
appears in a 14th-century manuscript,
now housed in St. John's College in England.
Here is its exact wording and spelling:

Fader Oure that art in hevene
halwed be Thi name,
Thi kyngdom come to,
Thi wille be doon
in erthe as in hevene,
oure eche daies bred gif us to day,
and forgive us our dettes,
as we forgive our detoures
and lede us nought into temptation
bote delivere us from yvel,
Amen.

Early Christians concluded the *Lord's Prayer*
with the words: "For thine is the kingdom,
the power, and the glory, now and forever."
Found in the Didache,
a first-century Christian guidebook, the ending
probably derives from David's prayer:
"Yours, O Lord, are grandeur and power,
majesty, splendor, and glory." (1 Chronicles 29:10)

TWOFOLD PERSPECTIVE

The Lord's Prayer has a double viewpoint—
3 "your" petitions and 3 "our" petitions:

    1 hallowed be your name,
    2 your kingdom come,
    3 your will be done,

    1 give us today our daily bread,
    2 forgive us the wrong,
    3 subject us not to the trial.

The 3 "your" petitions deal with the same event:
the coming of God's kingdom in its fullness.
Each approaches it from a slightly different angle.

The 3 "our" petitions shift the focus
from the coming of God's kingdom
to God's children, who await it.

CAPSULE SUMMARY

Many daily newspapers carry a feature
called the "News in Brief."
It summarizes the main stories of the day.

The Lord's Prayer is something like that.
It is the "Good News in Brief,"
grouping together and summarizing in prayer
the main points of Jesus' mission and message.

YOUR NAME	*"Father,* *I have revealed your name* *and I will continue to reveal it* *so that your love for me* *may live in them."* <div align="right">JOHN 17:26</div>
YOUR KINGDOM	*"May all be one as you, Father,* *are in me, and I in you."* <div align="right">JOHN 17:21</div>
YOUR WILL	*"Father . . . not our will* *but yours be done."* <div align="right">LUKE 22:42</div>
OUR BREAD	*"I myself am the living bread* *come down from heaven. . . .* *I have life* *because of the Father,* *so that the man* *who feeds on me* *will have life because of me."* <div align="right">JOHN 6:50, 57</div>
OUR FORGIVENESS	*"Father, forgive them;* *they do not know* *what they are doing."* <div align="right">LUKE 23:34</div>
OUR PROTECTION	*"Father most holy,* *protect them* *with your name . . .* *guard them* *from the evil one."* <div align="right">JOHN 17:11, 15</div>

OTHER PRAYER INSTRUCTIONS

Jesus' instructions on prayer
included several other practical points.
About the manner of praying, Jesus said:

"When you are praying do not . . .
stand and pray in the synagogues or on the
street corners in order to be noticed. . . .

Go to your room, close the door,
and pray to your Father in private."
MATTHEW 6:5-6

Jesus was not opposed to public prayer.
He prayed in the temple and synagogue himself.
What he opposed was turning prayer
into a public exhibition.

Concerning the words of prayer,
Jesus stressed that prayer has its origin
in the heart, not in what is said.

"In your prayers do not rattle on like pagans.
They think they will win a hearing
by sheer multiplication of words."
MATTHEW 6:7

The Four Gospels, I
BRUCE VAWTER

Probably the Gentiles acquired a reputation
for windy prayers with the Jews
owing to the multitude of names and attributions
under which they invoked Deity.
Jesus is also doubtless thinking
of the lengthy pagan formulas
to whose mechanical repetition
a quasi-magical efficacy was often attached.

Actually, prayer need not involve words at all.
Prayer can take 3 different forms:
meditation, contemplation, and conversation.
Often these forms occur intertwined
in one and the same prayer like strands of wire
coiled together in a cable.

Meditation is reflecting upon God,
or seeking to become aware of God's action
or presence in human life.
God's presence in human affairs
might be compared to TV signals
that are present everywhere.
Just as a TV set is needed

In Jesus' day, poor people lived in homes much like this one: a cave in the hillside with a walled-up front. A single door provided all natural light and air. Floors were simply clay, beaten hard by the family's many footsteps.

to bring the various signals into focus,
so meditation is needed
to bring God's presence into focus.

Contemplation is not thinking about God.
Rather, it is simply resting in God's presence.
It is like listening peacefully to a favorite song,
or sitting relaxed before some beautiful sight.

Conversation does deal with words, usually.
It is speaking to God from the heart,
or listening to God speak to us from Scripture
or in some other way.
In brief:

> meditation is thinking about God;
> contemplation is resting in God;
> conversation is speaking/listening to God.

Jesus also stressed perseverance in prayer.
He told this parable to illustrate the point:

"If one of you knows someone
who comes to him in the middle of the night
and says to him,
'Friend, lend me three loaves,
for a friend of mine has come in
from a long journey and I have nothing to offer him,'
and he from inside should reply,
'Leave me alone. The door is shut now
and my children and I are in bed.
I cannot get up to look after your needs'—
I tell you, even though he does not get up
and take care of the man because of friendship,
he will do so because of his persistence,
and give him as much as he needs."

LUKE 11:5–8

To appreciate Jesus' parable, we must recall
that Palestinians often journeyed at night
to avoid the discomfort of the desert sun.
Moreover, ancient hospitality was so sacred
that a host would do most anything for a guest.

The house described in the parable
is the typical one-room dwelling of the poor.
Sleeping mats were unrolled at night;
the floor became a wall-to-wall carpet of bodies.
To open the door and "dig out" some bread
was a gross inconvenience by any measure.

Palestinians baked bread only for the day.
Preservatives against staleness and mildew
were not yet a part of the baker's art.
Thus, the caller had no bread left from the day,
and there was a good chance
that his friend would not have any left either.

The Hardest Prayer

The film, "The Bridge Over the River Kwai,"
immortalized the Kwa Noi River in Thailand.
Along its banks, 12,000 POW's died of disease,
starvation, and brutality, building a railroad.
Working in heat that sometimes hit 120 degrees,
husky men became walking skeletons in weeks.
Morale was zero; something had to be done.
Two prisoners organized bible study groups.
The results were beyond belief:

134

The point of Jesus' parable
is not that God needs to be prodded or reminded
to help us.
Rather, it is that Christians must not lose heart
if prayers seem to go unanswered.

This leads to a final point Jesus made about
prayer:

"I give you my word,
if you are ready to believe that you will receive
whatever you ask for in prayer
it shall be done for you."

MARK 11:24

Jesus speaks here of the prayer of petition.
Concerning this kind of prayer,
it is important to keep in mind
that it presumes that our position is in accord
with God's fatherly concern for us and our needs.
It is equally important to keep in mind

that God often answers our prayers
in ways we do not recognize until later on in life.
An anonymous writer makes this point beautifully.

"I asked for health,
that I might do greater things;
I was given infirmity,
that I might do better things . . .
I asked for riches, that I might be happy;
I was given poverty, that I might be wise . . .
I asked for power,
that I might have the praise of men;
I was given weakness,
that I might feel the need of God . . .
I asked for all things, that I might enjoy life;
I was given life, that I might enjoy all things . . .
I got nothing I asked for,
but everything I hoped for.
Almost despite myself,
my unspoken prayers were answered.
I am among all men, most richly blessed."

"It Happened on the River Kwai"
ERNEST GORDON with CLARENCE HALL

We ceased thinking about ourselves as victims
of the same cruel jest and began to grasp the truth
that suffering
comes from human avarice and stupidity,
not from God,
and that the way out of suffering is through it,
not avoiding it or denying its existence. . . .

Nowhere was the change in attitude
more manifest than in our prayers. We learned
to pray for others more than for ourselves.
When we did pray for ourselves,
it was not to get something,
but to release some power within us.

Gradually we learned to pray
that hardest of all prayers: for our enemies. . . .

An incident that happened during
the final months of imprisonment revealed to me
how far we'd come from hatred. . . .
A trainload of enemy soldiers pulled in.
They were casualties from the fighting in Burma,
and in pitiful plight: indescribably filthy,
ragged, starving, their wounds full of maggots.

My men's action
was as instinctive as it was compassionate.
With no order from me
they moved over to clean the soldiers' wounds,
give them our own ration of rice,
share with them what little money they had.
To our men, these were no longer enemies,
but fellow sufferers.

This 3,500-year-old Canaanite stone relief depicts hands uplifted in prayer. It was unearthed at Hazor in 1956.

Discovering Prayer

Hungry For God
RALPH MARTIN

A real estate man I know
gets up early in the morning to pray;
an aerospace engineer
prays and reads Scripture on his lunch hour;
a production manager of a computing firm
prays after the children are in bed.

When something becomes important to us,
we don't leave it to chance;
we schedule it into our daily routine.
So it must be with prayer,
for the demands of modern living are so great
that if we don't have a schedule for prayer,
we probably won't pray.

Prayer Places

What is true of prayer time is also true
of a prayer place. The gospel says of Jesus:
"He went off to a lonely place in the desert;
there he was absorbed in prayer." (Mark 1:35)
Again, we read:
"Then Jesus went out to the mountain to pray."
(Luke 6:12)

A private place to pray has obvious advantages.
The important thing is that it helps us to pray.
Picking the right place is one of the keys
to effective prayer.

Prayer Postures

"The Magic of Good Posture"
WARREN YOUNG

How much would you give for a formula
that guaranteed to make you look younger,
brighter, more attractive—and feel that way too?
Probably a lot. Yet the secret
is built right into the human body, your body.

136

All you have to do is take a few minutes
every now and then to check on your posture.

Posture also plays a key role in our prayer.
The Acts of the Apostles says of Stephen:
"He fell on his knees and prayed." (7:60)
In the same book, Luke writes: "We all knelt
down on the beach and prayed." (21:5)

Kneeling was a popular posture in early times,
but it was by no means the only one.
Again, the best posture is the one that helps you
to pray better. Experimentation will be needed
to discover which posture works best.

Prayer Moods

The final step in disposing yourself for prayer
is to create the proper atmosphere or mood.
One method is the following:

Close your eyes
and concentrate on the sounds around you.
Let them penetrate freely and deeply.
Sounds distract you only when you fight them.
Monitor them until a reflective mood sets in.

Presence of God

As an arrow or a javelin takes its direction
from the start it gets, so does prayer.
The start is important.
The focus of prayer is the Lord,
and it is to him that we must turn our attention.
One way to do this
is by a reflection such as the following:

"Father, you are as real as the sounds
that surround me.
May each sound I hear
deepen my awareness of your real presence."

After praying in these words,
pause in a posture of openness to God's presence.
If God makes his presence felt,
as he does from time to time, remain in it

as long as it engages you prayerfully.
Do not be in a hurry to move on.

Prayer Styles

Most people need a kind of track to run on
when they first start to pray.
One such track is to meditate on a gospel event.
The procedure is simple.

Mentally, replay an episode from Jesus' life.
Enter into it as an active participant—
experiencing it with all 5 of your senses.

In other words,
you don't merely read the story of the blind man
being healed. (John 9:1–41)
You actually become the blind person.
You experience what he did when Jesus' fingers
touched his sightless eyes.
You experience what he did
when he saw Jesus' face for the first time.

After each prayer session
you end by speaking to Jesus or the Father
as the Spirit moves you.

Learning to Pray

The only way to learn to pray is by praying.
You can do this on your own,
but another person can be immensely helpful.
The person, who should be familiar with prayer
and the spiritual life, meets with the learner
on a regular basis—say 15 minutes each week.
The meetings help to motivate the learner
and to provide ongoing instruction in prayer
and the spiritual life.

This seventh-century mosaic at Madeba
is the oldest known map of Jerusalem.
Column Gate (modern Damascus Gate) is at top
with colonnade street leading from it,
dividing city.

Also visible is the Church of the Holy Sepulcher
(center of city, with dome to left),
and the Church of the Upper Room
(lower end of street, pitched roof to left).

PART FOUR
JERUSALEM MINISTRY

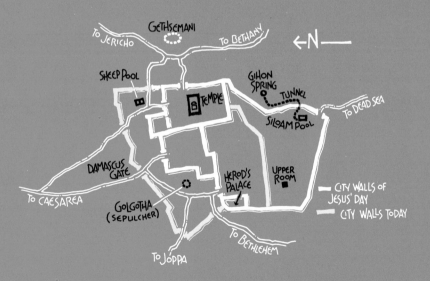

17

Hour of Jesus

NARRATOR   *Jesus came to the neighborhood*
of Caesarea Philippi.

JESUS   (to disciples)
             Who do people say
             that the Son of Man is?

DISCIPLES   *Some say John the Baptizer,*
             others Elijah,
             still others Jeremiah
             or one of the prophets.

JESUS   *And you,*
             who do you say I am?

PETER   *You are the Messiah,*
             the Son of the living God.
                        MATTHEW 16:13–16

This confession of faith
marked a turning point in the ministry of Jesus.
Matthew reports the events that followed it
with a special urgency and seriousness.

From that time on
Jesus started to indicate . . .
that he must go to Jerusalem . . .
and be put to death.

Jesus then said to his disciples:
"If a man wishes to come after me,
he must deny his very self,
take up his cross,
and begin to follow in my footsteps."
                        MATTHEW 16:21, 24

Six days later Jesus took Peter,
James, and his brother John
and led them up a high mountain
by themselves. He was transfigured
before their eyes. . . .

As they were coming down . . .
Jesus commanded them,
"Do not tell anyone of the vision
until the Son of Man rises." (17:1–9)

As Jesus
was starting to go to Jerusalem,
he took the Twelve aside. . . .
"Anyone among you who aspires to
greatness must serve the rest. . . .
Such is the case of the Son of Man
who has come
not to serve, but to give his life."
                        MATTHEW 20:17–27

Matthew's report of these events
is filled out in greater detail in John's gospel.
Whereas Matthew portrays the events
from the viewpoint of Jesus and his disciples,
John portrays them from the viewpoint
of religious leaders in Jerusalem.

The hostility between Jesus and these leaders
had stepped up noticeably in recent months.
It ballooned into a crisis situation
when word came that Jesus had raised Lazarus
from the dead. (John 11:1–44)
News of this event touched off excitement
even among conservative circles in Jerusalem.

The chief priests and the Pharisees
called a meeting of the Sanhedrin.
"What are we going to do," they said,
"with this man performing all sorts of signs?
If we let him go on like this,
the whole world will believe in him.
Then the Romans will come in and sweep away
our sanctuary and our nation. . . ."

"Hosannas" echo from Jerusalem's walls
as modern pilgrims celebrate
Jesus' Palm Sunday entry into the great city.

CELEBRATION

As they neared Bethpage and Bethany
on the Mount of Olives, close to Jerusalem,
Jesus sent off two of his disciples
with the instruction:
"Go to the village straight ahead of you,
and as soon as you enter it
you will find tethered there a colt on which
no one has ridden. Untie it and bring it. . . .

They brought the colt to Jesus
and threw their cloaks across its back,
and he sat on it.
Many people spread their cloaks on the road
while others spread reeds
which they had cut in the fields.
Those preceding him as well as those
who followed cried out: "Hosanna!
Blessed is he who comes in the name of the Lord!
Hosanna in the highest!"

MARK 11:1–10

The Jewish Passover was near,
which meant that many people from the country
went up to Jerusalem
for the Passover purification.
They were on the lookout for Jesus,
various people in the temple
saying to each other, "What do you think?
Is he likely to come for the feast?"
(The chief priests and the Pharisees
had given orders that anyone
who knew where he was should report it.)

JOHN 11:47–57

So the situation in Jerusalem was tense
as the Passover approached.
Would Jesus risk coming to the city for the feast,
now that a price tag appeared to be on his head?

The answer was not long in coming.
News broke that Jesus and his disciples
were on their way to Jerusalem from Jericho.

Carpeting the road with garments
was not unusual in the East.
The *Arabian Nights* mentions it several times.
Likewise, in early Jewish history,
the people honored Jehu this way
when he was anointed Israel's king. (2 Kings 9:13)
The disciples
also blanketed the road with branches from trees
(Matthew) and from fields (Mark).
Matthew and John tie the enthusiastic reception
to Zechariah's messianic prophecy:

Shout for joy, O daughter Jerusalem!
See, your king shall come to you;
a just savior is he,
Meek, and riding . . . on a colt.

ZECHARIAH 9:9

Luke concludes his report saying:

Pharisees in the crowd said to Jesus,
"Teacher, rebuke your disciples."

Damascus Gate
with the dome
of the Church of the Holy Sepulcher
visible in the photo.
The church encloses the traditional site
of Calvary and Jesus' tomb.

Jesus replied, "If they were to keep silence,
I tell you the very stones would cry out."

LUKE 19:39

Matthew adds:

As Jesus entered Jerusalem
the whole city was stirred to its depths,
demanding, "Who is this?"
And the crowd kept answering,
"This is the prophet Jesus from Nazareth."

MATTHEW 21:10–11

Jerusalem: Jesus' Day and Today

This aerial view
shows Jerusalem's Old City as it looks today.
The white-line overlay shows a probable
general location of the city walls in Jesus' day.

The "temple area" marks the exact site
of the temple in Jesus' time.
It now houses the famous Moslem mosque,
the Dome of the Rock.

Note that "Golgotha/Tomb"
(dome-roofed Church of the Holy Sepulcher)
lay outside the city walls in Jesus' day,
but inside the modern city walls.

One of the most attractive gates
leading into the modern Old City of Jerusalem
is the Damascus Gate.
The wall through which it passes
dates from the 16th century,
but rests on a wall dating from the 2nd century.

Left of the Damascus Gate is the entrance
to a huge cavern called Solomon's Quarries.
Legend says the temple building blocks
were cut from this quarry.
A writer describes his visit to the site.

In the Steps of the Master
H. V. MORTON

I went into the darkness, swinging my lantern,
and the path led steeply down into an enormous
entrance cave like a buried cathedral. . . .

It has been estimated that in ancient times
sufficient stone had been removed
from these quarries to build
the modern city of Jerusalem twice over.

It is a peculiar and unusual pure white stone,
soft to work but hardening rapidly when exposed
to the atmosphere.
The Arabs call these caverns the "cotton caves"
because they are so white. . . .

I propped the lantern on a ledge of rock,
and by the light of its candle
I read the extraordinarily detailed account
of the building of the Temple which you will find
in 2 Chronicles 2 and 1 Kings 5.

142

CONFRONTATION

As Jesus rode through the streets to the temple,
the crowds grew noisier and larger.
Movement had slowed to a snail's pace
during the last 100 yards.

When Jesus entered the precincts of the temple,
he was appalled by what he saw.
The court of the gentiles looked like a market.

Jesus entered the temple precincts
and drove out all those

engaged there in buying and selling.
He overturned the money-changers' tables
and the stalls of the dove-sellers,
saying to them: "Scripture has it,
'My house shall be called a house of prayer,'
but you are turning it into a den of thieves."

The blind and the lame came to Jesus
inside the temple area and he cured them.
The chief priests and the scribes
became indignant
when they observed the wonders he worked

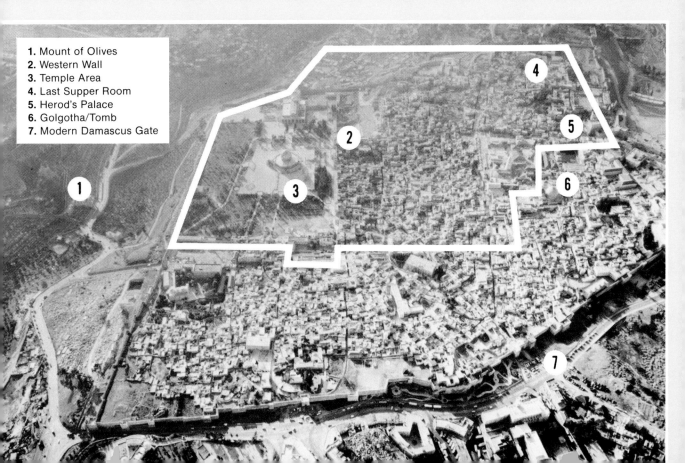

1. Mount of Olives
2. Western Wall
3. Temple Area
4. Last Supper Room
5. Herod's Palace
6. Golgotha/Tomb
7. Modern Damascus Gate

Jerusalem Temple

This schematic plan of the temple and its courts follows the general plan of Avi-Yonah's model, shown here. Biblical references pinpoint events that took place within them.

1 Holy of Holies

High Priest alone enters	Hebrews 9:7
Curtain torn	Mark 15:38

2 Holy Place

Zechariah enters	Luke 1:9

3 Court of Priests

Zechariah murdered	Matthew 23:35

4 Court of Israel (Men)

Boy Jesus	Luke 2:46
Bring your gift to altar	Matthew 5:23
Two men went to pray	Luke 18:10
Paul and gentiles enter	Acts 21:28

5 Court of Women

Mary purified	Luke 2:22
Jesus taught in treasury	John 8:20
Widow's mite	Luke 21:1–4

6 Court of Gentiles

Jesus on parapet	Luke 4:9
Jesus on Solomon's porch	John 10:23
Jesus expels merchants	Matthew 21:12
Beggar cured at gate	Acts 3:1–11

7 Curtain

8 Altar of Incense

9 Altar of Holocaust

10 Gate of Nicanor

11 Temple Treasury

12 Beautiful Gate

13 Gentile Barrier

14 Solomon's Porch

15 Western (Wailing) Wall

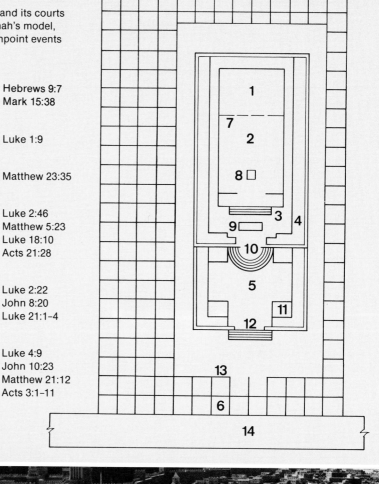

*and how the children were shouting out
in the temple precincts,
"Hosanna to the Son of David!"*

*"Do you hear what they are saying?"
the chief priests and scribes asked him.
Jesus answered them,
"Of course I do! Did you never read this:
'From the speech of infants and children
you have framed a hymn of praise'?"*

MATTHEW 21:12–16

To grasp the meaning of this "action parable,"
we need to know something about the temple
and its system of sacrifice.
The temple precincts was divided into 4 courts:

> the court of the priests,
> the court of the men,
> the court of the women,
> the court of the gentiles.

An imposing barrier separated
the court of the gentiles from the other courts.
On the barrier were warning signs.
Josephus describes them, but not until modern
times did archaeologists actually discover one.
Its seven-line inscription was chilling:

*No foreigner
is to go beyond the balustrade
and the plaza of the temple zone.
Whoever is caught doing so
will have himself to blame
for his death
which will follow.*

Money-changers and sellers were restricted
to the court of the gentiles.

Temple sacrifice explains
the presence of doves in the court of the gentiles.
Animals to be sacrificed
had to be free of any spot or blemish.

Thus, all animals had to be inspected.
It became simpler in the long run
to pre-inspect animals and sell them
right in the temple area.

Jesus of Nazareth
WILLIAM BARCLAY

*This seems harmless until it is realized
that there were times when a pair of doves
cost as little as five new pence
outside the Temple
and as much as seventy-five new pence inside it.
Jesus' wrath was therefore aroused
for two reasons.
The stalls where the sacrificial victims were sold
turned the Temple Court into a market place.
What should have been a place of prayer
had become a place of noisy bargaining.
Secondly, as we have seen, the poor pilgrims
were victims of a swindling racket.*

The money system produced similar problems.
The temple tax, which all had to pay,
could not be paid with coins bearing a portrait.

Jesus of Nazareth
WILLIAM BARCLAY

*Such portraits
were reckoned among the graven images
explicitly forbidden by the Law of Moses.
Hence while Tyrenian, Phoenician, Egyptian,
Greek and Roman coins
would serve for ordinary transactions,
they had to be changed into acceptable shekels
to pay the temple tax.*

145

These copper "mites" were minted during the rule of Pilate. Tiberius' name appears on the scroll side, the date of his rule on the wreath side. Jesus referred to this coin when praising a widow who put into the temple collection box "two small coins worth a few cents." (Mark 12:42)

It cost the pilgrim a coin called a ma'ah
to get his money changed,
a ma'ah *being the equivalent of a new penny.*
If changing the money involved getting change,
the pilgrim had to pay the money-changers
another penny for the service.

It was against these abuses
that Jesus' "action parable" was directed.
Matthew ends his report of the episode abruptly:

With that Jesus left them
and went out of the city to Bethany,
where he spent the night.

MATTHEW 21:17

CURSING THE FIG TREE

The next morning Jesus got up early
and set out again from Bethany to Jerusalem:

At dawn, as Jesus was returning to the city,
he felt hungry.
Seeing a fig tree by the roadside he went over to it,
but found nothing there except leaves.
He said to it,
"Never again shall you bear fruit!"

The disciples were dumbfounded
when they saw this. They asked,
"Why did the tree wither up so quickly?"
Jesus said:
"Believe me, if you trust and do not falter,
not only will you do what I did to the fig tree,
but if you say to this mountain,
'Be lifted up and thrown into the sea,'
even that will happen.
You will receive all that you pray for,
provided you have faith."

MATTHEW 21:18-22

Mark's gospel makes the cursing of the fig tree
even more surprising, saying:
"It was not the time for figs." (11:13)
This has caused some bible readers to wonder:
Isn't it unjust to curse a tree
for not producing fruit out of season?

In the Steps of the Master
H. V. MORTON

What Jesus was looking for were not figs
but green knobs about as big as an almond,
which Palestinian peasants eat today
and call tagsh.
These appear sometimes before the leaves,
but always in the budding time,
and after growing the size of nuts,
fall off to make way for the real fruit.
Therefore a tree without tagsh
will have no figs later on.

Jesus' curse of the fig tree was not to satisfy
an inner emotion.
A deeper, twofold reason was involved.

First, the curse acted as an "action parable"
to dramatize the power of faith.

Second, especially as Mark presents it,
the curse also acted as an "action prophecy"
to dramatize the fate of Israel unless it changed.

146

Jesus said: "There was a property owner who planted a vineyard . . . and erected a tower." Such towers acted as observation posts against thieves and wild animals. The one shown here illustrates what Jesus had in mind.

Prophets since Hosea had compared Israel
to a fig tree.
Jesus also used this comparison
in a previous parable:

*"A man had a fig tree growing in his vineyard,
and he came out looking for fruit on it
but did not find any.
He said to the vinedresser, 'Look here!
For three years now
I have come in search of fruit on this fig tree
and found none. Cut it down.
Why should it clutter up the ground?'*

*"In answer, the man said,
'Sir, leave it another year,
while I hoe around it and manure it;
then perhaps it will bear fruit.
If not, it shall be cut down.'"*

LUKE 13:6–9

By cursing the fig tree, Jesus dramatizes
that the time for bearing fruit
is rapidly drawing to an end for many in Israel.
They must open their hearts to God's kingdom
or "be cut down."

After the episode involving the fig tree,
Jesus and his disciples proceeded to the temple.

PARABLE OF THE TENANTS

Immediately after they arrived at the temple,
some religious leaders challenged Jesus
concerning his actions on the previous day.
A brief exchange followed and Jesus said:

*"There was a property owner
who planted a vineyard, put a hedge around it,
dug out a vat, and erected a tower.
Then he leased it out to tenant farmers
and went on a journey.*

*"When vintage time arrived
he dispatched his slaves to the tenants
to obtain his share of the grapes.
The tenants responded by seizing the slaves.
They beat one, killed another, and stoned a third.*

*"A second time
he dispatched even more slaves than before,
but they treated them the same way.*

Fig trees yielded their pear-shaped fruit twice a year. Early spring figs were usually eaten fresh. Late summer figs were usually dried, pressed into cakes, and served during the year. (1 Samuel 25:18)

This coin of Caesar
dates from Jesus' time.
The wording reads
from right to left.
"Ti [berius] *Caesar Divi
Aug* [gusti] *F* [ilius]
Augustus" (Tiberius Caesar,
august son of
the deified Augustus).

"Pontif Maxim"
(The Great Pontiff)

Caesar's Coin

After Jesus told the vineyard parable,
Luke says that the temple leaders sent "spies"
to trap Jesus into speaking against the Romans.

SPIES *May we pay tax to the emperor
or not?*

JESUS (recognizing the trap)
*Show me a coin. Whose head is this?
Whose inscription do you read?*

SPIES *Caesar's.*

JESUS *Then give to Caesar what is Caesar's,
but give to God what is God's.*
LUKE 20:22-25

Jews hated paying Roman taxes,
especially since it had to be done with a coin
bearing Caesar's "godlike" image and inscription.

To possess
a Roman coin was to admit a Roman obligation.
Thus, when the spies produced Caesar's coin
from their purse, they answered their own question.

*"Finally he sent his son to them, thinking,
'They will respect my son.'
When they saw the son,
the tenants said to one another,
'Here is the one who will inherit everything.
Let us kill him
and then we shall have his inheritance!'*

*"With that they seized him,
dragged him outside the vineyard,
and killed him.*

*"What do you suppose the owner of the vineyard
will do to those tenants when he comes?"*

*They replied,
"He will bring that wicked crowd to a bad end
and lease his vineyard out to others
who will see to it
that he has grapes at vintage time. . . ."*

*When the chief priests and the Pharisees
heard these parables,
they realized that he was speaking about them.*
MATTHEW 21:33-45

Jesus' parable, and the question attached to it,
forced the leaders to pass judgment on themselves:
"He will bring that wicked crowd to an end
and lease the vineyard out to others."

In other words, Jesus is saying
that the former leadership of Israel will end.
A new "lease" (covenant)
will install the disciples of Jesus
as the new leaders of Israel.

Matthew ends the confrontation saying:
"The Pharisees went off and began to plot
how they might trap Jesus in speech." (22:15)

18

Prophecy of Jesus

After Jesus' second straight day of confrontation
with religious leaders,
he and his disciples left the temple area.
They headed for the Mount of Olives.

As they walked along,
some disciples stopped momentarily
to admire the beauty of the temple buildings.
Jesus said:

"Do you see all these buildings?
I assure you,
not one stone will be left on another—
it will be torn down."

MATTHEW 24:2

Jesus' words
must have clapped like thunder
in his disciples' ears.
They must have wondered: "Is Jesus serious?"
No one said anything further
until they reached the Mount of Olives:

While Jesus was seated
on the Mount of Olives,
his disciples came up to him privately and said:
"Tell us, when will all this occur?
What will be the sign of your coming
and the end of the world?"

MATTHEW 24:3

Jesus responded by saying
that it would take place in 3 clear-cut stages.

FIRST STAGE

"Be on your guard! . . . Many will come . . .
attempting to impersonate me . . .
and they will deceive many. . . .
Nation will rise against nation. . . .
There will be famine and pestilence
and earthquakes in many places.
These are the early stages of the birth pangs.
They will hand you over to torture. . . .
Many will falter. . . .
The man who holds out to the end, however,
is the one who will see salvation.
This good news of the kingdom
will be proclaimed throughout the world. . . .
Only after that will the end come."

SECOND STAGE

"When you see the abominable
and destructive thing which the prophet Daniel
foretold standing on holy ground . . .
those in Judea must flee to the mountains.
If a man is on the roof terrace, he must not
come down to get anything out of his house. . . .
Keep praying that you will not have to flee
in winter or on a sabbath,
for those days will be filled with more anguish
than any from the beginning of the world. . . .
If anyone tells you at that time,
'Look, the Messiah is here,' or 'He is there,'
do not believe it. . . .
As the lightning from the east flashes to the west,
so will the coming of the Son of Man be.
Where the carcass lies, there the vultures gather."

THIRD STAGE

"Immediately after the stress of that period,
'the sun will be darkened . . . ,
the stars will fall from the sky. . . .'
Then the sign of the Son of Man will appear
in the sky, and 'all the clans of the earth

will strike their breasts' as they see
'the Son of Man coming on the clouds of heaven'
with power and great glory.
He will dispatch his angels . . .
and they will assemble his chosen
from the four winds. . . .
I assure you the present generation
will not pass away until all this takes place. . . .

"As for the exact day or hour, no one knows it,
neither the angels in heaven nor the Son,
but the Father only."

MATTHEW 24:4–36

EXPLANATION

Significantly,
Jesus did not begin by correcting his disciples,
who assumed that the end of the temple
automatically meant the end of the world.
The reason why he didn't is clear.

Even today as you stand on the Mount of Olives,
you are moved at the site of the Dome of the Rock.
But even this magnificent structure
can't compare to what the temple was like.

The Four Gospels, II
BRUCE VAWTER

The whiteness of the temple's massive stones
and the gold of its facade
made it one of the known wonders of the world,
and no Jew could look upon it
without feeling a natural surge of pride
in his race and religion.
Thus the shock . . . caused by Jesus' words.
Who could conceive a world without the temple?
The end of the temple
would mean the end of sacrifice,
and surely sacrifice would end
only with the world itself.

Jesus' answer indicated that the destruction
of Jerusalem and the temple would involve 3 stages.

FIRST STAGE

The signs for this stage would include
the appearance of false teachers, earthquakes,
famines, persecutions, worldwide preaching.
In later years, each sign came to pass:

false teachers appeared,	Galatians 1:7
earthquakes occurred,	Acts 16:25
a famine struck,	Acts 11:28
Christians were persecuted,	Acts 8:1
the gospel was worldwide.	Acts 18:1

SECOND STAGE

The sign for this stage was the appearance
"of the abominable and destructive thing
which Daniel the prophet had foretold
standing on holy ground."
Daniel's reference was to the desecration
of the temple by Antiochus in 168 B.C. (9:27, 12:11)

But the Book of Daniel was regarded
as a prophecy of future things to come
and, therefore, not yet ultimately fulfilled.
Later Christians interpreted
the "destructive thing" on "holy ground" to be
the "Roman armies" in the "Holy Land"
advancing toward Jerusalem and the temple.

The 4th-century historian, Eusebius, records
the Judaean Christians heeded Jesus' warning
and fled at the news of the approaching Romans.
History shows also that some of these refugees
eventually settled at Pella,
in the northern tip of the Jordan Valley.

Jesus' warning not to delay one's flight,
even to run back and pack a few belongings,
notes the speed with which his disciples were to act.
History bears out the importance of the warning.
The Roman advance came so fast that many
Jewish pilgrims, in Jerusalem for the Passover,
found themselves trapped in the city.

Tiny markets spill into the narrow, stepped streets of modern Jerusalem's Old City.

"Community ovens," like this one at El Jib, are still used in some rural areas.

Jerusalem, Jerusalem

Jesus wept over Jerusalem and said . . .
"Days will come upon you
when your enemies will encircle you. . . .
They will wipe you out,
you and your children within your walls."

LUKE 20:41–44

Like every Jew, Jesus loved Jerusalem deeply.
He loved its stone walls, its stepped streets,
its markets, and its people.
As late as the 1800s,
Jerusalem still retained many quaint features,
not unlike those of Jesus' Jerusalem.

A Diary of My Life in the Holy Land
A. E. BREEN

The grocer sells all kinds of dried fruits,
and olive and sesame oil. . . .
Almost all the buying and selling are done
in the street, as the shops are usually too small
to admit more than one person. . . .

The perfumers' street . . .
smells of Oriental spices a good way off.
All kinds of spices are sold on it, and the shops
are even more tiny than those of the grocers. . . .

Bakers are not confined to one street. . . .
They have their ovens in an out-of-the-way place,
partly so as not to annoy neighbors with smoke;
and partly because they require space for the
thorns and bushes with which they heat their ovens.
The inhabitants of the towns never bake bread
at home, but send the dough to the ovens.

151

Now stage two began to unfold in all its horror.
Roman armies, under Titus, attacked Jerusalem.
Titus placed his troops in the Mount of Olives
area and conducted his attack with care.
For, at first, Jerusalem's position was strong.
Eight miles of fortified wall ringed the city.

Titus' first tactic was to seal off the city,
keeping anyone from entering or leaving it.
Josephus tells
how the blockade affected the Jewish defenders.

Jewish Wars
FLAVIUS JOSEPHUS

*The alleys were piled high with the bodies
of the aged.
Children and young people, swollen from hunger,
wandered about like ghosts until they dropped.
Those who still survived were so far spent
that they couldn't bury anyone, and if they tried,
they fell dead upon the corpses themselves.
The misery was indescribable.
And as soon as even the shadow of something
edible appeared anywhere, a fight began over it,
and the best of friends fought each other for it.*
Some people attempted to flee from Jerusalem.

Jesus and His Times
HENRI DANIEL-ROPS

*Those who tried to escape the city
went straight into the arms of the Romans . . .
who sent them back with their hands cut off
if they were women,
or crucified them in full view of the city
if they were men. . . .*

*The agony was endured for a hundred days.
Although the third and the second wall had been
breached, the city would not surrender;
in many quarters, house to house fighting
was necessary for capitulation.*

*Titus hesitated to use fire. . . .
But in the end, he was forced to resort to it. . . .
Titus and his staff tried to limit the disaster. . . .
But the soldiers, exasperated by the resistance,
paid no heed.*

Jerusalem was transformed into a sea of fire.
In the end, all that was left was a vast graveyard
of charred bodies and buildings.

152

Standing near Rome's Colosseum
is the Arch of Titus, built in A.D. 80 to mark
Titus' victory over the Jews.
This bas relief panel shows laurel-crowned soldiers
carrying off the temple's 7-branched lampstand,
silver trumpets, and showbread table. (Exodus 25:23-40)

THIRD STAGE

Immediately after the stress of this period,
the sun will be darkened,
the moon will not shed her light,
the stars will fall from the sky. . . .
Then the sign of the Son of Man
will appear in the sky. . . .

MATTHEW 24:29-30

There is a running debate among Christians
concerning the third stage and its signs.
Some interpret Jesus' words about the sun,
moon, and stars literally.

Accordingly,
they say the third stage has not yet occurred.
But then they face an even bigger problem:
what about Jesus' words that
"the present generation will not pass away
until all this takes place"?
One solution is to say that Matthew's report
is in error on this point.

Saint Matthew
J.C.FENTON

Matthew believed that Jesus had taught
that he would return in glory
sometime within the years A.D. 30–100,
although Jesus himself
had not known the exact date of his coming;
and Matthew was probably right
in thinking that Jesus had taught this.
Nevertheless, the second coming did not happen
within this period.

Other Christians say Jesus intended his words
about the sun, moon, and stars
to be taken symbolically,
pointing out that the prophets frequently
used such expression in a symbolic sense
to describe catastrophic events.

The hand that stamped this tile
could have helped
to destroy Jerusalem.
After the city's destruction,
Titus left behind the
Legion of the Tenth Fretensis
to keep Jews from rebuilding.
This was the Legion's official stamp.

For example,
Isaiah describes Babylon's fall as follows:

The stars and constellations of the heavens
send forth no light;
the sun is dark when it rises,
the light of the moon does not shine.

ISAIAH 13:10

The Christians who follow this approach
also interpret the "coming of the Son of Man"
in a symbolic sense.
Old Testament writers commonly spoke of a
catastrophic event as a "visitation" of Yahweh.
Accordingly, the fall of Jerusalem is portrayed
as a "visitation" of the risen Christ.

The Gospel of St. Matthew
DAVID STANLEY

To the eye of faith, the fall of the Holy City . . .
is a manifestation of the power
of the exalted Christ
through the liberation of his Church
from the ties of Judaism.

Thus, Jesus' words concerning
the assembly of "the chosen from the four winds"
means the manifestation of Christianity
as it emerges everywhere over the earth.

"The Gospel According to Matthew"
JOHN L. McKENZIE

The coming of the Son of Man
as Matthew conceived it
could easily be the establishment of the community
of the Risen Son of Man as the new Israel
after the destruction of the Old Israel.

153

Regardless of which position you take,
everyone agrees that Jesus ends his discourse
with some remarks about the end of the world.

END OF THE WORLD

The last hours of human life on earth
have always been a concern of people.
The Sunday Express, a British newspaper,
filed this report on February 4, 1962:

*NEW DELHI, INDIA—Millions of Indians
knelt in prayer today waiting for the minutes
to tick away to doomsday.*

*For this is the weekend of the end of the world,
according to Hindu and Moslem astrologers.*

*The vital hours are from 12:05 P.M. Sunday
(Greenwich time) to 12:15 A.M. Monday.
During this time eight planets—earth, moon,
Mercury, sun, Venus, Mars, Jupiter
and Saturn—will be in one direct line
for the first time in four centuries.
And in the southern hemisphere
there will be a total eclipse of the sun.*

*Throughout India,
families are gathering together,
or going to huge nonstop prayer meetings.*

Will the end to human life on earth come slowly?
Or will it come suddenly?
Here's how one writer
presents the biblical answer to that question.

The inscription on this
"chair of Moses"
honors Judan, son of Ishmael,
as the one who built
the Chorazin synagogue.

THOMAS BLACKBURN

A San Francisco housewife said,
"I had just put the coffee on to boil
when I felt the whole house start to shake.
Then there was this terrific flash of lightning
and the whole sky lit up.
And I thought, my heavens!
The children are going to get soaking wet!"

A St. Louis schoolgirl had this to say.
"I was in history class. Mr. Fenkle's our teacher.
I leaned over to Sally—she's my girlfriend—
and whispered, 'Fenkle's awfully cute,'—
I mean Mr. Fenkle—

Silent Witness

Jesus' prophecy of Jerusalem's destruction
recalls a similar prophecy about Chorazin.
(Luke 10:13)

Today, the black basalt ruins of Chorazin
stand in silent testimony to Jesus' fateful words.
The town lies in a deserted spot about 2 miles
from Capernaum.

The synagogue ruins shown here
date from the 3rd century.
A prize find among the ruins
was a stone seat called the "chair of Moses."
Authorized teachers in synagogues
sat in this special chair.
Jesus alluded to it when he said:

"The scribes and the Pharisees
sit on the chair of Moses;
therefore do everything and observe everything
they tell you.
But do not follow their example."

MATTHEW 23:2

and anyhow I had just said that to Sally
when the whole place went dead still.
And I noticed something funny about the sky."

A sailor from New York had another version.
"I was in a bar on West 25th.
I was in a booth drinking beer with this blonde.
She wasn't so bad and things were just getting
interesting when all of a sudden the whole joint
started coming apart at the seams.
There was a real weird light in the sky."

Finally, a real-estate man from Florida said,
"You know, when you come right down to it,
the whole thing happened just like they said
it would:

"The day of the Lord will come like a thief,
and on that day
the heavens will vanish with a roar;
the elements will melt away in a blaze. . . .
What we await are new heavens and a new earth
where, according to his promise,
the justice of God will reside."

2 PETER 3:10-13

PARABLE OF THE BRIDESMAIDS

Jesus also compared the "day of the Lord"
to an ancient wedding celebration.

Spanning several days,
a highpoint of the celebration was the arrival
of the groom at the house of the bride.
Bridesmaids carrying torches welcomed him.

NARRATOR   *The reign of God can be likened to*
ten bridesmaids who took their torches
and went out to welcome the groom.
Five of them were foolish,
while the other five were sensible.
The foolish ones, in taking their
torches, brought no oil along,
but the sensible ones took flasks of oil

155

as well as their torches.
The groom delayed his coming,
so they began to nod,
then to fall asleep.
At midnight someone shouted,
'The groom is here!
Come out to greet him!'

FOOLISH   *Give us some of your oil.*
MAIDS   *Our torches are going out.*

SENSIBLE   *No, there may not be enough for you*
MAIDS   *and us.*
             You had better go to the dealers
             and buy yourselves some.

NARRATOR   *While they went off to buy it*
             the groom arrived
             and the ones who were ready
             went in to the wedding with him.
             Then the door was barred.
             Later the other bridesmaids came back.

FOOLISH   *Master, Master!*
MAIDS   *Open the door for us.*

GROOM   *I tell you, I do not know you.*
                          MATTHEW 25:1–12

Most people interpret Jesus' parable
as an allegory of the Christian community
waiting for Jesus' final coming.
The point of the parable is this:

Jesus' final coming
will take many people by complete surprise.
Some people (sensible maids) will be ready;
others (foolish maids) will not.
Those who are ready (have a supply of oil)
will enter the wedding with the groom (Jesus);
the others will be refused entry.

But what constitutes being "ready"?
In other words, what does "oil" stand for?

Since the meaning isn't clear from the parable,
we turn to the context of the parable for a clue.
The context is Jesus' "Fifth Discourse."
(Matthew 24:21–25:46)
A key theme of the discourse is helping others.
Jesus sums it up this way:

"Whenever you refused
to help one of these least important ones
you refused to help me."
                          MATTHEW 25:45

Unless Matthew is strangely inconsistent,
oil stands for "good works."

This dovetails with an earlier comparison,
where Jesus likens the goodness of one's works
to the brightness of oil burning in a lamp.
(Matthew 5:15–16)

A similar comparison
occurs in connection with Numbers 7:19.
It describes an offering of flour mixed with oil.
Rabbis compared
the study of the Torah to a flour offering,
saying it should be mixed with "good works."

PARABLE OF THE SILVER PIECES

Jesus told another parable
in the course of instructing his disciples
about the end of the world and his final coming.

A merchant was preparing to go on a long trip.
He gave his 3 servants silver pieces,
according to the ability of each. Then he left.

After a long absence, the merchant returned.
He called his servants.
Two servants, one given 2 thousand
and one given 5 thousand silver pieces,
reported excellent profits.
The merchant was delighted:

Cleverly done . . .
Since you were dependable in small matters

I will put you in charge of larger affairs.
Come, share your master's joy!

Then the man to whom he had given
a thousand silver pieces stepped forward:

"My lord," he said,
"I knew you were a hard man.
You reap where you did not sow
and gather where you did not scatter,
so out of fear I went off and buried
your thousand silver pieces in the ground.
Here is your money back."

His master exclaimed:
"You worthless, lazy lout!
You know I reap where I did not scatter.
All the more reason to deposit my money
with the bankers so that on my return
I could have had it back with interest.

"You there . . . .
Throw this worthless servant
into the darkness outside,
where he can wail and grind his teeth."

MATTHEW 25:24–30

Jesus' point is that his disciples
should use the time they have to do good works.
Moreover, they will be accountable
according to the ability and talent
that each has received.

TIME OF RECKONING

Jesus ended his instruction with a parable
about the moment of reckoning at the world's end.

A great king divided all peoples into 2 groups.
To one group he said:

I was hungry and you gave me food,
I was thirsty and you gave me drink.
I was a stranger and you welcomed me,
naked and you clothed me.

MATTHEW 25:35–36

When Lord?

adapted from
Wage Earner
REYNOLD HILLENBRAND

I was:

> *hungry . . .*
>> *and you taught me how to increase*
>> *farm production in Indonesia,*
>
> *thirsty . . .*
>> *and you helped me to dig wells*
>> *and build dams in arid countries,*
>
> *naked . . .*
>> *and you helped me to finance*
>> *textile mills in India,*
>
> *homeless . . .*
>> *and you promoted housing in Hong Kong*
>> *for refugee families,*
>
> *sick . . .*
>> *and you sent medicine to protect us*
>> *from the deforming disease of yaws,*
>
> *in prison . . .*
>> *in political and economic chains,*
>> *and you taught us self-government*
>> *and lifted us from poverty.*

PEOPLE: *Lord, when did we do these things?*

KING: *When you did them for these least*
of my brothers and sisters.

The people asked: "When did we do this?"
The king replied: "As often as you did it
for one of my least brothers, you did it for me."
Then the king turned to the other group.

Out of my sight. . . .
I was hungry and you gave me no food,
I was thirsty and you gave me no drink.
I was a stranger

and you gave me no welcome,
naked and you gave me no clothing.
I was ill and in prison
and you did not come to comfort me. . . .

As often as you neglected
to do it to one of these least ones,
you neglected to do it to me.

MATTHEW 25:41–45

Separation Time

Daytime finds this flock of sheep and goats
grubbing together for anything edible.

Saint Matthew
J. C. FENTON

They must be separated in the evening
because goats
have to be kept warm at night.
The sheep are more valuable than the goats,
and this is why, in the parable,

the sheep are placed on the right hand,
the place of honor.

MATTHEW 22:44, 26:64

Jesus' point:
During the daytime of life, good and bad people
will live side by side; but they will be separated
when the evening comes.
Separation also plays a prominent role
in Jesus' Parable of the Weeds and Wheat
and in his Parable of the Net. (Matthew 13:30, 49)

158

19

Cup of Jesus

Two novels by Elie Wiesel,
The Town Beyond the Wall and *A Beggar in Jerusalem*, illustrate the power of friendship.
In both cases,
the power flows not from the friend directly,
but from the memory of the friend.

The Living Reminder
HENRI J. M. NOUWEN

In The Town Beyond the Wall
it is Michael who lives through torture
but avoids madness because Pedro,
his absent friend, lives in his memory. . . .
And in A Beggar in Jerusalem
it is David who is sustained in his struggles
by the memory of his friend. . . .

In his novels Wiesel expresses the profound truth
that memory not only connects us with our past
but also keeps us alive in the present.
He touches here a mystery
deeply anchored in biblical tradition.
To remember
is not simply to look back at past events;
more importantly,
it is to bring these events into the present
and celebrate them in the here and now.
For Israel, remembrance meant participation.

Through liturgical or ritual remembrance,
Israel brought the past into the present.
In this way, Jews of later times shared in

God's blessings to the nation in earlier times.
It was with this understanding
that Jesus and his disciples prepared to celebrate
the Passover.

PASSOVER

Originally a feast by itself, the Passover
was later joined to the Unleavened Bread
to become a week-long festival. (2 Chronicles 35:17)
Thus Luke writes:

The feast of the Unleavened Bread
known as the Passover was drawing near . . .
on which it was appointed
to sacrifice the paschal lamb.
Accordingly, Jesus sent Peter and John off
with the instruction:

"Go and prepare our Passover supper for us. . . .
Just as you enter the city
you will come upon a man carrying a water jar.
Follow him into the house he enters
and say to the owner, 'The Teacher asks you:
Do you have a guest room
where I may eat the Passover with my disciples?'
That man will show you an upstairs room,
spacious and furnished.
It is there you are to prepare."

They went off
and found everything just as he had said.

LUKE 22:1-13

The secrecy of Jesus' instructions
may have stemmed from a concern
that an attempt may be made to arrest him.

The instructions to look for a man carrying
a water jar seem odd until we realize
that carrying water was a woman's job.
For a man to do it was unusual.
Thus, any male carrying water would stand out.

This stairway leads to an upper room
on the exact site an ancient tradition says
Jesus and his disciples ate the Last Supper.
This structure, however, dates only from about A.D. 1350.

"poured water into a basin and began to wash
his disciples' feet." (John 13:15)
This was customary at some ancient banquets,
but not the rule for Passover meals.
When Jesus had finished, he said:

"Do you understand what I just did for you?
You address me as 'Teacher' and 'Lord,'
and fittingly enough, for that is what I am.
But if I washed your feet—
I who am Teacher and Lord—
then you must wash each other's feet.
What I just did was to give you an example:
as I have done, so you must do."

JOHN 13:13–15

An ancient tradition says
the man carrying the jar was young Mark.
Tradition also says that the house with guest room
belonged to Mark's mother. (Acts 12:12)

PASSOVER MEAL

Normally, Jews ate 2 meals daily:
one about 10 A.M., the other late in the afternoon.
The Passover meal, however, was eaten at night,
after the appearance of the first stars.
Thus, everyone celebrated the meal
at the same time as one family.

As Jesus and his apostles awaited the first stars,
they would have seen Passover fires
blazing throughout the city.
Once the stars appeared, Jesus, acting as father,
began the Passover ceremonies.

Jesus took his place at the table,
and the apostles with him.
He said to them:
"I have greatly desired to eat this Passover
with you before I suffer.
I tell you, I will not eat again
until it is fulfilled in the kingdom of God."

LUKE 22:14–16

Instead of sitting, as at ordinary meals,
Jews reclined at the Passover supper
in the fashion of Greeks and Romans at banquets.
Possibly after the apostles had all reclined,
Jesus rose from the table,

For Jews, washing another's feet was humiliating.
No free citizen could be forced to do it;
it was a slave's job.
Jesus' action created a deep impression.

When finished, Jesus began the festive meal,
preparing the first of 4 ceremonial cups of wine.

Then taking a cup
Jesus offered a blessing in thanks and said:
"Take this and divide it among you;
I tell you, from now on
I will not drink of the fruit of the vine
until the coming of the reign of God."

LUKE 22:17–18

Red wine was usually used at Passover meals.
It recalled the blood-marked doorposts in Egypt
and the covenant blood at Mount Sinai.
Jesus drank from the cup and passed it.
Drinking from the same cup symbolized
and dramatized the close bond
that united those gathered for the Passover meal.

Next, the food was set before Jesus:
wild herbs, unleavened bread, and sauce

160

into which the bread and herbs were to be dipped.
Finally came the lamb.
When all the food was in place,
Jesus prepared the second ceremonial cup of wine.

Normal meals began with the breaking of bread.
The Passover meal, however,
began with the passing of herbs and sauce.
This change furnished the cue for the youngest
to inquire: "Why is tonight's meal different?"
In obedience to Exodus 12:26, the father then
explained the meaning of the Passover foods.

The bitter herbs, for example,
recalled the years of bitter slavery in Egypt.
The clay-colored sauce recalled
the long hours of brickmaking under the hot sun.
The unleavened bread recalled
the haste of Israel's departure from Egypt,
not even waiting for the dough to be leavened
for tomorrow's bread supply.
The lamb recalled the command to mark
the outer door frame of each house with blood—
a sign for the Lord to "pass over" the house
and spare its occupants during the tenth plague.

It was during the eating of the herbs and sauce
that Jesus said:
"One of you is about to betray me,
yes, one who is eating with me." (Mark 14:18)

Shortly after these deeply disturbing words,
Judas left the room.
This shocked some of the apostles,
until they remembered that Judas kept the purse.
Perhaps Jesus had instructed him
to make some offering to the poor.
It was customary to help the poor in this night.

JESUS INSTRUCTS THE APOSTLES

Once Judas had left, Jesus said . . .
"I am not to be with you much longer. . . .
Where I go you cannot come.

"I give you a new commandment:
Love one another.
Such as my love has been for you,
so must your love be for each other.
This is how all will know you are my disciples:
your love for one another."

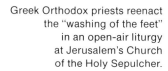

Greek Orthodox priests reenact
the "washing of the feet"
in an open-air liturgy
at Jerusalem's Church
of the Holy Sepulcher.

The bread Jesus broke at the Last Supper would have closely resembled these round loaves, which boys still sell in Jerusalem's streets.

"Lord," Simon Peter said to Jesus,
"why can I not follow you now?
I will lay down my life for you!"
Jesus answered,
"I tell you truly, the cock will not crow
before you have three times disowned me!"

JOHN 13:31–38

The disciples looked deeply troubled.
Jesus continued:

"Do not let your hearts be troubled. . . .
I am, indeed, going to prepare a place for you,
and I will come back to take you with me. . . .
This much
have I told you while I was still with you;
the Paraclete, the Holy Spirit
whom the Father will send in my name,
will instruct you in everything,
and remind you of all that I have told you.
'Peace' is my farewell to you,
my peace is my gift to you."

JOHN 14:1–27

JESUS PRAYS FOR HIS DISCIPLES

"Father, the hour has come. . . .
As you have sent me into the world,
so I have sent them into the world. . . .
I do not pray for them alone.
I pray also for those
who will believe in me through their word,
that all may be one
as you, Father, are in me, and I in you;
I pray that they may be one in us."

JOHN 16:32–17:21

After his prayer, Jesus began the singing
of the first half of the *Hallel,*
a signal that the preliminary festivities were over
and that the main meal was to begin.
In unison the group sang:

Blessed be the name of the Lord. . . .
From the rising to the setting of the sun
is the name of the Lord to be praised.

PSALM 113:2–3

JESUS GIVES HIS BODY

Jesus began the main body of the meal
by passing the second cup of wine
which had been prepared earlier.
It was followed by the breaking of the bread:

Taking bread and giving thanks,
Jesus broke it and gave it to them saying:
"This is my body to be given for you.
Do this as a remembrance of me."

LUKE 22:19

The apostles were struck by the blessing,
especially the reference to Jesus' body.
Some recalled that memorable day on the hillside
when Jesus said:

"I am the bread of life.
Your ancestors ate manna in the desert,
but they died. . . .
The bread I give is my flesh,
for the life of the world."

JOHN 6:49-51

When everyone had shared the bread,
Jesus prepared and passed the paschal lamb.
As he did,
the prophecy of Isaiah came to mind:

Like a lamb led to the slaughter . . .
he was cut off from the land of the living
and smitten for the sin of the people. . . .
And he shall take away the sins of many,
and win pardon for their offenses.

ISAIAH 53:7-12

The main meal was then eaten by all.

JESUS GIVES HIS BLOOD

After all had finished the main meal,
Jesus prepared the third ceremonial cup of wine:

After the supper,
Jesus took the cup, saying,
"This cup is the new covenant in my blood.
Do this, whenever you drink it,
in remembrance of me."

1 CORINTHIANS 11:25

The disciples were struck again
by Jesus' blessing, especially the words:
"This cup is the new covenant in my blood."

It recalled the Sinai covenant,
when Moses sprinkled blood on the people saying:
"This is the blood of the covenant
which the Lord has made with you." (Exodus 24:8)

This was part of what they were celebrating
around the table that night.
Was Jesus inaugurating the New Covenant?
New Covenant Blood? A New Covenant Meal?
Was this the great hour Jeremiah prophesied:

"The days are coming," says the Lord,
"when I will make a new covenant
with the house of Israel and
the house of Judah . . .
and write it upon their hearts;
I will be their God
and they shall be my people."

JEREMIAH 31:31-33

Before the disciples could do anything more
than plant the seeds to the questions,
Jesus intoned the second half of the Hallel.
The meal ended
with the drinking of a fourth cup of wine:

"The cup of salvation I will take,
and call upon the name of the Lord. . . .
Precious in the eyes of the Lord
is the death of his faithful ones. . . .

"I shall not die, but live,
and declare the works of the Lord. . . .
The stone which the builders rejected
has become the cornerstone.
By the Lord has this been done;
it is wonderful in our eyes."

PSALMS 116:13-15, 118:17-23

Mark concludes the Last Supper account
with these words:

After singing songs of praise,
they walked out to the Mount of Olives.

MARK 14:26

Archaeologists
date the remains of this stepped-street,
near the traditional site of the upper room,
back to about the first century.
Jesus and his disciples could have passed this way
en route to the Mount of Olives.

broke it and said,
"This is my body, which is for you.
Do this in remembrance of me."

In the same way,
after supper, he took the cup, saying,
"This cup is the new covenant in my blood.
Do this, whenever you drink it,
in remembrance of me."

"Every time, then,
you eat this bread and drink this cup,
you proclaim the death of the Lord
until he comes."

1 CORINTHIANS 11:23–26

Paul's words explain why Christians still gather
around the Lord's table to eat the Lord's Supper.

The Living Reminder
HENRI J. M. NOUWEN

As the disciples walked along in silence
under the stars with Jesus,
they must have been turning over many things
in their minds.
They were profoundly happy,
but it was a kind of bittersweet happiness.
Jesus had said too many sorrow-shadowed things
to allow unrestrained joy to reign in their hearts.
The final words of Jesus, especially,
kept drumming in their ears:
"Do this in remembrance of me."

INVITATION TO REMEMBER

Some years after the Last Supper,
Paul wrote to Christians in Corinth, Greece:

The Lord Jesus
on the night in which he was betrayed
took bread,
and after he had given thanks

We eat bread,
but not enough to take our hunger away;
we drink wine,
but not enough to take our thirst away;
we read from a book,
but not enough to take our ignorance away.

And what is the meaning behind these signs
and our celebration?

The simple signs,
which cannot satisfy our desires,
speak first of all of God's absence.
He has not yet returned. . . .
But even as we affirm his absence
we realize that he is already with us.
We say to each other:
"Eat and drink, this is his body and blood.". . .
Thus,
while remembering his promises in his absence
we discover and celebrate his presence
in our midst.

The great temptation of the ministry
is to celebrate only the presence of the Lord
while forgetting his absence.
Often the minister
is most concerned to make the people glad
and to create an atmosphere
of "I'm OK, you're OK."
But in this way everything gets filled up
and there is no empty space left for the
affirmation of our basic lack of fulfillment. . . .

Therefore, every time ministers call their people
around the table, they call them to experience
not only the Lord's presence
but his absence as well;
they call them to mourning as well as to feasting,
to sadness as well as to joy,
to longing as well as to satisfaction.

The kingdom of God is only in process;
it is not yet completed.
The vine is growing; it has not yet borne its fruit.

Eucharist in Pictures

This tabernacle door is a miniature catechism,
explaining how the eucharist was:

prefigured	John 2:6–9
promised	John 6:8–11, 24–27
instituted	Luke 22:19
celebrated	Luke 24:30

The horizontal wording quotes John 6:55.

"Caro mea vere cibus
(My body is real food)
sanguis meus vere potus."
(my blood is real drink.)

The vertical wording quotes John 6:58.

"Hic est panis qui
(This is the bread that)
de caelo descendit."
(came down from heaven.)

Promise of Jesus

"If anyone eats this bread he shall live forever."
JOHN 6:51

God's power
raises the decayed grain of wheat into a harvest
beyond belief.
God's goodness
places the harvest at the service of people.

God's word
changes some of the harvest into Christ's body.

In the same way, our bodies,
which have been nourished by the eucharist,
will be buried in the earth and decay.
But, at the appointed time, God's word
will raise them up to the glory of God the Father.
IRENAEUS, A.D. 200

20

Passion of Jesus

"The Friday Incident"

DRUE DUKE

My Sunday school teacher selected me
to represent our class of 13-year-olds
in a passion play. . . .

An internationally renowned troupe had asked
for local people to make up the crowd scene.
All week
I looked forward to my glamorous appearance
in a real stage play with famous actors.

An hour before curtain time,
all of us extras gathered. . . .
A tall, gray-haired director
introduced a dozen men wearing red turbans.

"These are your leaders," he announced.
"They will be placed among you.
Watch them. Do exactly as they do
and shout exactly what they shout.". . .
We were herded up the stairs to the area
behind the scenery. . . .

There are no words to describe my feelings
when a donkey was led into our midst
and I looked up at the man seated on it. . . .
I desperately wanted to touch him
but I could not move. This was Jesus! . . .

Excitement surged through me.
I was yelling as loudly as I could.
I forgot the audience and the stage.
This was Jesus and I was praising Him. . . .

All too quickly
the procession crossed the stage.

Once more we were grouped backstage,
the leaders pressing their fingers
against their lips to motion us to silence.
"We will be back on stage soon,"
a leader said in a harsh whisper. . . .
"Just shout what your leaders shout."

And then we went back on stage.
On an improvised balcony
stood the beautiful man
who had ridden the donkey.
Beside him
was a man in a purple robe with gold braid.

"Which do you choose?"
called the man in expensive clothes.
"Give us Barabbas," the crowd shouted.
I joined in, screaming with them.

"What shall I do then," boomed the voice
from the balcony,
"with Jesus who is called the Christ?"

"Crucify him!" the roar went up.
I yelled those terrible words. I know I did.
I heard myself shouting!

Suddenly I was cold.
I was shaking uncontrollably. . . .
I don't know when I started to cry,
but tears were streaming down my face
and I was moaning, "No, no, no!". . .

Many nights
I have lain awake in my bed,
reliving that horrible moment. . . .

True, it was only a role I was playing. . . .
But each time I remember,
I am made aware of one fact.
The crowd
which praised Jesus on Sunday
was the same crowd
which chose, five days later, to crucify Him.

PASSION ACCOUNTS

The record of Jesus' passion and death
was probably the first portion of the gospel
to develop as a complete unit.

One reason for early interest in Jesus' passion
was the emergence of rumors that threatened
the truth of what happened. (Matthew 28:11–15)

A second reason was the eucharistic meal
that Christians began to celebrate in response to
Jesus' instruction at the Last Supper.
Recalling Jesus' death and rising
became an important part of these celebrations.
The eucharistic meal, therefore,
played a key part in shaping the passion accounts.

The Gospel According to Luke
CARROLL STUHLMUELLER

Liturgical services demanded a solemnity,
a profound sense of adoration,
a stylization of language.
This tendency shows up in Matthew's account
of the passion. . . .
Matthew also reflects the evangelist's curiosity
about the last hours of Jesus.
Biographical details and anecdotes about Judas
or about Pilate and his wife are added.
Catechetical needs are also met by Matthew,
as he frequently matches prophecy and fulfillment.

"When you knock down the fruit of your olive trees,
you shall not go over the branches a second time;
let what remains for the alien, the orphan,
and the widow." (Deuteronomy 24:20)

The bible makes no mention of olives being eaten.
Apparently they were more valuable for their oil—
used in cooking, in lamps, and in medicines.

GETHSEMANI EVENTS

On the western slope of the Mount of Olives
still stands a grove of 8 ancient olive trees.
No one knows how old the trees are.

The Roman historian, Pliny, records the belief
that "olive trees never die."
He probably refers to the fact that new shoots
often emerge from old olive trunks.
These shoots produce a new growth
that matures and yields fruit
long after the parent tree has died and decayed.
It is possible that the 8 olive trees
mark the exact spot where Jesus' passion began.

After singing songs of praise,
Jesus and his disciples
walked out to the Mount of Olives . . .
to a place called Gethsemani.

MATTHEW 26:30, 36

Gethsemani means "olive press."
The name suggests that the place contained
an installation for extracting oil from olives.
The apparatus was probably housed in a cave—
perhaps one of those still visible there.

A stone wall guards 8 ancient olive trees on the Mount of Olives.
A 14th-century document describes a grove of 9 ancient trees
on the same spot. In 1942, one of the trees was cut down
to make room for a modern road. There is no way of knowing
if this grove marks the exact spot frequented by Jesus,
but it certainly lies in the vicinity of it.

Since Jesus was a frequent visitor to Gethsemani,
the plot may have belonged to a follower,
possibly a family of means, like Mark's.
Wealthy families frequently operated orchards
or farms outside the city walls.

Jesus said to his disciples,
"Stay here while I go over there and pray."
He took along Peter and Zebedee's two sons,
and began to experience sorrow and distress.
Then he said to them,
"My heart is nearly broken with sorrow.
Remain here and stay with me."

He advanced a little
and fell prostrate in prayer.
"My Father,
if it be possible, let this cup pass me by.
Still, let it be as you would have it, not as I."

MATTHEW 26:36–39

Jesus began his teaching career with prayer;
he begins his passion in the same way.
The 3 disciples who witnessed Jesus' ecstasy
now witnessed his agony. (Luke 9:28–36)

Jesus' prayer follows the same spirit
as the one he had taught his disciples earlier:
"Father . . . not my will but yours be done."

When Jesus returned to his disciples,
he found them asleep. He said to Peter,
"So you could not stay awake with me
for even one hour? Be on your guard,
and pray that you may not undergo the test.
The spirit is willing but nature is weak."

Withdrawing a second time, he began to pray:
"My Father, if this cannot pass me by
without my drinking it, your will be done!"
Once more, on his return, he found them asleep;
they could not keep their eyes open.

This "Rock of the Agony," now enclosed by the Church of All Nations, marks the place where tradition says Jesus prayed before his arrest: "Father . . . take this cup from me; yet not my will but yours be done." Jesus often spent the night at Gethsemani, which recalls Jesus' words: "The birds of the sky have nests, but the Son of Man has nowhere to lay his head."

He left them again . . . to pray a third time,
saying the same words as before.
Finally, he returned to his disciples and said . . .
"The hour is on us when the Son of Man
is to be handed over to the power of evil men.
Get up! . . . See, my betrayer is here."

MATTHEW 26:40-46

Luke says
Jesus' sweat "became like drops of blood." (22:44)
Paul calls Luke a "physician." (Colossians 4:14)
Such a detail would interest Luke.
Aristotle reports a similar phenomenon
in his lifetime.

ARREST OF JESUS

While Jesus was still speaking, Judas, one of the
Twelve, arrived accompanied by a great crowd
with swords and clubs.

He immediately went over to Jesus, said to him,
"Peace, Rabbi," and embraced him.
Jesus answered, "Friend, do what you are here for!"
At that moment they stepped forward
to lay hands on Jesus, and arrested him.
Suddenly one of those who accompanied Jesus
put his hand to his sword, drew it,
and slashed at the high priest's servant,
cutting off his ear.
Jesus said to him:
"Put back your sword where it belongs.

Those who use the sword
are sooner or later destroyed by it. . . ."

Then all the disciples deserted him and fled.

MATTHEW 26:47-56

The kiss of Judas was not an unusual gesture.
Orientals often greeted each other this way.

Peter's recourse to violence is quickly halted.
Luke, the physician, is the only evangelist to note
Jesus' healing of the ear.
John identifies the injured person as Malchus.

John adds a further detail that the others omit.
When Jesus identifies himself to the soldiers,
they react in a startled and stunned way:

"I am he," Jesus answered.
As Jesus said to them "I am he,"
the soldiers retreated slightly
and fell to the ground.

JOHN 18:4-6

Many have been intrigued by this report;
they note that the Romans Mark Antony and Marius
reputedly had a similar impact on assassins:

The Life of Christ
GUISEPPE RICCIOTTI

The sound of their voices was sufficient
to strike terror into men sent to murder them,

*but the latter were only individual assassins
in circumstances quite different.*

*It may very well be that in this instance,
the guards suddenly felt the full force of
Jesus' personality and were utterly dismayed. . . .
In any case it is obvious . . .
that John intends to picture it as miraculous,
thereby emphasizing the perfect freedom
with which Jesus accepted arrest.*

A final, surprising detail is recorded by Mark:

*There was a young man following Jesus
who was covered by nothing but a linen cloth.
As they seized him he left the cloth behind
and ran off naked.*

MARK 14:51–52

One speculation about this unusual detail
is that it is Mark's own identification of himself.
Indeed, Mark was just a youth when Jesus died.
The speculation takes on added interest
if Jesus ate the Last Supper at Mark's home
and if Gethsemani belonged to Mark's family.

A fitting signature to the events of Gethsemani
is John's note of Jesus' composure in the end.
One author comments on it in a striking way:

The Gospel of Luke
WILLIAM BARCLAY

*A famous pianist
said of Chopin's nocturne in C sharp minor,
"I must tell you about it. . . .
In this piece all is sorrow and trouble.
Oh such sorrow and trouble! . . .
until he begins to speak to God, to pray;
then it is all right."*

*That is the way it was with Jesus.
He went into Gethsemani in the dark;
he came out in the light—*

*because he talked with God.
He went into Gethsemani in agony;
he came out with peace in his soul—
because he talked with God.*

PETER'S DENIAL

*They led Jesus away under arrest
and brought him to the house of the high priest,
while Peter followed at a distance.
Later they lighted a fire in the middle
of the courtyard and were sitting beside it,
and Peter sat among them.*

*A servant girl
saw him sitting in the light of the fire.
She gazed at him intently, then said,
"This man was with him."
He denied it, saying, "Woman, I do not know him."*

*A little while later someone else saw him
and said, "You are one of them too."
But Peter said, "No, sir, not I!"
About an hour after that another spoke insistently:
"This man was certainly with him,
for he is a Galilean."
Peter responded, "My friend,
I do not know what you are talking about."
At the very moment he was saying this,
a cock crowed.
The Lord turned around and looked at Peter,
and Peter remembered the word
that the Lord had spoken to him,
"Before the cock crows today
you will deny me three times."
He went out and wept bitterly.*

LUKE 22:54–62

Mark explains that Peter was "warming himself"
in the courtyard. (15:67)
April nights in Jerusalem
can be miserably chilly,
as any modern tourist knows.

Concerning Peter's identification as a Galilean, Matthew reports:

Some bystanders came over to Peter and said,
"You are certainly one of them!
Even your accent gives you away!"

MATTHEW 26:73

The accent of a Galilean in Jerusalem stood out like the drawl of a Mississippi resident in Boston. A Talmud anecdote notes that Galileans pronounced the words for wool *(amar)*, wine *(hamar)*, lamb *(immar)*, and donkey *(hamor)* practically the same.

Mark, who wrote first, may have included Peter's denial of Jesus for special pastoral purposes. Writing for Christians under persecution in Rome, he may have wanted to remind them of the constant danger of apostasy.

More important, however, Mark's touching story would encourage those unfortunate Christians who, like Peter, denied Jesus under pressure. They, too, could hope for their Lord's forgiveness.

Matthew developed Mark's idea by contrasting Peter's sorrow to Judas' despair. (27:5) Godly sorrow brings repentance, worldly sorrow brings death. (2 Corinthians 7:10)

NIGHT SESSION

Matthew (26:59) and Mark (15:1) seem to imply that 2 trial sessions were held: one at night after Jesus' arrest, and another the next morning. Mention of a night meeting puzzles scholars. Jewish law forbade trial sessions at night where a person's fate was at stake.

Luke says nothing about a "night" trial but does imply a meeting of some kind. (22:66)

John could hold the key to a solution. (18:13-24) He suggests that the night session was a private, exploratory hearing before Annas, the former high priest. The morning session was the official, public trial before Caiaphas, the reigning high priest.

In any event, the main trial session began the next morning.

MORNING SESSION

At daybreak, the elders of the people,
the chief priests, and the scribes assembled again.
Once they had brought Jesus before the council,
they said, "Tell us, are you the Messiah?"
Jesus replied,
"If I tell you, you will not believe me,
and if I question you, you will not answer.
This much only will I say:
From now on,
the Son of Man will have his seat
at the right hand of the Power of God."

"So you are the Son of God?" they asked in a chorus.
Jesus answered, "It is you who say I am."
They said, "What need have we of witnesses?
We have heard it from his own mouth."

LUKE 22:63-71

Matthew adds:

At this the high priest tore his robes:
"He has blasphemed!
What further need have we of witnesses?
Remember, you heard this blasphemy.
What is your verdict?"
They answered, "He deserves death!"

MATTHEW 26:65-66

The high priest's charge of blasphemy puzzles some scholars. Claiming to be the messiah does not seem to be blasphemous in itself.

Perhaps the charge arose
from some deeper implication in Jesus' words.

"The Gospel of St. Matthew"
DAVID M. STANLEY

Caiaphas' query
probably refers to Jesus' messianic claims,
"Son of God" being a synonym for Messiah.

In reply, however, Jesus goes beyond
the question: he admits his messiahship,
then asserts his divinity of which "very soon"
evidence will be offered at his glorification,
when as God's Son
he takes his place "at the right hand of the power,"
a term for God.

Caiaphas appears, however vaguely,
to sense Jesus' deeper meaning and accuses him
of blasphemy.

After Caiaphas' charge, "the entire assembly
rose up and led Jesus before Pilate." (Luke 22:1)

TRIAL BY PILATE

The leaders started Jesus' prosecution saying,

"We found this man subverting our nation,
opposing the payment of taxes to Caesar,
and calling himself the Messiah, a king."
LUKE 22:2

The main thrust of the charges made to Pilate
were political, not religious.
Jesus was charged with being a political threat
to the authority and rule of Rome.

PILATE   (to Jesus)
Are you the King of the Jews?

JESUS   *Are you saying this on your own,*
or have others been telling you about me?

PILATE   *I am no Jew!*
It is your own people and the chief priests
who have handed you over to me.
What have you done?

JESUS   *My kingdom does not belong to this world.*
If my kingdom were of this world,
my subjects would be fighting to save me
from being handed over to the Jews.
As it is, my kingdom is not here.

PILATE   *So then you are a king?*

JESUS   *It is you who say I am a king.*
The reason I was born,
the reason why I came into the world
is to testify to the truth.
Anyone committed to truth hears my voice.

PILATE   *Truth! What does that mean?*

       (to priests)
Speaking for myself, I find no case
against this man.

NARRATOR   *[Pilate then tried to remove himself*
from the case
by sending Jesus to Herod. (Luke 23:7)
But this failed.
So Pilate tried another tactic.]

PILATE   (to crowd)
Recall your custom
whereby I release someone to you
at Passover time.
Do you want me to release to you
the king of the Jews?

CROWD   *We want Barabbas, not this one. . . .*

NARRATOR   *Pilate's next move was to take Jesus*
and have him scourged.
The soldiers then wove a crown of thorns
and fixed it on his head,
throwing around his shoulders
a cloak of purple. . . .
[Then Jesus was brought outside.]

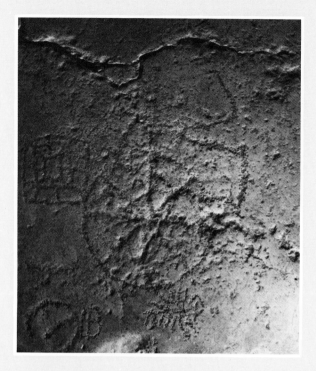

Gabbatha

Archaeologists found a huge stone pavement
near the temple area.
They date it to at least Hadrian's time, A.D. 135.

The discovery is especially interesting
in light of John 19:13.

*Pilate took a seat on a judges' bench at the place
called the Stone Pavement—Gabbatha in Hebrew.*

The stone, shown here, is part of that pavement.
Some identify the markings as the game of "King,"
described by the ancient writer Plautus.
Derived from a Saturnalia festival game,
where a man was crowned king before the festival,
paid mock honors during it, and killed after it,
the game was popular among off-duty soldiers.

Some suggest that such a game
could have inspired the soldiers to treat Jesus
as a mock king, paying him mock honors.

PILATE	*Look at the man!*
CROWD	*Crucify him! Crucify him!*
PILATE	*Take him and crucify him yourselves. I find no case against him.*
CROWD	*We have our law and according to that law he must die because he made himself God's Son.*
NARRATOR	*When Pilate heard this kind of talk, he was more afraid than ever.*
PILATE	(to Jesus) *Where do you come from?*
JESUS	(silence)
PILATE	*Do you refuse to speak to me? Do you not know that I have the power to release you and the power to crucify you?*
JESUS	*You would have no power over me whatever unless it was given you from above. That is why he who handed me over to you is guilty of the greater sin.*
NARRATOR	*After this, Pilate was eager to release him, but the Jews shouted, "If you free this man you are no 'Friend of Caesar.'"*

JOHN 18:33–19:12

Matthew says:

*Pilate finally realized
that he was making no impression
and that a riot was breaking out instead.
He called for water
and washed his hands in front of the crowd,
declaring as he did so,
"I am innocent of the blood of this man.
The responsibility is yours." (27:24)*

Pilate Inscription

In June 1961
archaeologists unearthed this dedication stone
while excavating an ancient amphitheater
near Caesarea-on-the-Sea.

The first line reads TIBERIEUM,
the second (PON) TIUS PILATUS,
the third (PRAEF) ECTUS IUDA (EAE).

The stone is part of a larger statement
of dedication to Tiberius Caesar
by Pontius Pilate, Prefect of Judea.
It is the only known occurrence of Pilate's name
in an ancient inscription.

Cross Inscription

יֵשׁוּעַ־דְמִן נְצְרַת מַלְכָּא דִיהוּדָיֵא

JESVS·NAZARENVS·REX·JUDAEORVM

IHCOYC·O·NAZΩPAIOC·O·BACIΛEYC·TΩN·IOYΔAIΩN

The script of the Dead Sea Scrolls
and the Latin and Greek inscriptions
on the excavated walls of lava-buried Pompeii
suggest the sign on Jesus' cross looked like this.
(The first line reads from right to left.)

Pilate considered the charges against Jesus:

> he subverts the nation,
> opposes payment of taxes,
> claims to be a king.

True, Jesus had criticized
the nation's leaders,
but on religious, not political, grounds.
He also discussed taxation, but didn't oppose it.
(Mark 2:13–17, Matthew 18:24–27)
He was called a king, but refused the title
in a political way. (John 1:49, 18:36)

Pilate's personal verdict on all 3 counts
was the same: "I find no case against him."

Whatever the reason,
perhaps his wife's dream (Matthew 27:19),
Pilate tried to avoid judging Jesus.
He tried to detour the responsibility to Herod.

He tried to invoke the "custom"
of releasing a prisoner to honor a great festival.
Finally, he had Jesus scourged,
hoping this would pacify Jesus' accusers.

When everything failed,
Pilate washed his hands of the ugly situation.
Handing Jesus over to the soldiers,
he had a sign made for Jesus' cross.
Written in Hebrew, Latin, and Greek, it read:

> *Jesus the Nazorean*
> *the King of the Jews.*

The chief priests of the Jews tried to tell Pilate,
"You should not have written, 'King of the Jews.'
Write instead,
'This man claimed to be King of the Jews.'"

Pilate answered,
"What I have written, I have written."

JOHN 19:21–22

The distance from Pilate's headquarters
to Calvary was probably about a quarter of a mile.
The streets were narrow and paved with stones.
Though often striated or grooved (as shown here),
the stones eventually became smooth and slippery
after decades of wear from feet and wheels.
Tradition says Jesus fell several times
en route to Calvary.

WAY OF THE CROSS

The solitary detail that Matthew records
concerning the march to Golgotha is noteworthy:

On the way out
they met a Cyrenian named Simon.
This man they pressed into service
to carry the cross.

MATTHEW 27:32

Mark identifies Simon
as the "father of Alexander and Rufus." (15:21)
Did this identification have a special meaning
for Christians in Rome, for whom Mark wrote?

A clue could lie in Paul's letter to the Romans:
"Greetings to Rufus . . . and his mother
who has been a mother to me as well." (16:13)

Some speculate that Simon became a Christian
after his experience of carrying Jesus' cross.
His family was now living in Rome
(Cyrene was in North Africa)
and could confirm Mark's passion account.

CRUCIFIXION OF JESUS

Upon arriving at a site called Golgotha
(a name which means Skull Place),
they gave Jesus a drink of wine flavored with gall
which he tasted but refused to drink.

When they had crucified him,
they divided his clothes among them
by casting lots. . . .
Two insurgents were crucified with him,
one at his right and one at his left.
People going by kept insulting him,
tossing their heads and saying:
"So you are the one
who was going to destroy the temple
and rebuild it in three days!
Save yourself, why don't you?
Come down off that cross if you are God's Son!"

The chief priests, the scribes,
and the elders also joined in the jeering:
"He saved others but cannot save himself!
So this is the king of Israel!
Let's see him come down from the cross
and then we will believe in him.
He relied on God;
let God rescue him now if he wants to.
After all, he claimed, 'I am God's Son.'"

The insurgents who had been crucified
with him kept taunting him in the same way.

MATTHEW 27:33–44

Golgotha lay outside the walls of Jerusalem.
It was also near a main road,
since Matthew speaks of "people going by."

Ancient Crucifixion

Bulldozers were clearing a Jerusalem hillside.
Suddenly, the work was stopped.
The site was honeycombed with burial caves
containing ancient ossuaries,
small stone coffins housing human bones.
One ossuary was especially interesting.
It contained the bones of a youth whose name,
Yehohanan, appeared in faded letters on the side.
The young man's heel bones
were pinned together by a 7-inch-long nail.

Working with this and other data, Nicu Haas,
a scholar from Jerusalem's Hebrew University,
reconstructed a surprisingly detailed picture
of Yehohanan (Hebrew for John).
He was probably a Jewish resistance fighter,
captured and crucified by the Romans.

"A Death in Jerusalem"
TIME

In his mid-20s at the time of his death,
he was of average height for the period (5 ft. 5 in.),
had delicate, pleasing features
that seemed to approach the Hellenistic ideal,
probably wore a beard, and apparently
had never performed any really arduous labor—
indicating his possible upper-class origins.

The nail was preserved by a freak accident.
It apparently wedged into a knot of olive wood
and could not be pulled out later.
Eventually, thinks Haas, the part of the cross
to which the feet were nailed
was removed and buried with the youth's body.

From pottery and other objects in the cave,
scholars put Yehohanan's death as early as A.D. 7.

Some experts think the discovery
sheds possible new light on Jesus' crucifixion.
Scholars have always felt uneasy about the way
that classical artists portrayed Jesus' death:
erect body, supported by nailed hands and feet.

Nailed hands would not support a buckling body.
Moreover, a sagging body would eventually
arrest breathing and cause rapid death.

Haas believes the new evidence
may point to a truer picture: seated body,
supported by nailed forearms and legs,
twisted under the body and nailed from the side.

The ossuaries
in this burial cave on the Mount of Olives
date from the first century.

Offering Jesus the gall-flavored drink
begins a series of Old Testament allusions:

gall drink,	Psalm 69:22
mockery of Jesus,	Psalm 22:8, 69:8
awaiting God's rescue,	Psalm 22:9
execution with criminals,	Isaiah 53:12
dicing for clothes,	Psalm 22:19
prayer: "My God, my God."	Psalm 22:2

Matthew's purpose in citing these is to affirm
that everything was being fulfilled as prophesied.

Holy Week pilgrims in Jerusalem retrace
the route of the cross.

DEATH OF JESUS

*From noon onward, there was darkness
over the whole land until midafternoon.
Then toward midafternoon
Jesus cried out in a loud tone,
"Eli, Eli, lema sabachthani?", that is,
"My God, my God, why have you forsaken me?"*

*This made some of the bystanders who heard it
remark, "He is invoking Elijah!"
Immediately one of them ran off and got a sponge.
He soaked it in cheap wine,
and sticking it on a reed, tried to make him drink.
Meanwhile the rest said, "Leave him alone.
Let's see whether Elijah comes to his rescue."
Once again Jesus cried out in a loud voice,
and gave up his spirit.*

*Suddenly the curtain of the sanctuary
was torn in two from top to bottom.
The earth quaked, boulders split, tombs opened.
Many bodies of saints
who had fallen asleep were raised.
After Jesus' resurrection
they came forth from their tombs
and entered the holy city and appeared to many.*

*The centurion and his men
who were keeping watch over Jesus
were terror-stricken at seeing the earthquake
and all that was happening,
and said, "Clearly, this was the Son of God!"*

MATTHEW 27:45-54

The darkness and the earthquakes are debated.
Some accept them as reported: they happened.
Others say Matthew intended them to be symbolic.
Such imagery, they say,
is typical of the way that ancient writers
sometimes report the deaths of great men.
For example, in his *Georgics*, Virgil says
that on the day of Caesar's death an eclipse
occurred "from the sixth hour till night."

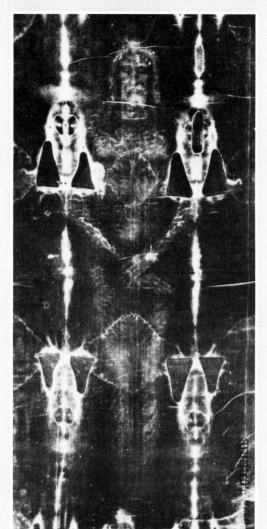

Image as it appears in photographic negative.
Triangles are patches sown over parts damaged
in a 16th-century fire.

Image of Jesus?

The Shroud of Turin is thought by some people
to be the burial wrapping of Jesus.
Without a doubt, a man's image is clearly visible
on the 14-by-3-foot linen cloth.
Moreover, bloodstains are clearly visible
around the wrists, feet, head, and side.

Brought to Turin, Italy in 1578,
little is known of the shroud's early history.
It first attracted worldwide attention in 1898
when Secondo Pia took a picture of it.
Pia's picture
showed the shroud as a photographic negative.

Some think the imprint could be a vaporgraph
caused by a chemical reaction.
Others think it could be a thermograph
caused by heat radiation.
Experiments have ruled out the possibility
that it is the work of a skilled artist.

The man must have been crucified before A.D. 300,
because after that crucifixion was outlawed
by Constantine.

Such literary symbolism, called poetic license,
aided readers to appreciate the unseen,
world-shaking implications of the event.

Others say that Matthew's purpose was to affirm
that the Day of Israel's Judgment,
which the prophets had carefully foretold,
is now fulfilled in its ultimate sense:

*On that day, says the Lord God,
I will make the sun set at midday
and cover the earth with darkness.*

AMOS 8:9

The bystanders misunderstand Jesus' *"Eli, Eli,"*
and think he is praying to Elijah.
Their response reflects a popular Jewish belief:
Elijah would herald and help the Messiah.
Another tradition said Elijah would aid good people
in the hour of their direst need.

John identified the "reed" as a hyssop stalk. (19:29)
Given John's eye for symbolism,
he is pointing to Exodus 12:22:
the saving blood
of the old Passover lamb prefigures
the saving blood of the new Passover lamb.

The tearing of the temple curtain
seems to have a deeper meaning also:
the old temple, symbol of God's presence,
is now at an end;
the reality of God's presence, Jesus' own body,
will be rebuilt in 3 days
to become the new temple of Jews and gentiles alike.
(Hebrews 10:19)

The opened tombs, from which the saints go forth
"after" Jesus' resurrection, are also debated.

Again, many readers accept this report literally.
Others say that Matthew merely attempts to portray,
in a visible way, the unseen ramifications
of Jesus' death and resurrection.
The just are freed from the sleep of death.
Jesus is the "first fruits of those
who have fallen asleep." (1 Corinthians 15:20)

But the overriding message of the crucifixion
is the man suspended between earth and sky:
"Clearly," says the Roman centurion,
"this man was the Son of God!" (Matthew 27:54)

During his days of preaching, Jesus had said:

"Just as Moses lifted up the serpent in the desert,
so must the Son of Man be lifted up,
that all who believe may have eternal life with him."
                                                        JOHN 2:14

An old Polish Jew
who survived the massacre of a Warsaw ghetto
said:

God in An Age of Atheism
S. PAUL SHILLING

As I looked at that man upon the cross . . .
I knew I must make up my mind once and for all,
and either take my stand beside him
and share in his undefeated faith in God . . .
or else fall finally into a bottomless pit
of bitterness, hatred,
and unutterable despair.

A modern writer was right:

Who is Christ?
ANTHONY PADOVANO

The suffering on the cross
is meant not for itself but for something else.
Christ does not suffer
because suffering is in itself a value
but because love without restraint
requires suffering. . . .
It is not the physical death of Jesus
which is redemptive
but the love of Jesus for us even unto death. . . .

The crucified Jesus is a sign . . .
that love may suffer but it overcomes. . . .
The man of faith has found [in Jesus]
a hope stronger than history
and a love mightier than death.

BURIAL OF JESUS

When evening fell a wealthy man
from Arimathea arrived, Joseph by name.
He was another of Jesus' disciples,
and had gone to request the body of Jesus.
Thereupon Pilate issued an order for its release.

Taking the body, Joseph wrapped it in fresh linen
and laid it in his own new tomb
which had been hewn from a formation of rock.
Then he rolled a huge stone
across the entrance of the tomb and went away.
                                                        MATTHEW 27:57-60

Modern Passion

Jesus' passion took on special meaning
for a modern prisoner.
Arrested for his religious belief,
he describes what followed.

"Those Who Lie in Jail"
TIME

I reached my prison
on the afternoon of the day of my arrest.
How long ago that was . . . I don't know,
because I am always in the dark.
On that day,
in complete darkness, I was led to this cell.
When the door closed behind me . . .
I was thinking of God,
and remembered to offer up my troubles
for his glory. . . .

I tried then to get to know something
of the place where I was.
I was already aware of much darkness
and of a smell . . .
from the place which I later found out
was where the drains of five lavatories
of the guards on the five floors above me
emptied themselves. . . .

I was able at first to get little sleep
because rats kept scurrying over me . . .
so I passed unforgettable moments
of intimate union with the crucifix,
which I conjured up before my mind.
My own had been removed at the prison gates.

Believe me all of you who are outside . . .
there is a face on the cross
which cannot be apprehended
save by those who lie in jail. . . .
God's happiness rests longer upon those
who have not light's distraction.

21

Rising of Jesus

Film director Cecil B. DeMille
described for a friend an incident that happened
on a lake in the northern woods in Maine.

The Amazing Results of Positive Thinking
NORMAN VINCENT PEALE

I looked down in the water. . . .
There in a world of mud and wet
were water beetles.
One crawled up on the gunwale,
stuck the talons on his legs into the woodwork
and died.
I let it alone and turned to my reading.
The sun was hot.

In about three hours
I noticed my water beetle again.
He was parched.
His back was cracking open.
I watched,
and out of the back of that dead beetle
I saw crawling a new form—
a moist head—then wings.
A most beautiful dragonfly. . . .

As I sat watching, it flew. . . .
It hovered over the surface,
just a few inches from the water beetles beneath.
They did not know it was there.

DeMille's beautiful experience in a Maine woods
may help us to approach
with renewed wonder the profound mystery
of the infinitely greater transformation
that took place 3 days after Jesus' death.

As the first day of the week was dawning,
Mary Magdalene came with the other Mary
to inspect the tomb.
Suddenly there was a mighty earthquake
as the angel of the Lord descended from heaven.
He came to the stone, rolled it back, and sat on it.
In appearance he resembled a flash of lightning
while his garments were white as snow.
The guards grew paralyzed with fear of him
and fell down like dead men.
Then the angel spoke, addressing the women:
"Do not be frightened.
I know you are looking for Jesus the crucified,
but he is not here.
He has been raised, exactly as he promised.
Come and see the place where he was laid.
Then go quickly and tell the disciples:
'He has been raised from the dead
and now goes ahead of you to Galilee,
where you will see him.'
That is the message I have for you."

They hurried away from the tomb
half-overjoyed, half-fearful,
and ran to carry the good news to his disciples.
Suddenly, without warning,
Jesus stood up before them and said, "Peace!"
The women came up and embraced his feet
and did him homage.
At this Jesus said to them,
"Do not be afraid!
Go and carry the news to my brothers
that they are to go to Galilee,
where they will see me."

As the women were returning,
some of the guards went into the city and reported
to the high priests all that had happened.
They, in turn, convened with the elders
and worked out their strategy, giving the soldiers
a large bribe with the instructions:

"This was the tree upon which the Lord, like a brave warrior
wounded in hands, feet and side, healed the wounds of sin. . . .
A tree once caused our death, but now a tree brings life."
Theodore the Studite

"You are to say,
'His disciples came during the night
and stole him while we were asleep.'
If any word of this gets to the procurator,
we will straighten it out with him
and keep you out of trouble."

The soldiers pocketed the money
and did as they had been instructed.
This is the story that circulates among the Jews
to this very day.

MATTHEW 28:1-15

Tomb robbing was not unusual in ancient times.
Striking evidence of this was unearthed
in Palestine in the form of an ancient decree.
Written in Greek and dating from about Jesus'
time, it makes tomb robbing a crime
punishable by death.

The charge that disciples stole Jesus' body
may have been credible at first,
but it diminished in impact as weeks stretched
into months, and months into years.

Now I See
ARNOLD LUNN

If the disciples had stolen the body,
they would have had the best reason for knowing
that Jesus had not fulfilled his promise
to rise from the dead,
and that he had died the death of a deluded fanatic
upon the cross. . . .

Is it conceivable that these twelve men
would have persisted to the end in maintaining
an elaborate conspiracy of falsehood . . . ?

Is it conceivable that men
would have faced death with radiant courage
in their efforts to propagate a doctrine
which they knew to be false?

"I really believe," writes Pascal, "those stories
whose writers get their throats cut."

The initial reaction of the disciples
to the resurrection of Jesus was disbelief:
"The story seemed like nonsense
and they refused to believe the women." (Luke 24:1)

183

But That I Can't Believe
JOHN A. T. ROBINSON

Jesus was someone
they had known and loved and lost.
They had shared with him
a depth of living
they had not guessed before.
All their hopes for a better life
were centered in him, and lost with him—
buried and sealed in the tomb.
It was all over.
They had been quickened by the vision
of what life could be,
but now they must face life as it was.
Back to reality!

And then it *happened. It came to them—*
rather, as they could only describe it,
he came to them.
The life they had known and shared
was not buried with him but alive in them.
Jesus was not a dead memory,
but a living presence.

One of the most dramatic appearances of Jesus
was to 2 disciples on Easter Sunday evening.
The 2 were returning by foot to Emmaus,
their home.
As they walked along,
they talked about the tragic weekend.

NARRATOR   *Jesus approached*
                and began to walk along with them.
                However, they were restrained
                from recognizing him.

JESUS   *What are you discussing*
                as you go on your way? . . .

NARRATOR   *[The disciples explained to him*
                the events of Good Friday.]

Wheel-like stones
once sealed ancient burial chambers.
Rolled down an inclined track,
stones often weighed as much as a ton.
Ironically,
this ancient Herod-family tomb in Jerusalem
was used to shelter the living
during the Arab-Israeli wars in 1948 and 1967.

DISCIPLES *Besides all this, today, the third day*
since these things happened,
some women of our group have just
brought some astonishing news.
They were at the tomb before dawn
and failed to find his body,
but returned with the tale
that they had seen a vision of angels
who declared he was alive.
Some of our number went to the tomb
and found it just as the women said;
but him they did not see.

JESUS *What little sense you have!*
How slow you are to believe all
that the prophets have announced!
Did not the Messiah have to undergo
all this so as to enter into his glory?

NARRATOR *Beginning, then, with Moses*
and all the prophets, he interpreted
for them every passage of Scripture
which referred to him.
By now they were near the village
to which they were going, and he acted
as if he were going farther. . . .

DISCIPLES *Stay with us. It is nearly evening—*
the day is practically over.

NARRATOR *So he went to stay with them.*
When he had seated himself
with them to eat, he took bread
and broke the bread
and began to distribute it to them.
With that their eyes were opened
and they recognized him; whereupon
he vanished from their sight.

DISCIPLES *Were not our hearts burning inside*
us as he talked to us on the road
and explained the Scriptures to us?

NARRATOR *They got up immediately*
and returned to Jerusalem
where they found the Eleven
and the rest of the company assembled.
They were greeted with,
"The Lord has been raised.
It is true! He has appeared to Simon."
Then the two disciples recounted
what had happened on the road
and how they had come to know him
in the breaking of the bread.

LUKE 24:15–35

RESURRECTED BODY

A repeating feature of Jesus' appearances
is his disciples' inability to recognize him.
When Jesus appeared to Mary Magdalene,
"she did not know him." (John 20:14)
When Jesus appeared to the Eleven in Jerusalem,
"they thought they were seeing a ghost." (Luke 24:37)
When he appeared on the seashore, "none of the
disciples knew it was Jesus." (John 21:5)

All this speaks to the nature of resurrection
and the resurrected body.
Jesus' resurrection was not a restoration to life,
such as happened to Jairus' daughter,
the son of the widow of Naim, and Lazarus.
With Jesus, it was not simply a case
of restoring life to a body.

The term "resurrection" designates
something no human being had yet experienced.
It is not the return to a former life,
but a quantum leap forward into a higher life.
In other words,
the body that rose on Easter Sunday morning
was radically different from the body
that was buried on Good Friday afternoon.

Paul compares the body before resurrection
to a seed planted in the earth. (1 Corinthians 15:37)

185

"It Is The Lord!"

After returning to Galilee as Jesus told them,
the disciples went fishing one night.
It turned out badly.
As they were heading for land, a stranger on shore
shouted to them to cast their nets one last time.
Reluctantly, they did.
The haul of fish was overwhelming.
John studied the stranger on shore and said:
"It is the Lord!"

When the disciples got the haul of fish on shore,
they saw that Jesus had prepared a fire
with fish laid on it and some bread.
At Jesus' invitation, they sat down and ate.

When they had eaten their meal,
Jesus said to Simon Peter, "Simon, son of John,
do you love me more than these?"
"Yes, Lord," he said, "you know that I love you."
At which Jesus said, "Feed my lambs."

A second time Jesus put his question,
"Simon, son of John, do you love me?"
"Yes, Lord," Peter said, "you know that I love you."
Jesus replied, "Tend my sheep."

A third time, Jesus asked. . . .
Peter was hurt because he asked him
a third time, "Do you love me?"

Sea of Galilee,
near the spot
where tradition says
Jesus breakfasted
with his disciples.

Church
marking
the traditional
breakfast site.

So he said to him: "Lord you know everything.
You know well that I love you."
Jesus said to him, "Feed my sheep."

JOHN 21:15-17

Peter's threefold testimony of love
erases from his heart his threefold denial of Jesus.
Jesus' threefold response to Peter
establishes him as the new shepherd of the flock.

The body after resurrection
differs as radically from the one before it
as does a seed from a plant:

When you sow
you do not sow the full-blown plant,
but a kernel of wheat or some other grain. . . .
So it is with the resurrection of the dead.
What is sown in the earth is subject to decay,
what rises is incorruptible.
What is sown is ignoble, what rises is glorious.
Weakness is sown, strength rises up.
A natural body is put down
and a spiritual body comes up.

1 CORINTHIANS 15:37, 42–44

Small wonder Jesus' disciples failed to recognize
him in his first resurrection appearances.

GLORIFIED BODY

Because he is risen, Jesus enjoys
a totally new relationship with his Father in heaven
and with his brothers and sisters on earth.
He is, in the words of the theologians,
in his "glorified state."

Who Do You Say I Am?
EDWARD J. CIUBA

For Jesus the resurrection established
a new relationship with God his Father. . . .
He was glorified,
that is, he became fully living and life-giving. . . .

This life-giving power
comes in the form of the Holy Spirit,
and a new relationship is established with us. . . .
Because of this,
our religious situation is fundamentally altered.
By the resurrection, his sonship becomes unique,
but also, by his life-giving power,
our sonship with God is established.

In him we have become
as adopted sons and daughters of God.
It is precisely through this sharing of his life,
his Spirit, that we are related in the Christian
community as brothers and sisters.
We become members of the one body of Christ.

Jesus rose in his glorified body
and it became the instrument
by which his Spirit was given to his followers.
This is what John talked of earlier in his gospel.
Recall the occasion:
the 7-day celebration of the Feast of Tabernacles.

During the feast,
water was taken each day from the Pool of Siloam
and carried in solemn procession to the temple.
There it was received with trumpet fanfare.
A priest then mixed it with wine
and poured it before the altar.

Each night of the feast,
2 giant towers, crowned with immense lamps,
were ceremoniously lit in the temple courts.
The flames leaped high in the starry sky,
illuminating the entire city.

Against this backdrop of colorful pageantry,
Jesus said to his followers:

"I am the light of the world.
No follower of mine shall ever walk in darkness;
no, he shall possess the light of life."

JOHN 8:12

And:

"If anyone thirsts, let him come to me;
let him drink who believes in me.
Scripture has it:
'From within him rivers of living water shall flow.'"

Here Jesus was referring to the Spirit
whom those
that came to believe in him were to receive.

"He Is Risen!"

The Winter of Our Discontent
JOHN STEINBECK

Aunt Deborah read the Scripture to me
like a daily newspaper
and I suppose that's the way she thought of it,
as something going on,
happening eternally but always exciting and new.
Every Easter, Jesus really rose from the dead,
an explosion, expected but nonetheless new.
It wasn't two thousand years ago to her;
it was now.

This same faith explodes
with newness and excitement each year
in Jerusalem's Church of the Holy Sepulcher.
Here, Armenians, Syrians, Greeks, and Copts
throng about Jesus' tomb
just as the bishop emerges with the Easter fire.

There was, of course, no Spirit yet,
since Jesus had not yet been glorified.
JOHN 7:37–39

But now Jesus was glorified.

Salvation History
NEAL FLANAGAN

The moment of that glorification
and the beginning of the era of the Holy Spirit
was the moment of Jesus' death.
As his side was pierced, blood and water flowed out.
The water is a Johannine symbol of the Spirit,
the effusion of the Spirit upon humanity
from the body of Christ. . . .

Once Christ
was glorified by his death and resurrection
he begins immediately to communicate the Spirit.
This he does first of all to the apostles
on the evening of Easter Sunday. . . .

Jesus breathed on them saying,
"Receive the Holy Spirit! . . ."

On Pentecost Sunday, fifty days later,
the Spirit was poured out upon the disciples
and manifested openly to the world.
This event fortified the first Christians
as witnesses to Christ
and constituted the external inauguration . . .
of the Kingdom of God on earth.

In A.D. 135,
Rome's Emperor Hadrian covered
the traditional sites
of Golgotha and Jesus' tomb
with a massive pavement.
Two centuries later,
Constantine removed it
and built the first
Church of the Holy Sepulcher.
This stairwell wall
belongs to the present church.
The carved graffiti
were left by pilgrims
nearly 1,000 years ago.

Jesus not only became life-giving himself,
but also empowered his disciples
to share in his life-giving mission to people.
He commissioned them to carry his life-giving
word and Spirit to all nations on earth.
This is the great message
with which Matthew ends his gospel:

The eleven disciples
make their way to Galilee, to the mountain
to which Jesus had summoned them.
At the sight of him,
those who had entertained doubts
fell down in homage.
Jesus came forward
and addressed them in these words:

"Full authority has been given me
both in heaven and on earth;
go, therefore,
and make disciples of all nations.
Baptize them in the name
of the Father
and of the Son
and of the Holy Spirit.
Teach them to carry out everything
I have commanded you.
And know that I am with you always,
until the end of the world!"

MATTHEW 28:16–20

This was the great moment.

An Analytical Approach
to the New Testament
F. B. RHEIN

From that time on the men of Palestine
who had been Christ's followers
never wavered from the faith. . . .

Off they went with burning urgency
to tell the news to all the world.
The Messiah had come.
Truly the Kingdom of God was at hand.

Their lives were led for that end,
and for that end alone.
No amount of persecution could stop them. . . .

Many were to find crosses of their own
on which to hang.
Some were torn apart by wild beasts in the arena.
Others were burned alive,
but the basic conviction remained unchanged.

Let Us Build Three Tents

The eleven disciples made their way to Galilee
to the mountain
to which Jesus had summoned them.

MATTHEW 28:16

Tradition identifies the mountain as Tabor.
Located 6 miles east of Nazareth,
it is the same mountain upon which tradition
places Jesus' transfiguration. (Luke 9:28–36)
Sixth-century Christians built 3 churches there
to fulfill Peter's desire to build 3 booths (tents)
in honor of Moses, Elijah, and Jesus.
Describing his visit to Tabor, a journalist says:

"The Years in Galilee"
HOWARD LaFAY

Long ago,
pilgrims climbed Mount Tabor on their knees;
now a road hairpins to the top.
There I found
the crumbling remains of a 13th-century
Saracen fortress enclosing a large basilica.
Within the church, a massive mosaic
depicts Jesus transfigured. I paid little heed.
Mosaics are, after all, but colored stones.

Yet, I soon noticed a shaft of light
pouring through a stained-glass window.
The light crept up the wall and caught the mosaic.
Suddenly the image of Jesus
shimmered with dazzling brilliance,
exploding into tiny, blinding bits of gold.
Then the light moved on. The moment passed.

Mount Tabor in Galilee.

22

Epilogue

Someone said:

Christians say that God is like this;
Jews say he is like that;
Moslems say that he is something else entirely.
I don't think any of them know what God is like.

One is reminded of a story learned in childhood:

"The Parable
of the Blind Man and the Elephant"
JOHN SAXE

It was six men of Indostan
To learning much inclined,
Who went to see the Elephant
(Though all of them were blind),
That each by observation
Might satisfy his mind.

Saxe then reports what happens.
The first blind man feels the elephant's side
and says he looks like a wall.
The second man feels the elephant's tusk
and says he looks like a spear.
The third man feels the elephant's trunk
and says he looks like a snake.
The fourth blind man feels the elephant's leg
and says he looks like a tree.
The fifth man feels the elephant's ear
and says he looks like a fan.
The last blind man feels the elephant's tail
and says he looks like a rope.
The parable ends:

And so these men of Indostan
Disputed loud and long.
Each in his own opinion
Exceeding stiff and strong.
Though each was partly in the right
They all were in the wrong!

Perhaps it would be better to say
that each was in the right—from his own viewpoint.
But each blind man was not completely right.
Only by dialoguing together could they get
a more accurate view of the elephant.

Many contend that the parable mirrors
the situation of religious groups and their diverse
viewpoints of God.
The question immediately arises:
"By what right do Christians, then,
claim to have a more privileged insight into God
than do other religious groups?"

The answer rests on the Christian's faith in Jesus.
Jesus claimed to know God as no other man ever did.
Jesus claimed much more;
he claimed a special kind of identity with God:

"Whoever has seen me
has seen the Father . . .
I am in the Father
and the Father is in me."

JOHN 14:9-10

No man in history ever claimed what Jesus did.
Mohammed acknowledged himself to be a sinner.
Buddha rejected any form of personal veneration.
No man in history ever dared to identify himself
with God in the way that Jesus did.

If Jesus was who he claimed to be,
then Christians can correctly claim privileged
access to a personally revealed knowledge of God.
The whole issue rises and falls on Jesus' question
to Peter: "Who do you say I am?"

Commenting on this all-important question,
a modern newsmagazine wrote of Jesus:

"... A Quest for the True Jesus"
NEWSWEEK

To the local authorities,
he was an itinerant Jewish preacher,
a carpenter's son from the province of Galilee
with a reputation for prophecy, wonder-working
and religious reform.

But to the authors of the New Testament ...
Jesus embodied the very incarnation of God
in human flesh.
They did not preach the philosophy of Jesus
but Jesus himself, the Christ,
the one in whom, they said,
God had revealed Himself to man. ...

This was a radical new religion,
blasphemous to the Hebrews,
ridiculous to the Greeks,
and subversive to the Romans.

Blasphemous, ridiculous, subversive—
these are apt words in talking about Jesus.
The reason is apparent.

Mere Christianity
C. S. LEWIS

A man who was merely a man
and said the sort of things Jesus said
would not be a great moral teacher.
He would either be ...
a madman or something worse.
You can shut Him up for a fool ...
or you can fall at His feet
and call him Lord and God.
But let us not come
with any patronizing nonsense
about His being a great human teacher.
He has not left that open to us.
He did not intend to.

And so Jesus' question to Peter returns:
"Who do you say I am?"

"... A Quest for the True Jesus"
NEWSWEEK

First-century Christians
used a variety of 'names' for Jesus.
They called him the Christ, or anointed one,
the Lord, Saviour, Son of Man, Messiah, Prophet—
by which they tried to describe, functionally,
what Jesus does for man.
Later, the church fathers tried to explain
who Jesus was
by using Greek philosophical concepts.
They said he was the second of three persons
of the divine trinity of Father, Son and Holy Spirit
possessed of both a human nature
and a divine nature—
meaning that he was at the same time
fully God and fully man. ...

"The difficulty,"
says Scripture scholar Leander Keck ...
"is that we don't know what it means to be divine."

Jesuit theologian Piet Fransen agrees. ...
"It is difficult to say in our age
what the divinity of Jesus can mean.
We are groping for a way to express it—
we just don't know."

Once again, the all-important question returns:
"Who do you say I am?"

No contemporary Christian can answer
that question without asking himself a prior one:
"How did Jesus' first followers answer it?"
For our answer will have to rest heavily
upon their testimony or it will rest on nothing.
We must trust the Pentecost community of Jesus'
first followers or have Jesus lost forever.
They are the privileged witnesses of Jesus.

The Gospels
clearly exhibited the faith of first-century Christians
that Jesus was a divine being, Son of God. . . .
Already in the sermon attributed to Peter
on Pentecost,
Jesus is identified with the Lord—
the Adonai of the Old Testament—
of whom it had been written
that he would pour forth His spirit upon all flesh
before manifesting Himself
as a universal judge at the end of time.

In terms of the theological vocabulary
available to Jewish Christians
at the moment the Church was born,
we could scarcely hope for, or even conceive,
a more forceful affirmation of Christ's divinity.

How did the apostles come by their conviction
that Jesus was Lord of all creation?
It was not just a matter of saying "yes"
to what Jesus had said about himself.
Nor was it a logical conclusion of his miracles.
True, Jesus cleared the way for his apostles
to recognize him.
But the final light of revelation or recognition
came from God:

"No mere man has revealed this to you,
but my heavenly Father."

MATTHEW 16:17

In other words, recognition of Jesus' divinity
is primarily a matter of grace.

"No one can say 'Jesus is Lord'
except in the Holy Spirit."

1 CORINTHIANS 12:3

It was the Holy Spirit who guided the apostles
to the fullness of truth about Jesus. (John 16:13)

Since
the apostles had not learned Jesus' divinity
through sheerly external evidences,
they did not seek to convince others
by strict proofs. . . .
The same is true of the writings of Paul. . . .

"My speech and my preaching
were not in the persuasive words of wisdom,
but in the demonstration of the Spirit and power,
that your faith might rest
not on the wisdom of men,
but on the power of God."

1 CORINTHIANS 2:4–5

The gospels do not try to "sell" or persuade.
Nor do they debate; they merely proclaim:

What we have seen and heard
we proclaim in turn to you
so that you may share life with us.

1 JOHN 1:3

And this is as it should be.
Pascal tells why: it preserves human freedom.
In other words:
"There is light enough for those who desire to see,
and obscurity enough
for those whose disposition is otherwise."

Jesus does not reveal his identity so clearly
as to leave no doubt about it.
Nor does he keep it so hidden
that the open-hearted searcher will miss it.
He satisfies both possibilities.

A modern Christian author
expresses the idea with this homespun analogy:

Jesus Christ
YVES CONGAR

Today, Ellen put a bright yellow headband
on her chestnut hair.
She knows that she is going to meet Roger.

Early Witness

The primitive Christian community
was not a memorial society
with its eyes fastened on a departed master;
it was a dynamic community
created around a living and present Lord.

JOHN KNOX

She says to herself:
if he feels about me as I feel about him,
he will understand.
Possibly he will not even notice:
Ellen will leave it at that. . . .
A simple sign, a signal:
If he loves me, he will understand!
The sign is the means best-adapted to lead someone
to declare himself, should he be so inclined,
while completely respecting
the spontaneous character of his freedom. . . .

God too presents his message in such a way
that there can be some justification
for not understanding it and rejecting it,
while a real possibility
of recognizing and accepting it remains. . . .
The visits of God are mingled darkness and light.

In the end,
each person is left with the awesome responsibility
of answering the question:
"Who is this Jesus?"

Perhaps, the most appropriate signature
to our study are the words of another searcher:

The Quest of the Historical Jesus
ALBERT SCHWEITZER

Jesus comes to us as One unknown,
without a name, as of old, by the lakeside.
He came to those men who knew him not.
He speaks to us the same word:
"Follow thou me!" and sets us to the tasks
which he has to fulfill in our time.
He commands.
And to those who obey him,
whether they be wise or simple,
he will reveal himself
in the toils, the conflicts, the sufferings
which they shall pass through in His fellowship,
and, as an ineffable mystery,
they shall learn in their own experience
who he is.

Modern Witness

<u>God of the Oppressed</u>
JAMES H. CONE

On Sunday morning, after spending six days
of struggling to create meaning out of life,
the people of Bearden would go to church
because they knew Jesus was going to be there. . . .
Sister Ora Wallace would line out a familiar hymn. . . .

Immediately, the entire congregation
would join her in the singing of the hymn,
because they felt the presence of Jesus. . . .
When the pastor would say,
"I know the Lord is in this place!
Can I get a witness?"
the people responded with shouts of praise saying
"Amen" and "Hallelujah."
Through song, prayer, and sermon
the community affirmed Jesus' presence
and their willingness to make it through
their troubled situation.
Some would smile and others would cry.
Another person,
depending upon the Spirit's effect on him,
would clap his hands and tap his feet. . . .
All of these expressions
were nothing but black people bearing witness
to Jesus' presence among them.
He was the divine power in their lives. . . .

How could black slaves know that they were
human beings when they were treated like cattle?
How could they know that they were somebody
when everything in their environment
said that they were nobody?
How could they know that they had value
that could not be defined in dollars and cents,
when the symbol of the auction block
was an ever-present reality?
Only because they knew that Christ
was present with them and that his presence
included the divine promise to come again
and take them to the "New Jerusalem."

REFERENCE NOTES

Part One

Wells, H. G. "The Three Greatest Men in History." Adapted from *The Outline of History.* New York: Doubleday & Company, Inc., 1970.

Toynbee, A. J. *A Study of History.* 2 vols. Abridged by D. C. Somervell. New York: Oxford University Press, 1954, vol. 1, p. 547.

Renan, Ernest. *The Life of Jesus.* New York: Belmont-Tower Books, 1972.

Dodd, Charles H. *The Founder of Christianity.* New York: Macmillan Publishing Co., Inc., 1970, pp. 7, 10, 11, 20.

Senior, Donald. *Jesus: A Gospel Portrait.* Cincinnati: Pflaum Standard Publishing, 1975, pp. 15–16.

Haley, Alex. *Roots.* New York: Doubleday & Company, Inc., 1976, pp. 547, 578.

Ahern, Barnabas M. *New Horizons.* Notre Dame, Ind.: Fides/Christian, pp. 83–84.

Davies, W. D. *Invitation to the New Testament.* New York: Doubleday & Company, Inc., 1966, p. 208.

Fenton, J. C. *Saint Matthew.* Pelican New Testament Commentaries. London: Penguin Books, Ltd., 1963, p. 16.

Caird, G. B. *Saint Luke.* Pelican New Testament Commentaries. London: Penguin Books, Ltd., 1963.

Senior, op. cit., pp. 26–27.

Dodd, op. cit., pp. 81–83.

Grollenberg, Luke H. *A New Look at an Old Book.* Translated by Richard Rutherford. New York: Paulist Press, p. 285.

McKenzie, John L. *Light on the Gospels.* Chicago: Thomas More Association, 1976, pp. 133–34.

Stanley, David. *A Modern Scriptural Approach to the Spiritual Exercises.* St. Louis: Institute of Jesuit Sources, pp. 112–13.

LaFay, Howard. "Where Jesus Walked." *National Geographic,* December 1967, pp. 74–77.

Haley, op. cit., pp. 2–3.

Stauffer, Ethelbert. *Jesus and His Story.* Translated by Richard and Clara Winston. New York: Alfred A. Knopf, Inc., 1960.

Scott, John M. "The Birthday of the Unconquerable Sun." *Today's Catholic Teacher,* November–December 1971, p. 18.

LaFay, Howard. *Everyday Life in Bible Times.* National Geographic Society, 1977.

Novak, Vincent. *Lord of History.* New York: Holt, Rinehart and Winston, Publishers, 1966, pp. 161–62.

Aschenbrenner, George A. "Hidden in Jesus Before the Father." *Review for Religious,* January 1975, p. 124.

Novak, op. cit., pp. 157–58.

Daniel-Rops, Henri. *Daily Life in the Time of Jesus.* New York: Hawthorn Books, Inc., 1962, p. 116.

Morton, H. V. *In the Steps of the Master.* New York: Dodd, Mead & Company, pp. 77–78.

Aschenbrenner, op. cit.

Barclay, William. *The Gospel of Luke.* Philadelphia: Westminster Press, 1957, p. 30.

Vicker, Ray. "Language of Christ Still Buys Loaves, Fishes in Maalula." *The Wall Street Journal,* May 3, 1976, p. 1.

Part 2

LaFay. "The Years in Galilee." *Everyday Life,* pp. 334–35.

Bruce, F. F. *New Testament History.* New York: Doubleday & Company, Inc., 1972, p. 156.

Byrd, Richard E. *Alone.* New York: G. P. Putnam's Sons, 1938, pp. 4–7, 295–96.

Muggeridge, Malcolm. *Jesus: The Man Who Lives.* New York: Harper & Row, Inc., 1975, p. 51.

Barclay, William. *Jesus of Nazareth.* Los Angeles: William Collins & World Publishers Co., 1977, pp. 19–21.

Alderson, Doug. "Why Drive When You Can Walk?" *Campus Life,* August–September 1976.

Daniel-Rops, op. cit., p. 192.

Frankl, Viktor. *Man's Search for Meaning.* Beacon Press, 1963.

Guthrie, Donald. *A Shorter Life of Christ.* Grand Rapids, Mich.: Zondervan Publishing Co., 1970, p. 20.

Kee, Howard C.; Young, Franklin W.; and Froelich, Karlfried. *Understanding the New Testament.* Englewood Cliffs, N.J.: Prentice-Hall, Inc., 1973, pp. 49–50.

McKenzie, John L. *Dictionary of the Bible.* Milwaukee: Bruce Publishing Co., 1965, p. 947.

Fletcher, Catherine. *Am I Free?* Niles, Ill.: Argus Communications, 1975, p. 9.

Blanton, Smiley M. D. "The Magic of Touch." *Guideposts,* 1965.

Brown, Raymond, and Stanley, David. "Aspects of New Testament Thought." *The Jerome Biblical Commentary.* Englewood Cliffs, N.J.: Prentice-Hall, Inc., 1968, p. 786–87.

Pilch, John J. "Towards Understanding Miracles in the Bible." *The Bible Today Reader,* April 1977, p. 1207.

Evely, Louis. *The Gospels Without Myth.* New York: Doubleday & Company, Inc., 1970, p. 86.

Barclay. *Jesus of Nazareth,* p. 88.

Navone, John. "Possession and Exorcism." *The Way,* 1975, pp. 164–65.

Stuhlmueller, Carroll. "The Gospel According to Luke." *The Jerome Biblical Commentary.* Englewood Cliffs, N.J.: Prentice-Hall, Inc., 1968, p. 155.

Senior, op. cit., p. 120.

Stuhlmueller, op. cit., pp. 154–58.

"The Exorcism Frenzy." *Newsweek,* February 11, 1974, p. 63.

Putman, John. "Jerusalem and the Last Days." *Everyday Life in Bible Times.* National Geographic Society, 1967, p. 359.

Cranston, Ruth. *The Miracle of Lourdes.* New York: McGraw-Hill Book Co.

Carrel, Alexis. *The Voyage to Lourdes.* Translated by Virgilia Peterson. New York: Harper & Row Publishers, Inc., 1950.

Ostroff, Roberta. "Meeting the Master of Suspense." *Flightime,* August 1974.

"Cloudburst at Petra." *Time,* April 19, 1963, p. 44.

Morton, op. cit., pp. 154–58.

Brown, Raymond. "The Parables of the Gospels." New York: Paulist Press, pp. 5–6.

Ahern, Barnabas M. "Gathering the Fragments: Of Fear and Scholarship." *Worship,* February 1961, pp. 163–64.

Brown, Raymond. *New Testament Essays.* Milwaukee: Bruce Publishing Co., 1965, p. 262.

Congar, Yves. *Jesus Christ.* New York: Herder and Herder, Inc., 1966, p. 116.

De Vaux, Roland. "The Qumran Story." *The Bible Today,* February 1966.

Ellis, Mel. "More Precious Than Pearl." *Wisconsin Trails,* December 1971.

Wasserman, Dale, and Darion, Joe. *Man of La Mancha.* New York: Random House, Inc., 1966, pp. 60–61.

Armstrong, April Oursler. *The Tales Christ Told.* Adapted from *The Greatest Story Ever Told: The Life of Christ* by Fulton Oursler, 1949. New York: Doubleday & Company, Inc., 1958, pp. 9, 17–18.

Davies, op. cit.

Part Three

Morton, op. cit., p. 415.

Stein, Joseph. *Fiddler on the Roof.* New York: Crown Publishers Inc., 1964.

Jeremias, Joachim. *The Parables of Jesus.* New York: Charles Scribner's Sons, 1972, p. 186.

Short, Robert L. *The Parables of Peanuts.* New York: Harper & Row Publishers, Inc., 1968, p. 164.

Bonhoeffer, Dietrich. *The Cost of Discipleship.* 2nd ed. New York: Macmillan Publishing Co., Inc., 1959.

Brown, Raymond. "The Beatitudes According to St. Luke." *The Bible Today Reader,* p. 306.

Senior, op. cit., p. 60.

Dodd, op. cit., pp. 91–92.

Vigeveno, Hank S. *Thirteen Men Who Changed the World*. Glendale, Calif.: Regal Book, 1966, p. 32.

Lazzarotti, Sal F. "Why Should I Get Involved?" *Guideposts*, June 1964.

Rauschenbusch, Walter. *Christianity and The Social Crisis*. New York: Macmillan Publishing Co., Inc., 1897, p. 204.

Craig, Mary. "Take Up Your Cross." *The Way*, January 1973.

"This Was Left Behind." *Newsweek*, November 29, 1955, pp. 30–31.

Dulles, Avery. *Apologetics and the Biblical Christ*. New York: Paulist-Newman Press, 1963, p. 39.

Vawter, Bruce. *The Four Gospels*. 2 vols. New York: Doubleday & Company, Inc., 1967.

Barclay. *Gospel of Luke*, p. 64.

Jeremias, op. cit.

Blanton, op. cit.

Jeremias, op. cit., p. 137.

Davies, op. cit., p. 195.

Hammarskjold, Dag. *Markings*. Translated by Lief Sjoberg and W. H. Auden. New York: Alfred A. Knopf, Inc., 1964, p. 197.

Wells, op. cit., p. 362.

King, Martin Luther, Jr. *Stride Toward Freedom*. New York: Harper & Row Publishers, Inc., 1958.

Wurmbrand, Richard. *In God's Underground*. Glendale, Calif.: Diane Publishing Co., 1968.

Kazantzakis, Nikos. *Report to Greco*. New York: Simon & Schuster, Inc., 1955, p. 54.

Dawes, Dorothy. "When You Pray, Say: Abba." *The Bible Today*. February 1972, p. 635.

Vawter, op. cit.

Gordon, Ernest, and Hall, Clarence. "It Happened One Night on the River Kwai." *Christian Herald*, June 1960.

Martin, Ralph. *Hungry for God*. New York: Doubleday & Company, Inc., 1974.

Young, Warren R. "The Magic of Good Posture." *Reader's Digest*, November 1971.

Part Four

Morton, op. cit., pp. 73–74.

Barclay. *Jesus of Nazareth*, pp. 81–82.

Vawter, op. cit.

Daniel-Rops, op. cit., pp. 453–54.

Fenton, op. cit., pp. 379–80.

Stanley, David. "The Gospel of St. Matthew." *New Testament Reading Guide*, p. 103.

McKenzie, John L. "The Gospel According to Matthew." *The Jerome Biblical Commentary*. Englewood Cliffs, N.J.: Prentice-Hall, Inc., 1968, p. 105.

Fenton, op. cit., p. 401.

Nouwen, Henri J.M. *The Living Reminder*. New York: Seabury Press, 1977, pp. 37–38, 45–47, 300.

Duke, Drew. "The Friday Incident." *Guideposts* 1974.

Stuhlmueller, op. cit.

Ricciotti, Guiseppe. *The Life of Christ*. Westminster, Md.: Christian Classics, 1952, p. 592.

Barclay. *Gospel of Luke*, p. 272.

Stanley, op. cit., p. 113.

"A Death in Jerusalem." *Time*, January 18, 1971.

Shilling, S. Paul. *God in an Age of Atheism*. Nashville, Tenn.: Abingdon Press, 1969, p. 187.

Padovano, Anthony. *Who Is Christ?* Notre Dame, Ind.: Ave Maria Press, 1967, pp. 88–90, 92–93.

"Those Who Lie in Jail." *Time*, April 30, 1951, pp. 71–72.

Peale, Norman Vincent. *The Amazing Results of Positive Thinking*. Englewood Cliffs, N.J.: Prentice-Hall, Inc., 1959.

Robinson, John A. T. *But That I Can't Believe*. New York: New American Library, 1967, p. 58.

Ciuba, Edward J. *Who Do You Say I Am?* New York: Alba House, 1974, pp. 142–43.

Steinbeck, John. *The Winter of Our Discontent.* New York: Viking Press, 1961, p. 56.

Flanagan, Neal. *Salvation History.* Mission, Kan.: Sheed & Ward, 1964, pp. 170–71.

Rhein, F. B. *An Analytical Approach to the New Testament.* New York: Barron's Educational Series, Inc., 1974, pp. 143–44.

LaFay. "The Years in Galilee." *Everyday Life,* p. 349.

". . . A Quest for the True Jesus." *Newsweek,* April 11, 1966, p. 71.

Lewis, C. S. *Mere Christianity.* New York: Macmillan Publishing Co., Inc., 1954, pp. 40–41.

Dulles, op. cit., pp. 68–69.

Congar, op. cit., pp. 124–25.

Cone, James H. *God of the Oppressed.* New York: Seabury Press, 1975, pp. 123–24.

INDEX (selective listings)

Names

Places

INDEX OF BIBLICAL CITATIONS
AND PASSAGES